She Called Me Woman

Nigeria's Queer Women Speak

She Called Me Woman

Nigeria's Queer Women Speak

Azeenarh Mohammed
Chitra Nagarajan
Rafeeat Aliyu

CASSAVA REPUBLIC

First published in 2018 by Cassava Republic Press
Abuja – London

A CIP catalogue record for this book is available from the National Library of Nigeria and British Library.

ISBN: 978-1-911115-59-5
eISBN: 978-1-911115-60-1

Designed and typeset by Cassava Republic Press
Cover & Art Direction by Maia Faddoul

Printed and bound in Great Britain by Bell and Bain Ltd, Glasgow

Distributed in Nigeria by Yellow Danfo
Distributed in the UK by Central Books Ltd.
Distributed in the US by Consortium Books

A project in partnership with The Initiative for Equal Rights, Nigeria

Table Of Contents

Introduction

It's un-Nigerian.
It's against our culture.
It's not allowed by our religion.
This thing isn't in us – it comes from over there.
I'm an African and there are some things I can never accept.

How often have you heard these phrases or others like them? How often have you said and thought them?

In recent years, hardly a day has gone by that we have not come across these arguments. Whether in the newspaper, on the radio, in church or mosque, in discussions with friends, eating with family, gisting at work or arguing on Facebook or Twitter, talk of queerness is everywhere. It seems everyone has an opinion, despite no one being or knowing 'a gay' – or rather, without admitting that they know someone or are themselves gay.

This book is a response to these discussions. It aims to correct the three types of erasure we see in these conversations.

The first is the erasure of queer people from the discussion about their own lives. Queer people are both hyper-visible and invisible, talked about but missing from the centre of the conversation. The voices and realities of the millions of queer

Nigerians (estimated to be more than the population of Lagos) are largely absent from the debate.

The second type of erasure is the rewriting of the rich histories and cultural traditions of diverse sexualities and gender norms in the land now known as Nigeria. Living outside gender norms and heterosexual relationships, or fluidity in gender identity, is not new. They may not be the same as those reflected in the language, films and TV shows of the west, as well as contemporary Nigerian cultural industries, but they are part of Nigerian history, culture and tradition, not in opposition to it.

The final erasure is the state of denial or conscious forgetting that many people engage in of their own experiences and those of people they know. Those things you did in secondary school, that unmarried uncle who lived with his friend until he died, the yan daudu you buy from or indeed the strong, powerful grandmother who had a wife to give her children – they hardly ever make it into private or public discourse.

These erasures mean our conversations are divorced from the truth of our reality and lived experience. Conversations about queerness frequently dehumanise and are dehumanising. Queer people are seen as the absolute and dangerous Other: predators set on converting others, corrupted by outside influences, or focused only on marriage. Adding to the confusion is a conflation of sexual orientation (the gender(s) – or none - you are attracted to), gender identity (the gender(s) – or none – with which you identify) and gender expression (ways in which you express your gender in a world where this is interpreted according to norms of what it means to be a man or woman).

We decided to put together this collection of twenty-five

narratives to correct the invisibility, the confusion, the cari-
caturisation and the writing out of history. We were inspired
by similar books such as *Bareed Mista3jil* by the organisation
Meem about Lebanon; *Facing the Mirror: Lesbian Writing
from India* edited by Ashwini Sukthankar; and *Tommy Boys,
Lesbian Men and Ancestral Wives: Female Same-Sex Practices
in Africa* edited by Ruth Morgan and Saskia Wierenga about
Kenya, Namibia, South Africa, Swaziland, Tanzania and
Uganda. Moved by the power of their stories and convinced
of the importance of documentation, we thought, *We need to
do something similar in Nigeria.* We wanted to tell the stories
we weren't hearing, to provide a space for voices, lives and
experiences missing and silenced from debate. Our audience
is two-fold: we address the general public to hold up a mirror
and show the richness and diversity of Nigerian society, and
we address the queer community to provide a platform to
speak and to see their lives reflected in full technicolour.

Our book focuses on queer women because they are often
missing and outside the frame even in conversations about
queerness, dominated as they are by queer men's experiences.
We recognise the fluidity of gender as a spectrum and this
is a theme in several narratives. The book shows a range of
attitudes towards the ways in which femininity is socialised
in Nigeria and not all of our narrators want to be or identify as
women (we use feminine pronouns only for those who identify
as female). However, we wanted to examine what it means
to exist at the intersections of queerness and femaleness.
In Nigeria, as in other countries, entrenched prejudice and
discrimination against people considered deviant and beyond
the norm when it comes to sexual orientation, gender identity
and/or gender expression (SOGI) occurs within a profoundly

patriarchal society. Although there is commonality between queer people, gender affects experiences, access to resources and perceptions. Women face further marginalisation because societal, cultural and economic structures manifest power and control in very different ways than for men. This is under-examined within public discourse and in community spaces, where the experiences, realities and voices of men who have sex with men dominate.

This book also tries to address the issue of marriage in queer and non-queer circles. When people talk of homosexuality, they automatically link this with whether 'gay' people can or should get married. The most recent legislation, although covering a range of prohibitions from 'registration of gay clubs, societies and organisations, their sustenance, processions and meetings' to 'the public show of same-sex amorous relationship' was given the name 'Same Sex Marriage Prohibition Act 2014' (SSMPA). The stories in this book challenge this focus on marriage, with many other experiences and concerns reflected and many narrators questioning the importance of marriage itself. They also show very human desires to have 'your person' and have that recognised by society and the people who matter to you, particularly in a country like Nigeria where marriage and children are so pivotal to social and cultural life.

A note on terminology

The narrators used a wide range of terms to describe themselves: lola, luadi, lakiriboto, same-sex, gay, lesbian, trans, bisexual, queer. We use the term queer as a catch-all in this introduction while keeping the terms the narrators used in the narratives.

Our methodology

We were not aiming to provide a comprehensive picture but rather snapshots of histories, experiences and realities. We reached out through networks to encourage as wide a range of narrators as possible to contribute. Our narrators come from and live in every geopolitical zone of Nigeria. They experience and identify with a range of sexual orientations, gender identities and gender expressions. They are of different ethnicities, religions and language groups. Although most narrators are middle class, all class backgrounds are represented. What proved most difficult was ensuring age diversity. We did not have many older women in our networks and those we knew were not interested in participating. In the end, the narrators fell within a narrower age window than we would have liked, from 20 to 42 years old when their interviews were conducted. We greatly regret not being able to include the voices of older narrators, which would have enriched the narrative and provided an opportunity to compare growing up queer at different periods in Nigeria's history.

The three of us travelled across Nigeria recording one-on-one interviews, asking questions ranging from childhood memories and first love to family relationships and experiences of work. The audio recordings were transcribed and written up into narratives. We then worked with the narrators to shape the narratives as they wished. We are conscious that there are contradictory statements within some of the narratives but feel one learns a great deal about the narrators and the way in which they perceive themselves from these inconsistencies. We have therefore reported these life histories as were told to us, and have made no attempt to iron out or 'tidy up' any contradictions in the narratives.

For a number of our narrators, opening up was a cathartic experience. Many shared experiences they had never previously spoken about. As a result, some looked to us for continued emotional support following the interview. Where relevant, we provided information about medical care, legal aid and counselling services. Unfortunately, discriminoatory attitudes and practices are common among service providers. Many narrators had never accessed these services before or had had bad experiences when they did so. We told them that services we recommended may not be friendly to them – for example, they could talk of sexual violence but might want to be careful about disclosing other issues – but they knew this without our even mentioning it.

It took substantial courage for many of the narrators to take part. They had the opportunity to withdraw at any stage up to publication and several of them did so. Those with whom we set up interviews sometimes did not show up. This was not necessarily because they had changed their minds. Two women in Maiduguri were due to be interviewed after a visit to their villages at the height of the violent conflict there. Nobody has heard from them since. We do not know what happened to them. Some narrators came to the interview location but could not bring themselves to enter. BM *(To Anyone Being Hated, Be Strong)*, who had tried to persuade friends to join the project, said 'I know at least ten people who are lesbian and bisexual but because they are married, they're not safe. They can't even be part of this project because they're going to jeopardise their marriage.'

Many narrators were concerned that their identities would be revealed, but some wanted their names to be known, saying they were tired of hiding. We have anonymised all narrators in the interests of standardisation and scrutinised narratives to remove identifying markers. We give only initials, along with ages and states where the narrator felt comfortable doing so. We asked narrators to self-identify where they were from and have listed all the places given if they provided more than one location. Having anonymity may not bode well for writing the history of a community that has been rendered invisible. However, we feel that the writing of experience and documenting of lives at the very least ensures that the lived experiences, if not the people of experience themselves, enter history.

Narratives start with a content note to allow the reader to make informed choices about whether to skip certain narratives. This is not an exact science. Many narratives discuss discrimination, hate speech, alienation and internal struggles. These issues are not reflected in content notes as, unfortunately, they tend to be a given. We do, however, give content notes for violence, including gender-based violence, intercommunal violence and forced medical treatment. In this way, we hope to make the book accessible to readers who find reading about particular issues traumatising due to personal experiences.

Key Emerging Themes

All too Nigerian, all too human!

Although the focus of this book is on queer women, some of the experiences and challenges narrators face apply to many Nigerians.

From TQ *(I Pray That Everyone Has Forgotten)*, whose family is from Gombe but grew up in Jos and Kano and now lives in

Abuja, to IX *(This Is What I Have Been Missing)* who says, 'I was born Yoruba but I grew up in a Hausa household in the north with a lot of Yoruba influence', many of the narrators have links to more than one part of the country, mirroring the realities of many Nigerians. CG *(There Is No One Way To Be A Woman)* says, 'I do not understand the concept of community because different people raised me.'

Narrators spoke of childhood memories: playing ten-ten and suwe; not being allowed to leave the compound for fear they would 'spoil'; being expected to always be reading and studying when they wanted to watch TV; experiencing bullying at school; and being warned off boys. They spoke of financial difficulties when parents lost jobs, interrupted schooling due to lack of money, time spent helping parents in their businesses and being sent out to hawk products to earn money for the family. The narratives contain stories of being brought up by the extended family and community, polygamous households, parents dying and fathers leaving, parents too busy working to spend time with children, strict parents and guardians, and love, laughter and close families.

Whereas some narrators remember knowing 'people like them' growing up, for others this only happened later in life. Girls dating girls was seen as normalised by many narrators, particularly those who attended same-sex boarding schools. According to DK *(Why Do I Have To Ask You To Consider Me Human?)*, 'We had a boarding house at the school and it was obvious some of the girls were dating each other ... Those girls were not treated any differently. In fact, they were seen as gods.' She goes on to say, 'The first time I saw two girls kissing was in my grandmother's house – my aunt and one of the girls.' That this was taking place does not mean it was always accepted – narrators and their classmates were also punished for relationships.

As adults, the narrators have different attitudes towards work. They talk of starting businesses, the stress of being an entrepreneur, relationships with colleagues and struggles to find work due to lack of social contacts or poor/no education. As TQ (*I Pray That Everyone Has Forgotten*) says, 'Anywhere I go, people say, "No work." Everywhere – no work, no work, no work. It's very hard. I'm tired.' However, a job does not guarantee income: 'they will go three or four months without paying you. How can I go home and ask people for money?' (JS, *Some Things You Do For Your Heart*). A recurring theme is the importance of money and the independence and freedom this brings. Narrators link providing for themselves with reduced attempts by family to control them. They feel this is particularly important for the queer community: 'The moment you do something with your life, nobody cares about your sexuality' (OW, *My Sexuality Is Just The Icing On The Cake*).

Religion comes up frequently. Some narrators had pastors and evangelists as parents, others were brought up in religious households and attended Islamiyya or church. Many are devout: 'I believe in God. I pray five times a day, every day. I respect my parents and I believe in the day of reckoning. I believe in good, bad, heaven and hell' (NT, *I Can Still Love More*). Others consider themselves spiritual rather than religious and are not tied to any particular religious institution: 'I believe in God and His existence, I just don't have to be in church to worship Him.' (RD, *If You Want Lesbian, Go to Room 24*).

A few narrators do not believe in God at all or have broken with religious practice, often due to experiences of hateful preaching or pressure to conform to gender norms: 'there was a particular day when the pastor started talking about homosexuality ... I was a serious Christian but I thought, *I'm done with this shit*' (VA, *Living A Double Life*). Others are critical of religion: 'For me, religion causes the problems we have in the world right now – the killings and everything else' (OW, *My Sexuality Is Just The Icing On The Cake*).

Given the history of violence in Nigeria ostensibly tied to religion, this point of view is not surprising. For example, both TQ *(I Pray That Everyone Has Forgotten)* and AG *(Everybody In J-Town Is Now A Lola)* talk of the Jos crisis and how it has affected their lives. AG's boyfriend was killed and TQ had to run away to safety.

Intercommunal violence is one of multiple issues that has caused psychological harm, even if it goes unnoticed for many Nigerians. Many narrators speak openly about trauma. They reflect honestly on mental health issues, loneliness and feeling alone, depression and suicide attempts. The culture of silence around mental health in Nigeria means narrators who experience difficulties did not know where to turn to get help or even how to name what was happening to them. BM *(To Anyone Being Hated, Be Strong)* highlights this lack of knowledge, saying, 'Here in Africa, you don't know what depression is. They just say, "She's not well. This one, ah, you know..."'

A few narrators speak of taking drugs and alcohol. While some say this was experimentation, others believe it was prompted by particular factors. At 15, when her boyfriend was killed, AG *(Everybody In J-Town Is Now A Lola)* 'started taking drugs, hard drugs, like codeine, white ashes ... They helped because there was no love.' Six years later, she is trying to break the addiction.

'I tried crack, I tried cocaine, to get my mind off things. I realised it felt better when I got high – or so I told myself' says BM *(To Anyone Being Hated, Be Strong)*, who struggled to deal with family reactions. 'When they started hating me, I hated myself even more... I went deeper into drugs.'

When narrators reflect on being Nigerian, hopes mix with realism. 'Nigeria is very disappointing' says OF *(Love Is Not Wrong)*.

'Somebody my age in another country would have a Masters, PhD and subsidised school fees. In other countries, somebody my age would be planning retirement, but in Nigeria, life is just starting.' says KZ *(This Is Not Our World)*. For many, attitudes towards Nigeria are linked with how they are treated in it, but some of these experiences are common to all Nigerians in different ways, irrespective of identity. Mixed with queerness, these socio-economic and cultural conflicts make for explosive and challenging living.

On being queer

Coming to an understanding of themselves took time for narrators, all of whom had gone through a period of internal struggle. Access to information via media and technology was important, whether this was seeing girls dating on Facebook, reading online articles about trans identities, having conversations on social media, being able to access dating websites or watching *The Ellen DeGeneres Show* on TV.

Some knew they were 'different' from a young age: 'I didn't know at 7 that I was a lesbian but I knew I wanted girls' (HK, *Same-Sex Relationships Are A Choice*). For others, reflections on same-sex attraction or gender identity was 'a gradual liberation' (NS, *Focusing On Joy*). Some saw queerness as integral to identity and used specific terms to describe themselves. Others took a different view: TQ (*I Pray That Everyone Has Forgotten*) says, 'I wouldn't put a word on my identity. It's just something I do.'

For some, having girlfriends and/or boyfriends started in school, sometimes with drama: 'I had three girlfriends in SS1. Two of them were best friends and I thought they knew that I was dating both of them' (KZ, *This Is Not Our World*). Many of the girls the narrators dated are now married with children. While some former girlfriends continue to date women, others have seemingly buried their past experiences.

Narrators talk of desire and attraction, taking different approaches to sex, from seeing sex as a way to boost love to finding it unimportant. They talk about good sex: 'After that night and during the next weeks, my friends got tired of me because I kept calling them like, "OMG I just had the best sex of my life." They were like, "WTF? You told me this story yesterday." I would be like, "Yeah, I need to tell you again. I do not know what she did but it was that good."' (FR, *I Don't Believe In Love*).

They talk about bad sex: 'We ended up having the most terrible sex. Terrible, terrible, terrible sex. In my mind, I was like, *What the hell is this?* I told her, "Let's just not bother." And that was the first time I was actually with a woman' (IX, *This Is What I Have Been Missing*).

They meet potential partners in a range of locations: the library, church, markets, parties, through friends and relatives, nightclubs and online. Many prefer connecting online first. This can be due to increased ease, clarity and variety, as well as the need to be careful when approaching other women.

The narrators take a range of views of relationships, from finding them exhausting, full of expectations or vowing never to love again after heartbreak, to valuing and finding support and acceptance. They discuss love, monogamy, sexual exploration, multiple partners, relationship breakdown and bereavement. Some are adamantly against marriage whereas thers long for it.

They speak of relationship challenges, including jealousy, infidelity, money issues, being torn between two people and the difficulty of finding time for friends. A number of narrators have had girlfriends marry men, often due to societal pressure rather than inclination.

Many narrators have had and continue to have relationships with men. Others tried being with men and see this as a stage they passed through. Some narrators take a harsh view of women who date both women and men, seeing bisexuality as synonymous with cheating. This view is widespread: 'Most of the time people think you are a cheat when you say you are bisexual' says NT *(I Can Still Love More)*. 'I met a girl online last year and I told her I was bisexual. She said she didn't think bisexuals could be faithful so nothing could happen between us. I wasn't too surprised. She was not the first to think or say it.'

Gender roles in relationships are frequently raised. Many narrators critique this: 'It is in a heterosexual relationship where you see a man and a woman, and gender roles are the whole problem in society.' (OW, *My Sexuality Is Just The Icing On The Cake*). However, others stress the need to have roles.

Unequal power dynamics play out along gendered lines. JS (Some things you do for your heart) insists that 'As the father of the family, I'm the one to dictate what happens in the relationship. No matter how busy you are, you have to tell me in advance that you are going out.' KZ *(This Is Not Our World)* characterises this as being because some women 'want to act and behave like men ... have two girlfriends, beat up their girlfriend, cheat, go drinking, get drunk, stay at home and be the king while the girl cooks, serves the drinks, washes their clothes and stuff.' Violence in same-sex relationships is not often discussed when talking of violence against women and girls but it comes up in many narratives.

The narratives also show a wide spectrum when it comes to gender identities, raising questions around the construction of gender itself in Nigeria. CG *(There Is No One Way To Be A Woman)* was confused by her gender: 'I never fit any of the things that people said women were ... I felt that I was not a woman.' This is unsurprising given the rigid socialisation process involved in becoming female. One of the narratives where this is most marked is *I Only Admire Girls.* Here, QM says, 'I used to run. I ran so much. But Islamically and in Hausaland, female children don't run. The way I ate, the way I sat, I didn't really behave as a female child. My father would say to stop that, that I'm a female child. Because of this, when I was growing up, I never saw myself as female. I saw myself as a male child.' QM's feelings may have been due to a longing for the freedom, possibilities and behaviour open to boys (she now identifies as female). She found it impossible to separate not conforming to social norms for girls from identifying as male. To her, the fact that she did all the things boys do meant she was male.

Some narrators have gender identities different from what they have been assigned. BM *(To Anyone Being Hated, Be Strong)* says, 'Honestly, I'm lesbian because I'm female and I'm here in this time and place ... I'm not happy. I'm not complete. I feel it's wrong when I'm on my period ... My folks and everybody will not accept me as transgender. I'm not ready for them to outright reject me. I love my mum and that would just kill her.' JP *(She Called Me "Woman")* says, 'I was always wishing. I wished I came out as a lady, oh I wished. I wished I was a lady, I wished I was a lady, I wished I was a lady!' She describes being shocked by a 1984 newspaper article on how 'A man had changed his sex to female' and details how she tried to answer the question, 'Was I gay or was I a woman?'

Many narrators talk about the need to be discreet and careful. Some feel they cannot be open with the people who matter to them, and have to lie when questioned or living in a state where 'it' is known but not spoken about. Narrators have had friends withdraw, family members beat them up, insult them, preach at them to change, threaten to report them to the police, take them for deliverance sessions to cast out the 'spirit of homosexuality' and attempt forced medical treatment to 'correct' them.

On the other hand, narrators also talk about complete acceptance from friends, family members fundamentally changing attitudes, having supportive fathers and mothers counselling them through heartbreak, teachers encouraging them to dress how they wish, taking partners to office weddings and parties, getting relationship advice from cousins and receiving counsel from priests.

Indeed, the positive reactions found in this book are a far cry from the dominant narrative in Nigeria that 'everyone hates gay people'. Narrators felt that acceptance by the older generation – socialised in earlier eras – and the younger generation – exposed to popular culture and social media – was higher than in middle-aged generations caught up in respectability politics and religious narratives. OW *(My Sexuality Is Just The Icing On The Cake)* believes, 'older people, not fifties or sixties but seventies and above, are more tolerant because it was normal in the culture back then – female–female and husbands having lots of wives and stuff going on between the wives.' What Nigerians actually think, particularly when it comes to their friends, children, grandchildren, siblings and others they love, seems to be a lot more varied than politicians and the media suppose.

Being women

The narratives also show what it means to be living in a patriarchal system. Narrators talk of girls being seen as unimportant, facing intense pressure to marry and the stigma of getting pregnant outside marriage. QM *(I Only Admire Girls)* states, 'As a Hausa girl, you cannot behave as a boy. When you behave like a boy, they despise you.

They don't see you as a real human being. They will always hate you.' A common theme is the pressure to conform to gender roles and norms whether this comes to behaviour, life choices, dressing or speech. Many of the narrators experience a lack of control over their lives due to a lack of financial power or others making decisions for them, whether this be fathers, brothers or husbands. JP *(She Called Me 'Woman')* finds her understanding of the power relations between women and men considerably changed since presenting as female: 'All the things that happen to women I now experience, especially the power play between sexes: men making passes at you and believing it is their right to have sex with you or rape you. Men calling you 'ashawo'. If you disagree with them or stand up to them, you must be a prostitute.'

A key way unequal power relations based on gender manifest is through violence against women and girls. When conducting the interviews, we were struck by just how many of our narrators had experienced sexual and gender-based violence. A 2014 national survey by the National Population Commission found that 24.8 per cent of women and 10.8 per cent of men aged 18–24 years had experienced sexual abuse before age 18. This prevalence is high but borne out by the experiences of our narrators. They also talk of sexual harassment at work, with pressure to dress in certain ways and to sleep with male bosses to get and keep employment. As discussed above, there are multiple examples of violence in relationships with other women, but narratives also contain accounts of violence perpetrated by men.

However, narratives also show women fighting back. For example, IX *(This Is What I Have Been Missing)* recounts the story of how her university Muslim Students Society threatened to tell a friend's parents about her boyfriend if she did not stop dating him: 'She just insulted the shit out of them. Her boyfriend was beside her. She kissed him and told them to go fuck themselves.'

Nigerian queer women speak

She Called Me Woman is full of stories of resistance and resilience. Narrators fight back against the discrimination they experience, whether this is due to their gender, queerness or both, to find internal strength and combat discrimination in personal lives and in society at large. Several narrators point out the hypocrisy of those who condemn them for 'immoral behaviour': 'She was preaching to me one day and I remember telling her, "Look, you have sex with your boyfriend. That is fornication. I am sleeping with a girl. Fine, that is lesbianism. We are going to the same hell, just different compartments"' (PD, *When I Die, I Just Want To Be Remembered*).

DK *(Why Do I Have To Ask You To Consider Me Human?)* sees attacks as a political power play: 'It all boils down to money or power. The 1 per cent who owns the wealth need to keep everybody so busy they won't notice ... They keep us busy so that we don't demand our power back. Somebody has to be vulnerable and victimised so that they, who feel powerless in other aspects of their lives, can feel powerful over others.'

Many narrators find it a revelation to find connection with others. VA *(Living A Double Life)* says, 'Now I can feel normal. It's not like being LGBT is abnormal or anything, but when you find people who are like you and you can relate to them, you think less about this burden of secrecy. You are able to get over that and face the struggle. It's a great thing.' Narrators also point to areas where the movement can improve. Problems include a sense of community being limited, generational differences, finding it difficult to trust one another, lack of understanding (particularly of trans and intersex issues), people of different religions and ethnicities not meeting each other and people just wanting to party but not rock the boat.

They see the situation in Nigeria getting both better and worse. Even though certain sexual acts were already criminalised before 2014, the passage of the Same Sex Marriage Prohibition Act (SSMPA) made some feel that they were seen as criminals, with one narrator pointing out that the penalties are more severe than for rape. These feelings are exacerbated by increased (negative) public discourse and preaching in places of worship. AG *(Everybody In J-Town Is Now A Lola)* says, 'Ten years ago, it wasn't really open. People didn't even know people like us existed. We could go out with a girl, hang out with her, hold her, but now it's crazy. People are very, very afraid.' Nevertheless, she goes on to talk about the openness she continues to experience in places like Jos, Abuja and Port Harcourt. Some narrators also feel that, conversely, the passage of the SSMPA has forced people to be open about their sexuality, to humanise and put a face to what is seen as the Other. HA *(I Convinced Myself I Wasn't A Lesbian)* 'wrote an article about being lesbian in Nigeria stating how the law couldn't criminalise sexuality' because she 'was determined to show everyone that gay people were everywhere and we were just as regular as they were.'

The narrators also see people having more exposure to new ideas through reading, social media and technology, and being more willing to be open than before. They see a generation learning to speak out. They want to see a stronger, bolder, more educated community whose members know their rights. As DK *(Why Do I Have To Ask You To Consider Me Human?)* says, 'I have a voice. Nobody can silence me.'

For the three of us, working on this book was an eye-opening experience. We were struck by the differences between the stories as well as the commonalities. It was an important reminder to us that not all queer experiences are the same. We expected more despair and loss, but instead we found joy and resilience. Although it was disappointing to note the number of people who wanted to leave the country, believing their chances at happiness existed somewhere other than Nigeria, it was affirming to see so many stories of triumph.

Our aim is for this book to add to conversations about gender and sexual norms in Nigeria, to introduce readers to queer people if they do not know any, and to introduce queer people to each other. We want readers to empathise with our narrators as they go through joys, heartbreaks and victories with them. We hope reading these stories makes the reader laugh, be surprised, feel angry, learn, reflect on their own opinions, feel moved, and be inspired.

— *Azeenarh Mohammed*
— *Chitra Nagarajan*
— *Rafeeat Aliyu*

She Called Me 'Woman'

'Oh jeez, I am beautiful! Even without make-up!'

Content note: sexual violence, physical violence, forced medical treatment, depression

I identify as a human being first. If anybody pushes, I say, 'Fine, I am a woman, a lady.' There was a time when someone said, 'Oh you are a trans woman.' I said, 'No, I am not a trans woman, I am a woman.' And then there was a time when someone was like, 'A trans woman is a woman, but to me, whatever name you call it, a trans woman is a man.' Hello! It is not just about your genitalia, please. But let me start from the beginning.

I remember living as a boy. It was fun initially because I was effeminate. I was 5 or 6 and my parents didn't seem to care that I loved playing with female things. I loved watching movies that included ladies' stuff and all those things ladies love to do. They were just there but I loved doing them. Then my father, a military man, left us – left me – when I was 9. My mum became a single parent to me and my two brothers, and life got really tough till I graduated from school.

In my teenage years, I was feminine. My trousers were unisex. I was more on the female side. I was always swaying when I walked, swinging my waist with reckless abandon because I didn't care what people said and because my mum showed me love and didn't seem to care either. I only started being concerned when she did, when it seemed as if there were external factors from her place of work, from society, saying, Why is your son like this? Why is your son like that? There was a time she would brush them all aside but then they started playing the religious card and all of a sudden it got to her. And she started giving it back to me.

Around that time, my younger brothers became huge, masculine, bearded men with deep voices. I, the first child, the first boy, was all feminine and gracious and my voice changed too. I sang in the choir and my voice went to sopralto, a higher key. When one of my brothers who used to sing that high key became baritone/tenor, all the questions started coming out. What is going on? I would ask myself the same thing. Somewhere along the line, my body and I went through different processes. At the age of 16, I started battling with depression. Even though I knew I was attracted to men, I had not acted on that because we had been taught that homosexuality was a sin. I was still trying to figure myself out.

I was always wishing. I wished I came out as a lady, oh I wished. I wished I was a lady, I wished I was a lady, I wished I was a lady! You know all these kinds of wishes. I wished, I wished, I wished I was a lady. And at times, I would look into the mirror and try to accentuate my looks, then realise, Oh jeez, I am beautiful! Even without make-up!

One day in 2001, while I was in school, a guy walked up to me with an old newspaper. He said, 'Read it. It is for you,' and walked away. This person had never spoken to me before.

I picked up the newspaper and what did I see? A man had changed his sex to female. I looked at the date: 1984. And I was like, is what I have been wishing for real? I read through it with excitement, and there was even a picture. I was shocked! As of then, my quest for knowledge began. I went back to the guy who'd given me the paper and he said I should go do my research. I did, and I realised that anything is possible. No more wishful thinking followed by depression because you think it's impossible. One day while doing research, I saw a book called *Middlesex* on Oprah. It's about a trans woman and I was like, *Wow, so this is actually real.* I continued googling.

I was fighting with external pressure and at the same time, I was trying to know who I was. What was happening with me? Was I gay or was I a woman? I was afraid of acting on my sexual impulses because I knew I was attracted to men. I was trying to know myself and get through the confusion and conflict. My mind was going, *No I am not gay, I am a lady ... No, you are gay ... uh uh, how else?* And I thought my case might be more than that, that there must be something else. But at that point, I was always trying to know, trying to understand, trying to find *me.*

I came out to my mum when I was twenty years old. I just walked up to her in the room and said 'Mum, I think I want to have a sex change. Not think. I know I want to. I am more like a lady and this is who I am.' I started talking and talking and talking.

And she said, 'I think it is a demon speaking through you.' She tried to change my mind and made my brothers beat me up on the spot. I will never forget that day because it was just before my birthday. I didn't even have to come out to my brothers. She told them. It was a circle. They brought me there and she was screaming 'This is what your brother said o, haaay.' My brother was like, 'Really? No!' They were 18 and 16 at that point. They called me all sorts of names: 'You are a disgrace to us ... You are urgh ... You are this, you are that.'

The once beautiful mum who was my angel became my demon and my brothers became her bulldogs, her emissaries. They had grown bigger than me, over six feet tall and quite macho. If you looked at them, you would quiver at the sight. There was no day they didn't beat me, their first-born 'brother'.

I became less and less comfortable at home. When I wanted to clear my head, I would go to school and hear things like 'obirin-asuko', a Yoruba term that means boy-girl. Or 'obirin-okurin'; those kinds of terms. And they were used in a friendly way. So to me, it seemed as if the people at school were the ones who were okay, treating me like I was okay. But when I got home, I would only get a fight from my family.

When I entered university, I breathed a deep sigh of relief. It wasn't a nice environment but at least it made me mingle with people. People who seemed to appreciate me as a person. I met people who, if they saw you being harassed, would say, 'Hey, stop am.' These people didn't come up to you and say, 'Let's be friends.' But anytime they had the opportunity to defend you, they would defend you and walk away.

I was staying in Sultan Bello, a male hostel at the University of Ibadan, and it was so adventurous. People often wondered, 'Is that a boy, or is that a girl?' 'Na boy, abi na girl?' And I just walked without giving a hoot. Sometimes I would wear bum shorts because I loved to flaunt my legs, right from when I was living as a boy. And guys would hit on me. They knew I was a boy and yet they still came to me.

What I loved then was that I was doing what they call

'shakara' – show off. I was not interested in a relationship or even sex; I just loved myself. And so a guy would come up and express himself saying, 'I like you.' When I said no, he'd hurl insults at me – your papa, your mama – in frustration at being turned down. Some of them would then go to their girlfriends and say, 'That guy na fag; he approached me.' A lot of people frown at homosexuality and transsexuality, but so many of them are in their closets.

I didn't give a hoot. I realised that I had to be strong for myself. You will not touch a small part of me and get away with it. I will retaliate on the spot so that you know I am not weak. They tend to harass the community. When the victim backs down, they keep doing it. They keep harassing us. But when you stand out and face them, they tend to back off. It doesn't mean I didn't have enemies at university, but at least everybody knew me as that beautiful boy. Some people would want to connect with me. Some would run from across the street to touch me. I felt like I belonged, contrary to what my family said, that people would stone me. Yes, when I was at home I had such experiences. Even while I was in school, I had such experiences, but they were not much.

Sultan Bello was a male hall but they hosted something called Ms Bello, where men dressed as women, like a drag or something. Macho guys would put up their pictures and everybody would come laugh. Even the Vice Chancellor sometimes attended. It was a very nice social event. They told me that I could do the Ms Bello, so I put up my picture and all the contestants backed off because I was exceptional. They said, 'No, this is Ms Bello, s/he has the crown.'

That was a beautiful day I will not forget, because it was the first time I expressed myself as a lady to the full glare of everyone. Other halls came: Independence, Idia, Queens, Kuti, Melambi, Tedder. I was the only one competing for the crown. It was the first time I expressed myself with my hair, make-up and outfit, and I glowed. They said the Ms Bello should dance to a song, so I played *Crazy in Love* by Beyoncé and oh my goodness! I danced freely. I shook my bum, my tiny bum. I did everything. And because the show was within the hall space, it lasted till two in the morning.

When it was over I removed the feminine attire, the make-up and everything I'd used to express my true self, and went back to the life where I couldn't express myself. I became sad, but that memory lingered. If this kind of thing could happen, then I could see the future. It meant that there would come a time when I could live in that dream, not just enjoy it once, remove it, and drop it on the side.

I was so excited that I called my mum, who I had not spoken to for a long time, and told her, 'Guess what? I did this thing and it was so exciting ...'

But she was antagonistic. Before I could say Jack Robinson I started receiving threatening messages: Oh you have started sleeping with men eh, ooohhhh, you have now sold your star, homosexual, blah blah blah. I said I had not started sleeping with men. I had not even had a boyfriend. I'd just expressed myself. The woman in me was crying for release and she came back! I felt sad. I became depressed. Later, I realised that my mum was communicating with L___, one of my best friends. L___ just turned her back on me and started insulting me.

But I was lucky; some people stood up for me. One of those people was the supervisor in charge of my project, Professor M___. I was scared of her at first, but she made me feel free.

I remember the day L___ stabbed me in the back. She said

'No, no, no. You can't take pictures with us cos we are taking a final-year picture. Are you a he, a she or an it? In fact, you are a disgrace to your mother!' I told Professor M___. When I entered her office, she was combing her gold hair and looking at her reflection on her laptop. I told her what had happened and she said, 'Nobody has the right to infringe upon your rights!' Then she looked at me and said, 'I have heard so much about you. Why don't you start wearing earrings, necklaces and other jewellery? Please, express your feminine side!'

I looked at her and thought, *Shoo, is it this woman who is telling me this?* I was impressed. In my final year, I started putting on earrings and strutting my stuff. Professor M___ even made me meet some social workers at school.

Another person who looked out for me was I___. She was a poet and a dancer. She was the mother I never had and she made me super strong. She was a phenomenal person. She taught me dance. She taught me choreography. She taught me to be bold about who I was. She called me 'Woman' even before I started to. I could not accept it at the time, but I was always free around her. She was strict and disciplined, yet open. People didn't understand her, but I did. If she screamed at me, I understood. She used to call me 'JP', which means 'sweet to have' in Yoruba, and was always telling me, 'Look, the world is bigger than what you think, JP.'

There was a day in 2009 when my mum used my brothers to beat me. They locked me up inside the room, but at 11pm, I___, who was in Ibadan, rescued me. She called a doctor who was a friend, told him how to get to our place and he got me out of the house.

I had to move on. I didn't go back home. During the holidays, I stayed at the hostel. They normally didn't send people away because there were 400-level[1] students who wanted to do projects. My mum would say, 'Come back home. You're sleeping with a man,' but I just ignored it all. Sometimes I received text messages from my friends, from people who were at home. I ignored them too.

Some people at school were transphobic but at least the people who stood up were like, 'No, uhm uhm, let her be.' A person who detested me once gathered the whole department for the kind of meeting where students discuss departmental issues, but this time they were castigating, talking rubbish about me. A lecturer came in and annulled the whole thing. He called me and told me what they were saying.

For the most part, though, I was favoured. I am eternally grateful to UI. I doubt if there are other schools like the University of Ibadan. I had one HOD who took a shine to me and other people who cared about me. In fact, all the women who groomed me were powerful and wild in a positive way. The wires in their brains used to touch. They thought outside the box. They were strong and hated injustice. Sometimes they were super aggressive. Somehow, I fell under the tutelage of such women.

When I was finishing university, it was assumed that I wouldn't do my NYSC[2]. But I served in Kaduna State. Note, I had not had any surgery but I was presenting as female by then and everybody was like, 'Oh, she has had the surgery.' I just had to keep it mute. But deep down I was freaked out by the fact that when I went to serve, I would stay in an all-female space. *Oh my goodness,* I thought. *How am I going to do it? Oh my God!* But I did. I was lucky because I was given the last hall in the female hostel and there were only ten of us. The halls are spacious with lots of bunks so I could do whatever I had to do.

In the past, I'd acted Ms Bello but now I was living the dream. So when people tried to convince me to contest for Ms NYSC, I refused. They would have to dress me up and we might reach a stage where I'd stand naked before a couple of people. So I said no.

During my service, there was a guy who was pampering me. My clothes were washed. Everything I needed was sorted out. I dared not tell this person that I was trans. To this day, he still doesn't know, but he was so interested in me, spoiling me with everything I needed. Other men would also make passes at me, but I could not tell them, 'Look, this is who I am.' Some of them, I would see them and like them. Some of them would come up to me and say, 'I love you' and all I could do was watch with teary eyes and say to myself, *I wish I could tell you who I am.* They would look at me like I was a heartbreaker, mean or wicked. But all that time, I was thinking, *I can't say anything.*

When I finally started working, men were still making passes at me. I knew I was attracted to men. I started accepting myself, understanding myself a little bit. Around that time, I had a two-bedroom flat all to myself, so there was that privacy and that happiness. At least I was no longer acting the dream, even though getting to that stage had not been easy.

To date, my mum still has not accepted me. I am not really bothered about that. One of my brothers turned against her and started protecting me. He said, 'For goodness sake, nobody wants to be persecuted. Nobody wants to go on the streets and see people stoned. Nobody wants it so don't make it look like that for my sister.' He refers to me by the proper pronoun. 'Please take care of my sister,' he will tell me.

'Please be careful of mummy. Mummy is still on your neck. Be careful. If she invites you somewhere, please don't go.' When I am financially challenged, he will send money to me. This was someone who was an attacking bulldog, pinning me down with his strength. He said he did his own research and started studying and studying.

When I was still in school, my family told him they wanted to take me to the hospital to have my hormones measured and get female hormones so I could live as a woman. I knew that was a lie but they tricked him. They hired a cab and took me to the psych ward in LASUTH[3]. My brother was like, 'You people told me we were going to the place where they will check her hormones. What am I seeing here?'

'I told you,' I said, but he could not see it. He wanted to give them some benefit of the doubt.

But inside, he noticed that one of the nurses gripped my hand, not with care, but in a tight fist. When they started taking me away, he flared up. 'This is not the deal. This is not what you told me. Oh my goodness, you wanted to operate on her.'

It wasn't long before they called the doctor in charge of psychiatry. By the time he came, they had registered me as male, so he asked, 'Who is Mr. So-and-so?' When he saw this female-presenting person, he said, 'Oh, I understand.' He asked me for my name, I told him, and he accepted it. And the tables turned.

He took me inside his office to talk. He was not trying to change my mind; he was talking to me to make peace. He said, 'I have come across these cases. From the look of things, it's your family that needs psychiatric evaluation. I am going to call them in.'

They claimed that they wanted to give me male hormones. The doctor said, 'Do you know what you are talking about? To give male hormones, you have to obtain consent. Or else she could commit suicide.'

They kept saying, 'We don't care, we just want ...'

'Wait, you don't care?' he said. 'You don't care about her life?' He printed a document on intersexuality and transsexuality and gave it to them. 'Go and read,' he told them. From that moment on, my younger brother started shifting ground. That doctor played a big role.

My mum and brother tried again when a doctor from the UK came to join the discussion. She didn't know who I was and said, 'This lady is beautiful. What's going on?' My mum and my brother shouted my birth name. The UK doctor said, 'Oh, we understand. Did we give them anything on intersex and transsexuality?' They said, 'We did but they seem to be very stubborn.'

The doctors said that from the look of things, they needed to give me female hormones and take me to Israel to do a sex change. The doctors were talking about doing it free of charge and my mum and brother stopped taking me to the hospital. They continued their persecution but this time they could not go far with it as my younger brother refused to participate. Their bulldog wasn't there to attack me any more. He said to them, 'No, you were not straightforward. It seems as if you were wrong all this while. You people don't want to face the truth.' Since then he has evolved. He calls me his sister. From the way he talks now, my brother has really changed for the good. My mum is always afraid of laying a hand on me because of him.

I still maintain contact with my mum. I am just careful

with her. The last time I saw her was June 2014 but she called me last month. Sometimes she talks to me once a week. It depends. Sometimes she pretends. She refers to me as 'she' but I know it is a 'he' in her head. I was in a relationship last year. She came and ruined it. She tried to make the guy sabotage me. I got wind of it so the guy and I went our separate ways. We'd been together for a year and he'd abused my mind, always threatening to out me. That was after I went to Belgium.

Everything changed in Belgium. When you change environments, you get some fresh air. You go out and see people who appreciate you. Even looking at you is enough of a compliment. My eyes opened and I tasted the forbidden fruit of freedom. Now I know what is good and bad.

Over time, I have had lots of people stand up for me. I can't pick one but let me tell you about some of them.

A long time ago, I wanted to seek asylum and leave Nigeria, but I never knew the processes. So I went to the Dutch embassy and they helped me. They asked if I had a degree and I said I did. They said, 'You are a trans woman and you have a degree. Do you know how many people have degrees and are presenting as women?' So they put me in touch with Z___. He looked at me twice and said there was no way he would let me go out. 'You are going to work with us,' he said, and that is how I got my first job. He made me feel free. We could fight. I could express myself and say, 'No, this is wrong.' He treated me like everyone else, without being personal about it.

I eventually got another job, but you know how it is when you go to work and it is boring because you are not doing anything serious and nothing is challenging you? I got my salary working on HIV and AIDS but those were not the primary needs of the trans community. I got that job expecting to attend to trans needs, but I wasn't, so I left.

Z___ and I organised a conference on trans and intersex people. Now, we are trying to get a sub-grant to start an organisation focused on trans and intersex people in Nigeria. I am vocal. I am ready to flaunt who I am unapologetically. If you want to tell me rubbish, I'll give it back to you. And I realised that the trans and intersex community has been marginalised and put aside. Many trans women and trans men are seen as lesbian or gay and so they are not fully understood. Most people, even those who work in this field, do not know anything about trans or intersex issues. I was talking to one who believed that a trans person must switch and look either feminine or masculine in presentation. What of those who are intersex, I asked. They assumed the person must have two genitalia, and I was like, Oh my goodness! You are so wrong! I explained the definition of an MSM according to a trans. 'An MSM is a trans man who is attracted to a man,' I said. 'A trans MSM – that is someone who went from female to male – is a woman to you, but to this person, they are male and they sleep with men.'

I am a one-partner person. With my first crush, I couldn't say anything as it was someone I tripped for when I was seven. I fell in love for the first time in university. He was bisexual but wouldn't accept his sexuality. He was also the first person I kissed. We separated when we went to serve. The last time we saw each other was five years ago, and once in a while he still calls me. I think sometimes he wishes we did not break up, but I moved on a long time ago.

I never really had a steady date back then because I was

being security conscious. I met my current partner online. We got chatting for a long time before we met in person. It took a long time for me to tell him who I was because we were always talking about sexuality and other things. I said I was not interested in a relationship with him but that my friend might be. He asked who the friend was. I told him it was a trans woman and he got the gist: 'A trans woman, really? I would love to meet such a person.' Whenever we chatted, he asked about the trans woman, saying he would love to meet her. So I said, 'Okay, you must not disappoint her.' I gave him a fake name and my other number. But when I saw his number calling I would not pick.

One day I told him I was the trans woman. He didn't believe me. I said, 'Yes I am a trans woman,' and started explaining things to him. 'And the number you gave to me?' he asked. I said, 'That is my number' and he was like, 'So that's why you didn't pick.' I said, 'Yes, that is why I didn't pick.'

He travelled from Port Harcourt to meet me here in Abuja. I have a very good relationship with him and he has been supportive. I feel very loved by him. For someone to say, 'Look, you don't have to do the surgery to be accepted,' is an encouraging thing. In my previous relationships, I couldn't even stand naked in front of someone or feel free walking around. Most times, trans people don't like what is between their legs, especially when they have not transitioned. Now I am indifferent because my partner tells me, 'Look, I am not interested in what is between your legs. With or without surgery, you are okay.' I can walk freely without someone saying, 'Don't remind me that I am sleeping with a guy' or 'It makes me feel like I am sleeping with a guy.' My partner has even gone as far as trying to introduce me to his mum and grandmum.

He is unshakable and tells me, 'Who cares when they come to know who you are?' Because many of our mutual friends are his family members, I'm always asking, 'What if people find out?' He says, 'Come out. Let them send me whatever. Let them say they disown me. I don't care.' So we moved on and got this far. When I asked him what he'd do if his parents found out about me, he said, 'I will bullshit them and be with you. As a matter of fact, I think it is high time you started flaunting.' Now I am the one telling him to slow down. He has been wonderful, if not perfect. I feel free with him.

As with life, everything has this ripple effect, this domino effect. All the things that happen to women I now experience, especially the power play between sexes: men making passes at you and believing it is their right to have sex with you or rape you. Men calling you 'ashawo'. If you disagree with them or stand up to them, you must be a prostitute. I didn't understand, before, how a woman could get raped and not scream or speak out. Now I understand. People say, 'Ah, she is a woman. She should have screamed. She should have fought back.' I look at them in consternation. They are talking from the point of view of a man with masculine strength. I now know that it is not a woman's fault. It is not our fault.

I was nearly raped as a guy and I stood my ground. But when I was living as a woman, the same thing happened and the person nearly conquered me. I had just met this person, and he wanted to get me tipsy but I refused. I was fully confident in my strength and thought he couldn't try rubbish with me. I didn't realise that I was no longer as strong. Since my place was close by, I thought it was okay to walk home even though he was complaining. When we got to the end of the junction to get a cab, this guy turned and slapped me, held me and dragged me to a waiting bike. This happened fast and I was in shock. When I came to myself, I started whispering to the bike driver, 'This guy wants to rape me. You have a sister. You have a mother. Help me.' The driver stopped and the would-be rapist started beating me, saying 'Imagine o, my wife is misbehaving.' But the bike man turned and started fighting the rapist. Passersby heard the sounds, and helped me get away. I was just thinking, *Ah, he mustn't find out who I am. If he can be this violent, he shouldn't know. He mustn't know.*

Sometimes when I'm sick, I can't go to the hospital because they ask me all manner of questions: When was your last period? Have you had any abortions? All these questions that don't apply. You can't open your mouth and tell them that you are a trans woman. I don't come out to doctors. I did once, a long time ago, but Nigerian doctors like playing politics. They said that I would have to take hormones for a very long time before the effects would even start manifesting. Then the price: they said that to take hormones for a month would cost N300,000. When I came to Kaduna State for NYSC, I priced all those hormones and they cost less than N30,000. I was shocked. It was affordable. I took them once and the effects showed faster than what I'd expected. But I stopped taking hormones after that first time. I chose to plan for the future, to get ready and restart. When I start I will not take it for a long time. Probably one year, two years to three years and I will stop. I always pass for female anyway. I became patient. When the time comes, I will take the hormones.

I used to want surgery but now I am indifferent. Patience is the most important lesson I have learned in life. You will get what you want. Never lose focus. No matter what, never lose focus, ever.

Another thing I am proud of is me. I am not a proud person, but I love the fact that I am confident. Even when I was living as a guy, no one could come and spit trash to me or try to break my spirit, no, uh uh. I do not let it happen.

I am not a religious person. I am a spiritual person. They say that religion is the opium of the masses and some people play that religious card too often. They go, 'The Bible says' or 'The Quran says God hates your type.' To beat religion at its game, you have to study it. What did the scripture say? What did it mean? What was it implying? I tell people the Bible is like a pharmacy. In it you find expired goods and you find recent stuff. Study it like it is the law. You need to understand it so they can't twist it. I can't imagine going to a Bible that says that if you have a stubborn child throw him off the edge of a cliff or something. It also says that it is a sin to eat crayfish or wear garments made of more than one fabric. So if you want to bring the religious card to me, I will go and study that religion very well so I can give it back to you, with facts.

In the future, I see myself living with my partner. We would have adopted kids, probably two, have cats and dogs and be in Nigeria, probably Abuja. I want to bring up my children so they respect all people and it will be easy for them to relate to me. My children will be able to tell me if they are gay or lesbian or trans or whatever. If people are homophobic and transphobic, I will be BIASphobic. My kids will realise that they have to respect everybody. I will lay this foundation in my children so that they pass it on to the next generation.

Outside family, I am focused on this NGO we are starting. I hope it gives birth to other NGOs and trans and intersex issues are taken seriously all over the country. I hope Nigeria becomes a tolerant place for everyone over the next fifty years.

When I was younger, I was always hoping I could live as a woman. I used to play with Barbie dolls and pray my hair was like theirs. I am very happy that dream was actualised even though I lost friends. Looking back now, I realise that I am better than them. I have moved on in life. That taught me a lesson. No one can be your best friend except you.

– JP, age 33, Lagos/Ogun /Abuja

---

1   400-level = Fourth year at university

2   NYSC = National Youth Service Corps

3   LASUTH = Lagos State University Teaching Hospital

I Pray That Everyone Has Forgotten

'I wouldn't put a word on my identity. It's just something I do.'

Content Note: Intercommunal Violence, Physical Violence

My family is from Gombe but I was born and brought up in Jos. I stay in Abuja now.

I can remember just a little from when I was small. We are six – four brothers and two sisters. I'm the last. As a child, I was very friendly. I spoke like a parrot, seriously. My mum was busy, always doing housework and selling small provisions at home. People came in all the time to buy rice, beans, oil and many other things. I was excited when there was a knock at the door – this meant I had to check what it was the person wanted, get it and sell it to them. It was almost like playing. My mum was a busy type but my dad was always there with us. He played with us whenever he was at home. He made sure we felt his presence as a dad. Even now, he is both my dad and my friend. He is the most important person in my life.

We were happy in Jos but everything changed when they closed down the shop my dad worked at. That's when things started getting hard for us. My siblings had to move from home and get jobs so that they could help the family. That's why I didn't start JSS1[1] until I was 11. I found it very difficult because I didn't have the foundation. I had to start from the bottom, so it was not easy, but I tried harder and I picked it up.

And then the Jos crisis started. It was terrible. Very, very terrible. We suffered a lot, running helter-skelter, seeing things we couldn't forget, seeing how people kill, seeing people die every day ... All the killings and bomb blasts, here and there. You would be moving and scared. We had to relocate because we were Christians and our house was close to a mosque. In Jos, Christians and Muslims are separate. You can't stay together. We went to the house of a family friend of my dad's. In that area, we were all Christians. The house was full because we were two families. You didn't really sleep at night, scared that something might happen. You'd hear people shouting and screaming. You'd see them running and you would start running too, not knowing where to, just running because you were scared and confused. It was horrible.

I moved to Kano when I was 15 or 16. My brother was there and I had to stay with him and his wife after they got married to help them in the house. Kano was better than the conflict in Jos but I found it difficult to live in too. We Christians had to behave like the Muslims so peace could reign. You had to fast during their fasting period. We women had to be careful what we wore. It's a big case if you're caught by the Hisbah Board!

I had lots of friends at school though. I'm a noisy type and everywhere I enter, people like me. I don't bear malice. If you do something to me, I'll tell you and be done with it. I'm friendly, free and open-minded.

There was a girl I liked at school. I don't really know how it started; I just found myself in it. What I felt for her was definitely more than friendship. I loved everything about her.

There were so many girls in relationships with each other at school. Some would tell me how they felt about me. I never gave anyone a chance because I liked that one girl, but for years I didn't say anything. I was worried. How would she look at me? Would she feel the same way? Would she be mad at me? Would we start having problems? Maybe she wasn't that type? I was thinking about so many things that I did not have the courage to speak my mind.

At the end of our last semester at school, we had to be free. We started sharing our feelings. And she told me that she felt the same. What was on my mind was on hers too. She liked me and I liked her the whole time but we were both pretending. I'd been waiting for her to say it and she'd been waiting for me.

One day after that conversation, I went to her house. She called me sweet, sweet names. I was confused and surprised. She wanted something to happen but she was leaving Kano and I didn't want to start something I couldn't finish. Even now, the love is still there. We call each other and speak.

Some years later, I met my girlfriend. We bumped into each other at a market. I dropped the nylon I was holding and she picked it up for me. She apologised and I told her, 'Okay, no problem.' She told me that she loved the way I talked; could she get my contact? I gave it to her.

She called me in the night asking where I stayed and if she could visit me. I said, 'Why not?' So I gave her an appointment. She came one afternoon and we gisted for hours. Things happened from there, just like that. We kissed. We did lots of crazy things. I can't explain what happened. It was the first time I had ever done anything with another girl. And it felt good.

When we finished, I looked at her and she looked at me. I had never liked a man, even before. I can tell when a man is handsome but nothing else is in my mind. But I was still very, very surprised.

We're still together. It has been four or five years now. Our relationship is perfect. It's good to have someone who loves you back. You will feel happy whenever you're with that person. M___ is very caring. If I'm sick, she will be sick. She makes me crazy because she's so caring and friendly.

All was well until her uncle caught us. We were alone in her house and he came in and saw us. He screamed and gave her the beating of her life. I had to run out of the house. He told her dad. Everybody in her family now knows. He told my brother and his wife too. My brother asked me if it was true. I said it was and that it was the only thing that made me happy. I wouldn't be happy with a man. I didn't hide anything from my brother. I told him the truth.

It has affected my relationship with him. Even though we talk and gist, he looks at me without the respect he had before. He told me that he would keep praying for me to stop this thing. He said he knew it was not me, that it was a spirit and I should work on it. Everybody was mad at us. I was scared. I had to leave Kano and move to Abuja.

It's really hard in Abuja. I had a job as a cook for a family in Kano, but I've been looking for work ever since I came to Abuja. Anywhere I go, people say, 'No work.' Everywhere – no work, no work, no work. It's very hard. I'm tired.

For M___, it's not been easy. They chased her out of

the house after what happened. She's on her own now, struggling for survival. She is in contact with her family but the relationship isn't there any more. I feel bad. She passes through a lot for my sake. I shouldn't have left her in the first place.

Every day, her mum calls her and tells her that she should stop all this nonsense. That's why she had to find a guy and they're dating now. I've spoken to him on the phone. He thinks I'm just her friend in Abuja. He's a cool guy. He's trying his best to see that she gets back home. He tells her dad and mum that they should please forgive her. They didn't tell him what actually happened, but he's still pleading on her behalf for the relationship to go back to what it was before.

He said that he's going to marry her. I feel bad but I'll be happy for her. There's nothing I can do. If she gets married, I can't be with her. I'll have to move on with my life.

I've met someone here in Abuja. M___ knows. I met C___ at a friend's party. I was sitting down and she sent one of her friends to say hi to me. He told me that his friend wanted to meet me. I thought it was a man, so I told him, 'Sorry, no.' He pointed to her and said, 'That's the lady there.' I walked up to her, sat down and we started gisting. She took my number. Since then, things started going on.

My mind is split in two. For me, a relationship is about an emotional connection. Maybe you have sex once in a while, when you feel like it. I don't love somebody because I want to have sex but because I like them naturally.

I feel very serious with both women. I'm confused. One mind is saying I should date only one, but I love the both of them. I feel like I'm cheating on both of them but there's nothing I can do. Every day I'll sit down and think, *Which one?* I really think it's M___. She's perfect. If I get a job for her in Abuja, she will definitely leave Kano. But I'm still looking for work so how can I tell her to come to Abuja? If I can find work, maybe I should get to know people and ask them if there is any vacancy for her. She works in a shop in Kano and I could find something like that for her here. If M___ was in Abuja, I would not be with C___. But she's not here and I need someone.

I wouldn't put a word on my identity. It's just something I do. Most of my friends know I am in a relationship with another woman. They're cool with it but I don't want my family to know. How I wish I could tell them my mind, who I really am and what I really want. I feel like I'm hiding an important thing in my life from them. It's bad. I'm supposed to tell them. We should discuss it as a family. But I can't. I'm scared of what will happen if I do that. My dad would disown me and my mum would be even worse. It would change how they treat me. My family is very close and I don't want to destroy that relationship.

I'm a devout Christian. Anything I do, I put God first. I don't play with prayer. But it's difficult. In most churches now, preaching against homosexuality is the only thing they know how to talk about. I sit there thinking, *They're wasting their time.* At times, it pisses me off when I hear people talking about it, criticising people who are doing it. It makes me feel very bad because I'm one of them. I feel as if I'm the worst sinner. I think, *How will this thing that I have started end?* But what I'm doing is not wrong. Or it's wrong but we can't help it.

My ideal future is settling down and having kids with someone I love. Marrying a woman? How I wish it could happen. I can't date a guy. I don't even think of marrying any man. But being married to my girlfriend would make such a difference. You know you will be together with the person you love for your entire life. I would love to have children but it's not possible. At times, I think about playing with my own kid. I would be open with them. I would teach them awareness. I would tell them not to have prejudice.

I'm planning to go to Kano next month to see M___. Yesterday, I sat down and imagined what it would be like. Will people look at me and call me all sorts of names? How can I look at my brother and his wife? How can I go to M___'s house to even look at her? I disappointed her by running away. I just pray that nothing is going to happen. I pray that everyone has forgotten.

– TQ, age 27, Gombe / Plateau

---

1   JSS1 = Junior Secondary School 1

Love Is Not Wrong

'Loving another person and that person loving me back – I do not see how that is a bad thing.'

A regular day for me is waking up, going to work, hanging out with my girlfriend, heading home. I wake up around six and make breakfast. I shower, go to the office, then work, work, work, although I sometimes take a break. My girlfriend finishes work at 5pm, so from then onwards it is girlfriend time. Usually she meets me at the office, then we go find somewhere to hang out. Some days, I go home early and other days I stay out. We also have date nights, usually on Fridays.

The most important people in my life have been my siblings and my mum. I grew up with my siblings and we are very close. I do not talk to them as often as I should but they are important to me. I have a hard time explaining to people that although I am not good at keeping in touch, it does not mean I love you any less.

My formative years were in a state in the south-south of Nigeria, which was then outside the country. I also lived in the north with my parents. Those days revolved around waking up to go to school, extracurricular lessons, then going home to play until it was time for dinner, then bed. One time we were supposed to have the end-of-year party at school but I got the dates mixed up so I went dressed in my fancy clothes while everybody else was in uniform. The other kids laughed at me but I was already there so the teachers just let me be in school like that for the day. It wasn't nice and it did not feel good.

While growing up, there was mostly school work and chores. I was responsible for stuff like washing plates, cooking and cleaning. I cooked for the house. I later realised that if you're asked to do anything and you fuck it up at first, they will never ask you again. But if you do it well, you're hooked for life. That is the mistake I made. I cooked well when I was asked and I have been cooking for the family ever since.

Even as a kid I did not like pink or girly stuff, but I liked video games. I still do. I liked to ride bicycles. I didn't really get into books till JSS3[1] or SS1[2]. I was also getting into music. At that point, it was reggae, patios, that kind of thing. Then I came across rap albums like *Rappers' Delight* and I was like, *Oh wow!* Which led to my Eminem phase. I think I can still sing Eminem songs in my sleep. I listened to Foxy Brown – whose lyrics were very explicit for that time – Coolio, Biggie, Ice Cube ... but I didn't listen to Tupac until much later. I also listened to a lot of TLC's *CrazySexyCool* album.

I had a later phase where I was sort of girly, then secondary school happened and I felt very awkward. I tried to be girly around JSS1 and it somehow didn't fit. My whole JSS1 was awkward but by JSS3 I had found myself and I was like nah, no more awkward.

I dated this dude from JSS2[3] to JSS3. I was dared to kiss him one day. I did. We started hanging out. He liked to play and I liked to play so that was good. It was a full-on kiss but it wasn't my first. I was a naughty, curious child and I had kissed way before that. I had kissed about four boys by then. Some were in my class in primary school and some were friends at home. We'd kissed and never talked about it afterwards. It was more about kids being childish, probably after we saw something on TV.

The first person I had a crush on was my family friend, some dude. He was very quiet and I think that was what I liked about him. I was in primary school so I was really young and quite curious. He was one of those I kissed a couple of times. We used to play hide and seek and he used to like to hide with me so we would kiss. It never became more than that and the most we did was hold hands. Eventually we left primary school and I guess that was how we grew out of it.

But those were all close-mouthed kisses and anything before French kisses doesn't count. My first French kiss was in JSS1 and it was terrible! Funny enough, I didn't like him. He annoyed me. But we got to talking one day in the library. We had this farm so we went to the farm to make out and I hated it. Too much tongue, too much everything! And he had a smell about him. It wasn't a bad smell per se, just weird. Long after that, I could still smell it. Thank God it didn't put me off kissing.

My first female crush was not until SS3[4]. Quite late, I know. After dating my then boyfriend, I wasn't interested in anyone till I fell for her in SS3. And it was more like a *Huh, what is happening to me?* kind of thing. I was quite confused about it. I was confused about who I was; that awkward teenage angst. I can't say what it was about her but we used to talk a lot. We were friends in SS1 but we never really used to talk, and only said hi until we got to SS3. I started talking to her, then one day realised I was attracted to her. I started thinking about her, wanting to be with her. I would write in my diary and question myself: *What is happening to me?* She was and still is my friend but I didn't tell her about this until a couple of years later when I started dating someone else.

I also wrote poetry. I think every teenager feels like they have some deep things to talk about. I can't even remember what I wrote but I tried to make the stuff I wrote about her vague. Even when I wrote in my diary, I wrote in code. You can't write that kind of thing in the open. So I would change names and everything.

There was already this stigma then. I remember the first time I heard that slur cos I went to a mixed school and those things never used to come up. But there was this junior girl in JSS3 who had apparently been caught with another girl. All they did was touch. I think they were making out when they were caught. They said she had been with many girls. They made it seem like she went on a rampage and was just pressing girls. I didn't think it was such a big deal. I kept thinking, *Why is everybody angry?* She didn't force any of these girls to do anything so why did they make it seem like that? Making out means the other person participated.

Anyway, I don't think it went all the way to school authorities but all the students were talking about it and she was punished. She had a strong personality so I don't think she was fazed but I guess it still affected her cos she was young, regardless of how strong her personality was. Most of the homophobia I experienced was in school. People did not say it to my face; they said it behind me. Other people just had something to talk about. I have a couple of friends who stopped talking to me. But I didn't really mind those people because I felt that I still had friends who supported me, so fuck the rest. To this day I do not even know where they are. I feel that if you can stop talking to someone, that friendship is meaningless.

The first time I kissed a girl was in SS3. The same girl I had a crush on. The circumstances were weird because even though she was straight, she suggested we practice kissing. It was a proper kiss and because I already had a crush on her, I was like *yeeeaaahhh!!!* After that, I wanted to practice again but I was too chicken to ask.

My first relationship with a girl was in my first year of university. We were together for three years. I used to see her around. She always said hello to me and kept asking me to come visit her. I came over once, then invited her to my place. We started hanging out and one day she asked if she could kiss me. I was like, 'Okay' and that was how that happened.

I have to have conversations with you and make a connection before I can be romantically involved. With her, it had already progressed. I was already attracted to her when that happened. She was really pretty and we had spent a lot of time just talking and getting to know each other. We were just kissing and making out, and we didn't have sex for a really long time.

She had been with girls before and wanted to take it to the next level. I was not sure I wanted to. I was still not sure about my sexuality. I can't believe I wasted so much time! She still teases me about it. I think it was partly because of my upbringing; growing up you hear about so many things you shouldn't do. I wasn't so sexual then.

She was the first girl I was with but I had been with a guy before. I had wanted to get rid of my virginity so I picked a guy for the job. I went to his room. We were young adults so it wasn't that hard, but it was horrible. It didn't hurt. It was just uncomfortable. After we were done, I packed my things and was just like, 'See you later.' I felt more like, *Is that all?* I didn't have second thoughts but it lacked the oomph.

I was expecting fireworks and there were none. But I found fireworks when I was dating my girlfriend, when I became more sexually aware, I guess. We would hold hands and we moved in together so I guess we were pretty out there. We would never make out in public but it was obvious that we were together.

The relationship was rocky. I didn't really have a lot of relationships with guys, cos it never worked out but because my girlfriend and I were on and off, I'd have flings. I like to believe that I followed the principle of it; when we were on, I was faithful but when we weren't, I had those flings. I felt like I needed to do or try something different and that was all part of my experimentation. But, after the break-up I stopped dating men. It was a bad break-up and I was really low so I had to sit down and evaluate everything. I finally accepted myself. I eventually met a nice girl and that went well ... till it didn't.

I practice monogamy now but I have cheated in the past. I think I have cheated enough to know that I shouldn't. Even if you don't get caught, it still fucks up your relationship: you have done something so you are always suspecting the other person of doing something too.

My girlfriend and I have been together for over two years now. I met her while hanging out at a restaurant in town with a friend. There was this girl with my friend, like a shining light. We got to talking and I could tell she was into me so I got her number. She lived close to where I worked so I asked if I could take her to her workplace and see her after work. We started seeing each other every day after work. This went on for a while.

There was that initial lust but I wanted to be sure it wasn't just lust. I wanted to be sure that I would like to spend time with her. And even though we were not yet dating, we were hooking up. Hooking up is part of the decision-making because what if you agree to date but find that the sex is not happening? I doubt it would work out. She asked me out a couple of days after we started talking but I had just got out of a relationship so I wasn't ready to jump into another one. I told her to wait and, exactly a month later, I said yes.

The best part of being in a relationship is having someone to talk to and disturb. Having a person you can call when you see something random on the road, when you are sad, or just having someone who understands you, to an extent, and takes your bullshit. The hard part is that I like my alone time. What my girlfriend doesn't like about me is my need to be alone sometimes. I sometimes forget that I have to consider that I am in a relationship with someone and I can't just pick up and zap.

I do not think there is any difference between dating men and dating women. People are people. You just need to know the kind of person you are, what you can handle and what you can handle from the other person. I think people expect you to be a certain way when you are dating men and a different way when you are dating women. I think that's bullshit.

This is also something that I find with women. When you are a tomboy, they expect you to act like a man, but I don't think that is how it should be. I shouldn't have to pay all your bills if I take you out. I am a woman, even if I like to wear pants.

Thank God my girlfriend and I have no gender roles in our relationship. I am tomboyish in my dressing because I like to be comfortable but there are days when I wear a skirt. I own a few skirts and dresses and I have days when I want to wear something different, even though those days come maybe once or twice a year. I don't wear make-up, just lip balm and sometimes I use black eye pencil. She recently shaped my eyebrows. She said she was trying to define them. She is cool like that. But she likes dresses. She has tons of clothes and I think half of her wardrobe is more than my full wardrobe. She is more feminine-presenting but that still doesn't give us gender roles. For an outsider, I guess it might look that way but, to us, not at all.

Indoors, my friends are tired of me cos my girlfriend and I are always showing affection as long as we are among people who we know and are comfortable with. But in Nigeria, if I go out with my girlfriend, I try not to be affectionate because you just don't know. Like if we go clubbing, we do not dance with each other. We kind of dance apart. Around certain people, we also try not to call each other by pet names, which is really hard because it is subconscious. We just generally try not to be obvious.

I had an incident where someone saw me with a girl. I do not know where or when but the person brought the news home and there was this whole issue. My mum made me laugh when she said it was something that happens in secondary school, that it was something I was supposed to get over. I guess that was how she saw it – you leave it behind when you leave school. I just told her I had heard her. That was the end of that conversation. I think in some parts of their heads they know, but they are afraid to have the conversation.

I am out to my siblings. In my early twenties, one of my siblings straight up asked me and I said yes. My other siblings and I never officially had the conversation. I always felt that if I ever dated someone serious enough, I would introduce her to them. Finally, I met someone who I was serious with so I told them. One of my siblings said she had been waiting for me to tell her. Even though she knew about it, she didn't want to bring it up. I told her she was wasting time cos everyone asked me since. I then introduced her to my girlfriend and they talked over the phone.

The first person I actually sat down with and thought, *Fuck it, I am just going to tell*, was a good friend. I told her I had a girlfriend. And she was cool. I really like how she handled it. She didn't make it seem any different from anyone. She didn't ask me any questions and she was just like, 'That is cool.' There was no issue and it was totally normal, like if I had a boyfriend. And since then she has been a very, very close friend.

I don't have any close friends I am not out to. It is not worth it. I feel like I have to pretend to the world and at home so why add the people I choose to be around me? All my close friends know. I know there is a queer community. I know where to find them but I am not really part of the community yet. I would like to do more stuff with them. I have only gone to two queer events and I quite enjoyed them, especially the last one. The event itself wasn't wow but I was comfortable. I was happy and I could dance with my girlfriend in public. That was what I enjoyed most.

When I was younger and I imagined the future, I figured I would be on my own by now. I definitely imagined having more money but the harsh reality isn't so. I knew I would follow my passion, which is very important, so that part is not too different.

Ten years from now, I imagine I will be married. I want a dog, although my girlfriend doesn't, so maybe I will settle for a turtle. I think turtles are low maintenance, as they do not move around much. My girlfriend wants a kid but I am not sure yet. I do not know what I feel about kids, but if we end up having any, it'll be just one. I don't think I want more than that.

I most likely will not be living here. I don't think I want to be married and still be hiding. My girlfriend and I have talked about moving abroad, but wherever we end up has to be gay-friendly. In a perfect world, I will be in Nigeria. I will have my girlfriend in Nigeria, have my family in Nigeria, have my work, my life – everything here.

But Nigeria is very disappointing. I try to block out the part about the same-sex law. All I know about the law is that if they catch you, you are going to jail for fourteen years. You and the people around you. I heard rape gets fewer years in prison. I guess the legislature just wants to be busy by doing something. I do not think we will ever get rid of this law. And if we do, it'll take, like, a hundred years. I feel like we are too wrong – in policies, priorities, everything.

I know fourteen years stands out but even before the act came out, it wasn't any different. Nothing has changed for me because whatever I was doing before, I am still doing now. They have just brought it into the limelight. I guess the effect of the law is that people need to hide more, but I was already hiding. The law has made me a little more careful but that is about all. I guess it would have more of an effect on people with a different lifestyle.

The kind of lifestyle I live is more of a secluded one. I meet the same friends, in the same circle so I do not exactly have to sit down in groups of people who are homophobic. I make a conscious effort to distance myself from homophobic people. I can meet you and if I can tell you are intolerant, I will not hang out with you – except perhaps on social media. Sometimes, when I get tired of that, I get angry, pissed off and switch off my phone.

It also helps that, in my line of work, there is less judgement. My work is like an expression of self so we have fewer people judging. I am not saying there isn't judgement, but there is less of it in our community. I even know a couple of queer people in my line of work.

I believe in God but not religion. I think it divides people and I do not like that about religion. I also do not believe God is going to smite me for loving. Loving another person and that person loving me back – I do not see how that is a bad thing. If you kill somebody, steal from somebody or do something without a person's consent, then that is wrong. But love is not wrong.

– OF, age 30, Abuja

---

1   JSS3 = Junior Secondary School 3

2   SS1 = Senior Secondary 1

3   JSS2 = Junior Secondary School 2

4   SS3 = Senior Secondary 3

I Only Admire Girls

'A lot has happened – both the things I remember and the ones I do not.'

Content Note: Early and Forced Marriage, Domestic Violence And Abuse, Forced Seclusion, Sexual Violence.

I'm so very excited because I've never told anyone my story before. At last I have somebody to tell my story to, somebody to share my pains with.

I grew up in a family where we were many and mostly girls. As girls from Hausaland, we lacked rights. You don't have rights to do anything until your parents say. When you get married, you still don't have rights unless your husband says so. The only right you have is when your husband divorces you and you have the right to marry another husband.

Once you reach the age of 14 or 15, they expect you to get married. If you don't get married, you will be hated. Even when you are married, the husband will not treat you right. He will always let you know you can't do this unless he says so. You don't go to school unless he agrees to it. I never wanted to get married but my dad became angry and forced me. I thought that the man I was married off to would beat me up. So I ran away.

Right now I'm scared, because when the first person came to marry me and I said I would not marry him, my dad made sure I never sat outside for two months. I was indoors at home. They didn't allow me to do anything. It's not that my mother doesn't show concern but she is under my dad. Whatever she does is what he asks her to do. I'm scared of communicating with them because I do not want anything that will make me feel uncomfortable. Where I am right now I feel safe, but at home I don't feel safe because nobody wants to listen to me. Nobody wants to know what I want and what I don't want.

It is like this for many women I know. I grew up in a village in Zamfara. My father had two wives, who are still living with him. He had four wives before. He divorced the two others. He said they didn't respect him and abide by his rules and regulations. The last one he divorced because she went to see her family and he had not asked her to do that. So he said she should go back to her mother. She left with nothing. She had four children and had to leave them behind. Men will say they are theirs and not allow you to take even one. The other wife had six children but one was late so five remained. She also had to leave them and go.

We are twenty-four children in total between the four wives. I started hawking when I was 6. My mother would send me to sell things. I used to sell groundnuts and sometimes ingredients for soup, especially in the dry season. When I started, it was inside the village. I later started crossing over to other villages.

I didn't like hawking because people want to take advantage of you. I was 8 years old when this started. Sometimes, you will go to sell things, even to the old men you think are your father. They will claim to be buying something from you. At the same time, they will be using their hand to touch you.

When I was 13, I was almost raped by some guys while going back to my village. It was with the help of an old man that I was able to get back. I told my parents. They said people do not do such things and I should keep quiet. They insisted I continue to hawk.

My sisters also went to hawk. They had their own experiences. I have a sister who was raped. I was 8 then. She is my elder sister, older than me by three years, I think. They married her to a man who had three wives. He had children older than her. The community did not know about the rape but my father told the man. When the man agreed to marry her, she said she did not want to marry him. My father said she had no choice because she had been raped and no one would want to marry her.

She is not all right. She's suffering ... When the man beats her and she comes back home, my parents say she has no right to come back home, that it's her husband and she should go back. The man also does not feed them. The other wives, their children have grown. They always bring food for their mother. But my sister, her kids have not grown up enough to give to her. Even at their little age, their father will say she should be asking the younger ones, her daughters, to go hawking. He will not let her outside. Her children go outside but he does not allow them to go to school. He will say he has no money so she should give them something to hawk so they can bring money for her to cook. Because of the experience she had, she says no. That keeps on causing problems.

So, my childhood was full of hawking and Arabic school. I went to Arabic school as far back as I can remember, although, sometimes I would go and play instead of going there. They taught us how a female child should behave and how a male child should behave. They would keep on telling us that a female child should always abide by the rules of her parents. It did not allow you to express yourself.

I first started feeling different from the other children at school when I was 9 years old. I was hard-working but didn't use make-up or do things as a female. I would always farm. I would push the truck. When I carried water, females would take one gallon, but I would take two and carry with both hands. Sometimes, I would climb on top of the horse and ride. They didn't believe a female child could do that. I used to run. I ran so much. But Islamically and in Hausaland, female children don't run. The way I ate, the way I sat, I didn't really behave as a female child. My father would say, stop that, that I'm a female child. Because of this, when I was growing up, I never saw myself as female. I saw myself as a male child.

The first time I saw a girl and liked her, I was 13 or 14. I used to tell her, 'You're beautiful. I like you.' Sometimes I would tell her, 'I admire your eyes, I like the way your lips are, I like the way you are, your structure. Everything about you looks good.' I used to say, 'Will you be my friend?' That is how it is normally. When I see a girl I like, I will think, *let me ask her if she will be my friend.*

I only admire girls. No matter how much people see how handsome a boy is, I don't see it. I will always say, 'Kai, he's not fine.' Sometimes, they will say, 'Ah, this boy is cute.' I will say, 'No! He looks rough.' But if it is a girl, I will say, 'Look at this girl. She is beautiful. I like this girl.' I have never said 'I like this boy.'

I didn't know anybody else like me except for one friend who also told me she did not feel like a girl. I told her, 'You look beautiful.' She said she had been looking at me too, that

I look beautiful. I said, 'Wow. So we have the same feelings then.' She said, yes, she liked me. I said I liked her too; let's be friends. And we became friends. We shared our feelings. When I was sad, she would hug me and say, 'Don't be sad.' A lot happened between us. She was the first one. Sometimes, she would tell me she liked me a lot. Sometimes she would say, 'Let's run away.'

But she opened up to her parents and was beaten. As in everybody, not only her mother, beat her. They called her names. So she left home. I did not have the courage to leave home at that time. I didn't know where to go and who to go to. She had a nephew who was educated so she left to stay with him in Abuja. Me, I did not know anybody. It was quite unfortunate.

After that, I knew nobody like me. I used to tell my friends that I did not feel like a female and I did not want to get married. They would say I should stop saying that. That it is not good to say it. I thought I was a male child but nobody wanted to believe me. It was only me who always saw it like that.

That was the reason I was married out. My parents thought I was behaving like a boy and so I had to get married. I never knew how they started the arrangements. One day they told me, 'You're going to be married by next week.' Just like that. I said, 'Married?' They said, 'Yes.' I said, 'But my sisters are here. They're not yet married.' I said I would not marry him, but here in the north, they do not give us that listening ear. They believe that if you say you don't want to get married, you are not a good person. They don't even listen. They say you don't have any right to say you don't want to do anything. They said I must get married. That the way I behaved scared them.

I didn't know him. I didn't know what he was like. We met the day we were married. He was older than me. He was not educated. He sold all these foodstuffs. I was the third wife. I stayed with him for three years or so. It was hell. The first time I left the house, he used this local vigilante to get me. He beat me up in their presence. The next thing he did was to make sure, just in case I went outside, that there would be somebody to ask me, 'Where are you going?' I was inside the house for two years without coming out.

Sometimes we fought. There was never peace. I was never happy. My father said I must stay, so I did not have anywhere to go. Even the security people would say, no, it's a family matter, they don't need to intervene, that you should go home and settle it. If you went home, that would not settle it. It would remain the same. He would not even take care of me. He wanted me to stay at home. Even when I was sick, I had no right to go to hospital. He would just go out and buy some drugs.

Not even only me. I have seen other women suffer the same thing. They are not given ears that listen. Nobody listens to them. Nobody wants to intervene. Nobody wants to talk.

I had a friend. She died two years ago because of her husband. She was not feeling fine but he did not allow her to go to the hospital. He said she should be treated inside the house. She died because of the illness. If she had been given the opportunity to go to hospital, she would have been fine. But we are not given that opportunity. As a Hausa girl, you cannot go out. As a Hausa girl, you cannot behave as a boy. When you behave like a boy, they despise you. They don't see you as a real human being. They will always hate you. When you say you don't want to get married, everybody will hate you. They will even give you names. If you go to school, they will say your parents are not good people. You have to get married, because that is where your life ends.

The day I got the courage to leave, he had beaten me up to such an extent that I had to go. I did not take anything because I did not want anybody to stop me. I trekked from the village up to the road. Somebody took me in his car and brought me to ___. He said, 'This is ___,' and dropped me. I had never been there before. I did not even know the name of the area. I asked somebody who told me the name. I told her I was looking for a place to sleep and that I had not eaten. She took me and introduced me to D___. He was sitting in front of her house with his friends. He said he was not scared, that he had seen people like me and loved helping them. He took me in and looked after me.

A week afterwards, that man got to know I was in ___. I do not know how. In the presence of D___, he slapped me. He said, 'I have divorced you' three times. I said, 'Okay, since you have said that, I am so happy. After all, I have not been happy with this marriage and I was not even interested in getting married.' I told D___ that for this thing to end, he had to take me to a distant place, where nobody would know where I was staying. That is how I came to be in the place I am now.

I never wanted to tell D___ anything initially. It was only when he told me that he had some people like me that I decided to trust and talk to him. They were the ones who have been helping me take care of my health and found me somewhere to stay. They will come by to see me and know how I am doing. It's really hard now, but in Zamfara everything was worse. I was still in his house. At least now I feel a little safer.

The happiest thing about my life is that I have left. I am now free.

It is not easy though. A lot has happened – both the things I remember and the ones I do not. There was a day when I went to the sharia court with one of my friends as her mother was overseeing a case. The mother said the father could take his remaining children but she would take the girl. Because the girl was brilliant, the mother was going to give all that she had for her to go to school. The father said no. The court said the mother did not have rights over the child.

While I was there, I saw cases of women accused of lesbianism. Some were even beaten. I asked one girl, 'What happened? How come you are here?' She said somebody gave information that she had liked another woman. The community beat her up and brought her to the police. Even though they didn't even catch her in the act, they beat her up. The police said she was caught in the act. She had no lawyer. The judge said, 'Is there evidence?' There should be witnesses and evidence. But she was convicted and taken to prison. Islamically, the person will be stoned to death, but when it is in the courts, they sentence you to some years. My pain did not allow me to wait to find out her sentence. I said I had to go home, even though my friend told me I should not go as it was some distance.

I have met girls like me here. They are the only friends I have now as I do not want anybody to have a link to where I am or know where I am staying. I am no longer in touch with my family, not even my mother. Sometimes my friends and I support each other and sometimes we talk. I am not so close to them. I just try to hide myself. I do not want to be in a situation where I will involve anyone in trouble. They too are hiding and scared. Most of my friends need help. Most of them have been married but didn't want to marry. I have a friend who was getting married and took this medicine and died. She said she would rather die than be married.

I want to help my fellow people so they will not go through the same torture I went through. I want them to know their rights and what they are able to do for themselves. Nobody has the right to tell them what they must or must not do. I want them to believe in themselves. I want them to have the courage to say no to what they do not want even if they are being forced into it. It is better to leave a life where you will not be happy.

There was a man telling others that whenever they saw a girl who behaved like a boy or liked a fellow woman, they should spit on her. I asked my friend, 'Why is this person judging? Why is he trying to take laws into his hands? He's not God. It's God that creates people so why is he trying to stop people like this? What have we done to him?'

Since then, whenever I see people saying things like that, I think they are not good people. They hate us. They hate us so much they will not buy anything from us. They will not even allow us to come close to them. They think we are harmful, that we can harm them. But that is not true. We do not harm people. They are the ones harming us. I want to let them know this is just the way we are. We are good people. This is how God created us. We are not the ones who created ourselves. They should not judge us with what other people say. They should know that it is only God who can judge.

– *QM, age 20, Zamfara*

This is What I have Been Missing

'It was the first time I experienced love.'

Content Note: Forced Outing

My family brings me the most joy and happiness. It's quite difficult right now though. I'm from the north, I'm Muslim and it's very complicated being gay. I grew up in two cultures. My father is Yoruba and my mother is Hausa. So, I was born Yoruba but I grew up in a Hausa household in the north with a lot of Yoruba influence. My household was liberal – my father was liberal. Those restrictions of growing up in the north – we didn't really have that.

My childhood was loving, close. I am the last child. I have many sisters but just one brother, and he was my favourite. My earliest memories are of sleeping on my father's shoulder and actually bullying my mum away. My parents were there for us. They didn't go to school and education was important to them. They tried as much as possible for us to go to the best schools. We didn't have a lot but we had each other. I lost my dad in 1998. It's still difficult. I lost my mum in 2011.

I was a stubborn child. I've always been different. I wanted to dress like a boy, ride bicycles, play football, play basketball

– and nobody raised an eyebrow. They just thought, *She's like that.* Nobody really cared.

I wanted to try everything. I think I tried smoking weed in JSS1. I tried alcohol in JSS3. The only thing I wasn't adventurous towards was sex. I knew from a young age that it was not something anybody should rush into.

When I went to secondary school, everybody was dating and having sex. It was weird to me. I knew something was wrong but I didn't even know the meaning of the word 'gay' then. So, I went on with life and normal secondary-school dating. I dated boys. It was the only thing I knew but it never worked for me. I never had the desire to be with men, never felt that electricity everyone was talking about.

Going to university was a drastic change. I left my state, which is quite liberal in comparison and went to an eastern part of the north. There, if you are a Muslim and you wear trousers, they pick on you. The culture shock was disturbing to say the least. I didn't understand the environment. There were lots of things you couldn't do once they knew you were Muslim. There were lots of parties – and alcohol at these parties. You couldn't drink openly if you were Muslim, and they usually knew who the Muslims were.

The Muslim Students Society (MSS) was big and strong at that university. They were specifically focused on women. You know how it is now in the north. They believe it's a man's world. They take religion and interpret it according to what works for them. For example, I had this friend who was dating a boy. The MSS told her they'd heard she'd been going around, kissing the boy and everything. They said if she didn't stop, they were going to send a letter to her parents. The girl looked at them and you know how Hausa people can be: she just insulted the shit out of them. Her boyfriend was beside her. She kissed him and told them to go fuck themselves.

They also talked to me. Even in uni, I still dated men. I was dating this Christian guy and MSS called me for a meeting to ask me why. They see you on the road and just stop you and start talking to you. At 300-level[1], we stopped living in school and got our flats. One day, they came to preach to us about living on our own and about how men would have access to us. What difference did it make that we were living alone? After all, when we were staying in hostel we could easily go to a guy's house.

The environment really affected me. I ended up not going to a lot of my classes and sleeping a lot. I was just partying and getting high. Obviously, I failed. When I was in my fourth year I decided, This is enough. If you don't leave, you're going to be here for a very long time. You'll end up graduating at third class.

I got my transcript and I went to a more liberal school. This uni was a much nicer, calmer environment. People liked me a lot and I made lots of friends. The MSS might have been there but I never encountered them. They weren't stopping girls and telling them what not to do.

I wanted to do architecture or civil engineering but I didn't get them when I transferred. I ended up studying building. It was not something I ever wanted to do but it was the most amazing decision I've made in my life. Building was fantastic. It was easy for me to visualise how buildings were made. I really enjoyed it. I did very well in school.

I was the one of the oldest in my class because I had to go back to my second year. I had already done all the partying and everything in my previous uni, so I was calmer. I just wanted to be done with school. I would just chill in my house. I would invite people and we'd sit down and talk.

At the time, I had been dating a man for seven years. It was the only serious relationship I've ever had with a man. I'd started dating him in my first year of university. He was seven years older. It was good for me. Well, the sex was terrible, obviously, but the relationship itself was very good. I cannot fault it.

We met through one of my cousins. Everybody in the family knew we were dating. His sisters knew me. His mother never liked me. She wanted him to marry someone from a rich home, like him. It was that kind of relationship. He was living in the UK but used to come back to Nigeria a lot. When he finally moved back, he told me he wanted to get married. I was still in uni and obviously not ready. He told me it was not a problem, then three weeks later said he couldn't wait any longer: 'If you want to get married, just tell me. Let's get this over with.' A couple of months later, he was married. He had been dating her at the same time he was dating me.

I was devastated. Everybody kept on calling me to say sorry, like somebody had died. But it was at this same time that I started finding out about my sexuality, so it was a good thing. I would have been miserable in the marriage. At least now we are still good friends.

I still didn't know what was wrong with me but at least I was getting more exposed to people and ideas. The first time I definitely liked someone was just after secondary school, when I was 16 or 17. I realised my relationship with my best friend was a little weird for her because people around us made comments and laughed at me. We were uncomfortable but she never walked out. I guess she understood the attention was harmless. Later on, I realised I had been very attracted to her. I think she knew. I started questioning myself but we Nigerians can be in denial for a long time. I pushed it aside. I forgot about it until later when I was at university. In the years in between, I cannot say if I liked any girl. I don't know if I would call it attraction or just friendship. I can't say it was attraction, attraction, attraction. I don't know even now. I eventually decided to start researching. The first picture I saw on Facebook of a girl and another girl dating, it was like an epiphany: *Oh! This is what is different about me!*

I had a lot of internal struggles around this. Number one, religion. Two, family. I knew that if my mum should ever find out, it would absolutely kill her. I never wanted her to find out. It was really important for me to keep quiet about it. To be honest, my mum's death made it easier for me to be more open.

In my fourth year, I met a girl. She was in the same department, a year ahead of me. We became friends. She was my first kiss, the first time I ever did anything with a girl. We just made out. It was fantastic until she freaked out and went, 'Stop. Stop. Stop.' I asked her what was wrong. She said nothing was wrong but that I should leave her house. When I kept asking, she told me she had a pact with her boyfriend to prove to him I liked her. She called him and said, 'I told you she was gay.'

I was devastated. Sad. I liked her. I really did. Our friendship went from being very close to just saying hello. Looking back on it now, she knew I liked her and she took advantage of it. I gave her money, credit and many other things. I did a lot for her. We were both at uni so it wasn't as if I had a lot – and of course I never got that money back.

After that kiss I was willing to accept myself. *It's really obvious that you like girls.* I stopped fighting it. I was twenty-six years old.

I met this other girl after about a year. I didn't know much. For me, it was, 'You're a girl, you're into girls, I would like to meet you.' She was a little too much like me. We ended up having the most terrible sex. Terrible, terrible, terrible sex. In my mind, I was like, *What the hell is this?* I told her, 'Let's just not bother.' And that was the first time I was actually with a woman.

Sometime later, my university room-mate brought a friend to the house. She was so pretty. She had more experience. She had gone to a boarding school. They like to pretend they were playing around but we all know they had relationships. We ended up making out a lot of times but we knew we could not be anything more. She's more into boys than girls. That was the first time I was with another girl and liked it. From there, I just went with it.

I had a Facebook friend who had a girlfriend. She was on my BBM and we would talk about everything. One day, she said, 'Okay, I know you don't want anybody to find out about this, and I would never do that to you, but I want to introduce you to someone.' I told her to go ahead. She introduced me to this girl who ended up being my first love. It was the first time I experienced love. The first time I thought, *Oh, wow, this is what I've been missing all this while.*

I had just finished uni and was doing my NYSC. She was in Calabar. I didn't have a lot of money and couldn't go to see her. I didn't have a place of my own. We didn't have anywhere to be private. She wanted me to grow faster than I was willing to grow. She wanted me to be bold but I was not willing to allow even my best friend to know I was gay. She didn't understand. We ended up breaking up even though I loved her a lot.

After her, I was a nuisance to society for a long time. I think it was more of an experimental stage for me. I was open to a lot of things. I was just sleeping around with random girls.

The next real relationship was with my ex. It was amazing while it lasted. We're still good friends. She was studying in Ghana. She's still very much in the closet. Even though her immediate older sister knows, she's scared of her parents finding out. She's always been, 'Oh, this is not something God would want.' She was in that denial stage. I think it was getting too intense for her and it was difficult with the distance too. One time, we both travelled to Lagos to meet. On the last day, she said we should break up.

I begged her for a year. A full year. She kept saying no. I didn't know what was in her head. Recently, she tried to explain it. She said she had gone through a nasty heartbreak before and was not in the right place to date anybody. She was broken and she knew it. After a year of me begging her and her saying no, we became friends.

I like relationships generally. They are good for me. They keep me grounded but I'm currently in a relationship I don't want to be in. I'm ashamed to say, at my age, that I was pressured into it. One day my friend's girlfriend was all, 'I know who to hook you up with!' She showed me a picture of a very nice-looking girl who she went to school with, so I told her she could give her my pin. I thought we were going to chat for a while. I was just getting to know her. Three weeks later, she goes, 'I should come visit you.' I go, 'Okay ... You can come if you want.' When she came, my friends made a lot of effort to impress her because they thought I had made up my mind to date her.

Later, they said that if I had told them I was not sure, they wouldn't have made so much effort. One of my friends doesn't stay out late but she ended up going out with us, dancing, sacrificing, just because she wanted to be with me, trying to impress the girl she thought I wanted to date. The next day, my friend cooked and invited us over because she wanted to meet this girl. I was trying to explain to my friends that if we were to date, we were rushing into it. But they felt they had wasted their time. Everybody around me sees something in her that I obviously don't. They believe she will be good for me. I told myself that being girlfriends is just a label. It's just a title, right?

She's a very nice girl. She likes me a lot but I don't like her that much. At least she lives in the south. At least she's not here. At least we just talk on the phone and I don't have to see her. It's not fair on her because I think she knows how I feel. Yesterday on chat, she sent me a message at 3am saying I make her very unhappy. When I asked her why, she replied, 'One minute you are sweet to me and the next minute you are very mean.'

I honestly don't do it on purpose but she doesn't understand me. She's much younger. She's in her twenties. We don't have a lot to talk about. She does a lot of things I don't see the need for. For example, she calls me and I go, 'Hey, how are you?' She doesn't say she's fine. She just goes, 'Where are you?' Is she a police officer? Things like that get to me. Even if you want to know, there's a better way of asking these questions, but for her, it's just me being difficult. Sometimes she pings me. Just ping, ping. You don't have to ping me. If I'm by my phone, I'll reply to you. If I'm not close to my phone, I will call you when I get back. She keeps on asking me if I've eaten. I'm like, 'You realise I'm an adult right? If I'm hungry, I'll eat.' I have a problem with these types of questions. I don't see the need. I keep on having to tell her not to do it again. She gets really sad and I feel bad for her.

I want to ride it out because I know she's getting pissed about a lot of things. I'm hoping she will break up with me soon. At least that way I can say, 'You see, it wasn't my fault. I didn't do anything wrong.' I know it's not nice but unfortunately, that's where things are.

She's so different from the women I like. I really like smart women. I like women who can cook. I like women I can have conversations with. I don't mean just normal gist. I need somebody I can relate to about life outside the relationship. I think it's quite irritating not to have any ambition. Be passionate about something! Intelligence is important but physical appearance not so much. I'd go for a slimmer kind of girl, but it doesn't really matter. I don't want to date any girl who's into men. I think it's confusing and unhealthy. I'm very conscious of my health. If you are having sex with another person you're at risk, so having sex with two people ... I can't do that.

Usually, I like to be the one taking care of the other person in a relationship. Even sexually, I like to do all the pleasing. It gives me joy. I mean, we do strike a balance but I usually do things like that more. Sex is very important to me. I try not to have terrible sex!

A couple of my colleagues know about me. I like my job. I work in a place where, if you are willing to learn, you will learn a lot. You'll see me having a meeting with somebody talking about technology. When did I become this person? A year ago, I couldn't do that, so it's nice. A while back, I was having a conversation with one of my colleagues. She knew I was angry. It was about the time I was still begging my ex. One day when I was on the phone, she saw my face and asked what was happening. I said, 'Man, I've been begging my ex for like a year.' She was like 'Oh, just leave the boy now, it's obvious that—' And I just couldn't lie to her. I told her 'Oh, it's a she.' She was like, 'I'm sorry?' I told her, 'It's a she.' She was like 'Oh wow, okay … Maybe you should just leave her alone.' She was in shock for like thirty minutes to an hour. But she's so cool about it. We hang out together every day. We go drinking. We go dancing. We do everything together.

Another colleague also likes girls. When I saw her, I just knew and she knew also. One day, she said, 'You like girls, right?' and I said, 'You like girls, right?' And that was it. With the rest of my colleagues, they're not as exposed and I don't think they notice a whole lot of things.

If they knew … Well, I know one is quite homophobic because of the kinds of statements he makes but I don't think it would be a problem. When they passed the Marriage Bill in America, he had a lot to say, 'This is the end of America. These people are mad!' I said, 'You live in Nigeria. You most likely will never go to America. So why is it a problem to you?' And he was all, 'No, but this thing is a curse.' This is a Yoruba boy; you know how they think.

I stopped at some point because he kept on bringing religion into it. He's Christian and I'm Muslim and things like that are quite sensitive. I didn't want it to be a religious debate so I let it go. The only thing I told him was that if a gay girl should walk up to me right now (him assuming I'm straight) and tell me I'm sexy and she wants to be with me, I'd think it was a huge compliment. And he goes, 'How?' I told him, 'Somebody thinks you're sexy. Isn't that a compliment?' And he kept quiet. I said, 'For me, straight people should not have a problem as long as a gay person is not trying to forcefully have sex with you.' That shut him down and he kept quiet.

My friends are fantastic though. All of them know and nobody has a problem. They just tell me to be careful, not to let my family know and things like that. One actually ended up being with a girl for a bit. I think she has always been curious so she tried it out. They're cool about it. My friends have been very supportive.

The biggest problem my sexuality has caused me is with family. Family. Family. Family. My brother is very homophobic. Any time he sees Ellen DeGeneres on TV, he goes, 'Shegiya yar wuta' which means, 'Bastard. She is going to hell.' The first time I heard it, I asked him, 'Why so harsh?' He told me he did not know what was wrong with this woman. Is it because she's a lesbian that she's always dressing like a guy?

I looked at myself and said, 'Dude, don't I look like I'm dressed like a guy?'

'Oh it's you, you've always been like that,' he said.

'What makes you think that she has never been like that?'

'Oh, she's a lesbian.'

I thought, *If only you knew* – and walked away.

A couple of months ago, somebody called my sister to say she saw me kissing someone. This was not true – boy or girl, I cannot kiss anybody outside in public. So my sister called me, laughing and said 'Ah, I just heard something funny about you, that they saw you kissing a girl … Don't worry. I don't believe them. It was just quite funny and I had to tell you.'

I said, 'You know people think I'm gay because of the way I walk, right?'

She said, 'Yes and the way you dress. But you grew up like that. Nobody really cares in the family. Okay, bye!' She dropped the phone and that was the end.

But then! Around Eid, my brother came back from ___, where he lives. Somebody he didn't know called him to ask, 'Sorry, is I___ your sister?'

He said, 'Yes.'

'Do you know what she's doing?'

'She works.'

'Um, are you keeping an eye on her?'

'She's an adult. Why do I need to do that?'

'Well, I'm not trying to cause a problem with your family but I want you to know your sister is gay. I don't have proof, but she's slept with my girlfriend. Since she's slept with her, I don't even understand our relationship any more. She's confused the girl.'

He called a couple of people. 'Oh well, I've never seen her with anybody but we've heard that ... but it's not confirmed.' He called my sister and told her to give me an ultimatum: Resign from my job, move back to ___ and stay at home jobless or know that he and I do not have a relationship any more. My family all live back at home, except for him, so the idea was that would I move back, live with them and they could control me.

My brother was my favourite growing up, so it was disappointing that he couldn't talk to me but had to call my sister to ask her to give me this ultimatum. He didn't even have the conversation with me directly. He just listened to these people and believed them. Since my brother was not willing to talk to me, my cousins would call me instead. One of them is my brother's best friend. He called a friend of mine and asked questions. I told her to tell him to be very careful, that if he doesn't want any disrespect, he should just leave me be. I tell all my cousins that they should leave me alone. I'm not their sister. They should stay out of my business.

Then my sister started calling friends to ask, 'Do you know if I___ is doing anything I should know about?' People started calling me, 'What's happening in your family? Why are they calling?'

I told my sister, 'Don't do that. You're making me look bad. They'll think something is wrong, more than what it is.'

'Ah, it's because I care about you. I'm trying to find the truth.'

I said, 'You can find out all the truth you want but don't call people randomly.' I told my sister, 'I'm not leaving my job. I'm not going to move home where, if I want to buy deodorant for N600, I'll have to ask, "Please give me 600." I cannot do that. Not right now. Not at this age. I will not move back. Tell him I said that.'

My sister was crying, 'This is a big issue! Everybody is saying you're a lesbian.'

I couldn't tell her it was true but I said, 'Wait. Even if I was a lesbian now, if I move to ___, what is it going to change? Do you think I'm going to stop being a lesbian? All of you go to work! There are plenty lesbians in ___.'

She was quiet for a while. For a month she tried to convince me to move back home. She said, 'I don't need to know if it's true or not, I just want you to do the right thing.'

I travelled home for Eid and the only conversation I had

with my brother was, 'Good morning and welcome.' That was it. My sister and I don't have the relationship we used to. We used to talk a lot and we were the closest in the family but it's a little bit shaky right now. The strangest thing is, I sat down for over two hours trying to think of somebody I'd been with who has a boyfriend. I cannot think of anybody. So, I don't even trust the story. The last few months have been difficult but I try as much as possible not to think about it. It will take a while but I will ride it out.

The problem is that we have a lot of culture and it's mixed with religion in most parts of Nigeria. It's different for Muslims and Christians. I know they're talking about this a lot in the churches now but you don't have a lot of talk in Muslim societies about any kind of sex, so we don't have the kind of dialogue that they do.

I am a Muslim so I try not to think about it from that aspect. Islam says, don't act like the opposite sex. For me, a woman, I should not act like a man. A man should not act like a woman. Don't be with anybody of the same sex. They talk about men mostly. I don't think women were so open at that time. For me, being gay is being gay; it doesn't matter what your sex is.

I know it's wrong. I know it's bad. I think about it sometimes but I don't really struggle with it religiously. After all, I'm not the greatest Muslim. I try to pray as much as I can and I fast. I have complete faith in my religion. It's something I can never change. I want to be married to a Muslim with the same background, ideology and teachings. But, I drink, I smoke and I like girls. I try not to do things that are wrong because I'm already doing a lot of wrong things. I still do these things, but yeah, I would like to stop soon.

I do think it's becoming more known now. People are more willing to show their sexuality than before. You see a lot of girls with girlfriends who go out for dinner and everything. That was impossible a couple of years ago. We have social media now. We have exposure. A lot of people have access to more reading materials and more information. They know it's nothing abnormal. They know they are just that way. And then, with the SSMPA, people felt they had to come out and say this is what being gay is like. I know a lot of people who are quite open about their sexuality, especially in Lagos. They are comfortable in their own skin. They are not trying to hide who they are.

This is both men and women and, in some ways, it's more difficult for men. Straight people are more likely to accept lesbianism. A few days ago, I was at a table, the only girl among guys. We were having a conversation and homosexuality came up. I asked a simple question – 'If a gay guy was sitting at this table, what would you do?' Somebody said he would walk away. I said, 'Why? Why would you not sit down with a gay guy? He's having a drink. We're having normal conversations.' I asked, 'What if it's a girl and she's a lesbian?' They were like, 'Oh! We'd probably ask her if we could join.' It's not seen as that serious for women. It's seen as something they will get out of, if you give them time. It's seen as more extreme for men. I can't really explain why they see it that way but I think it's because of the sexual act that most people find it disgusting.

I know a lot of other queer women. We are friends. One of my best friends is gay. There's a sense of community, but only to some extent. It cannot be central because there are some tomboys in particular who a lot of people don't want to be around, even me. They are always trying to talk to a girl. I think they are unnecessarily out there. I always see them in the club and I'm like, 'What is she doing?' They try to be friends with me and I just walk away. I don't want to be friends with them. If you're not civilised to a certain level, we can't be friends. Just be normal about it. That's the only problem I have with some people in the community. Apart from that, it's nice.

In the future, I want to get married and have children. I love relationships. They keep me grounded. They make me more focused. They make me want to succeed more. I want to make you happy and for you to have a better life. When I'm not in a relationship, I don't know how to save, I just do whatever, so I know it's good for me. I love kids. My nephews are my world. If I have kids, I don't want my sexuality to influence theirs. I mean, me growing up in a straight household didn't stop me from being gay but I know a lot of people who are like us but are married now because it's what is expected. I wouldn't have an issue if my children were gay; I just want them to be their own people.

As much as I want to do it now in Nigeria, I can't get married to a woman and I can't have kids with a woman. I don't see the life I want to live happening for me in Nigeria. So, I think I want to leave, probably go to Canada or somewhere. It's going to take a very long time for Nigerians to reach the stage I want my life to be in. Nigeria is not ready right now. Maybe in fifty years or more, a long time from now. At the moment, religion does not allow us to accept things, no matter how much we want to try. Nigerians are too religious. They are not spiritual. Everything, even the smallest thing, they are like, God did this, God did that. It's frustrating. I know a couple of people who have been threatened because of their sexuality. In some places, it can be dangerous. It's kind of impossible to stop a homophobic person from being homophobic but they need to give us a chance – and please not be violent.

– IX, age 31, Kaduna

---

1   300-level = Third year at university

Focusing On Joy

'Yes, I am queer. I am black. I am American. I come from a Nigerian–Jamaican heritage. I am Igbo. All those are main parts of my identity but I'm so much more complex than what those identity labels indicate.'

Content Note: Racism

I was born in Illinois and grew up in the US South. I am interested in education, history and in connecting with extended family based here in Imo State. My mum is Jamaican and my dad is Nigerian. Most of my immediate family are in the States but I have family in Canada and England. My grandmother lives in Georgia. Including my parents, there are seven of us in my family. Both my parents work in the medical field so I grew up upper-middle class and attended a private high school and college.

I was born in a suburb of Chicago. Before they had children, my parents lived there for years. One of my earliest memories of snow was there. Almost every morning, when I would have been about 2 years old, I came down the stairs to my grandmother making porridge. I really loved that Caribbean tradition of porridge in the morning.

When we moved to New Orleans, we lived in an apartment surrounded by my parents' friends and I felt like part of a community. I loved it because it was fun. I remember my dad always wearing scrubs because he was doing his residency. Every night my siblings and I would climb on him when he was sitting on the couch. We broke all the pockets on his scrubs because we'd put our feet in them to climb.

When I was in my mum's womb, she thought something was wrong because I was so quiet she could barely feel me. After I was born, it kind of continued. I was always sleeping. Even if I was hungry, no one would know. I remember spending a lot of time alone. I stayed up late and would be in my closet drawing or building things in my own little world. For a big part of my childhood, if someone asked me what I wanted to do, I would say I wanted to be an actress or artist. I used to write storybooks all the time. I would write down my dreams when I woke up or draw illustrations. Outside the house, like in school, I was shy but could be pretty talkative once I got comfortable with others.

I struggled at school for a long time because part of me was terrified. Some of it had to do with confidence, and the other was because I did not understand why I was there. Maybe it was due to the type of learner I was. I had a short attention span and it was hard for me to sit at a desk to focus. A lot of it had to do with the fact that the quality of teaching in some of my schools and classes was bad.

At home, I was often the centre of attention among my siblings. I was very dramatic and would create projects and plays all day long, and then force everyone to perform in them. I would get mad if they did not take it seriously. I loved doing things in groups. Sometimes I would wake up with this fear of being left out if I heard people walking around and talking downstairs. If I had homework to do, I would do it in the middle of the kitchen where I was surrounded by people.

I was probably a 'tomboy' for a long time, although I hate using the word because it implies girls don't naturally do things perceived as boy-like. I did a lot of so-called girly things too. My whole family is really athletic so we played a whole lot of sports. My sister and I were competitive gymnasts. I had a lot of body awareness as a kid. I felt like being a girl meant trying to prove to the boys that I could be better than them. There was this silent competition with my brother. I spent my days hanging out with him and my male cousins who were around my age. I would walk around with only my shorts on and no top at all, just like them. We would measure and compare our muscles. My sisters did it too. I was very proud of strength and power and was trying to assert that over them, especially when we were fighting. At school, when we played games where boys had to catch girls, I would take it seriously: 'Girls, we have to beat them.' It was a real sport to me, but to other girls it was just a way to be caught by boys. I thought that was horrible. We were so much better than the boys.

For as long as I can remember, I walked around with my shirt off. Then puberty hit and one day it was like, *Oh, what is this knob on the left?* I thought something was very wrong so I went downstairs and told my mum, 'You have to feel this; something is wrong.' She was cooking and did not feel it. She just looked over and said, 'They are just growing because the left breast grows first.' I was like, 'What do you mean?' She explained, 'You are just growing breasts.' I was so devastated and embarrassed.

From that day on, I always wore shirts. Puberty made me aware of other people's perceptions of my body. I could no longer walk around showing my chest. Instead, I had to hide myself. I was not prepared for it. The responsibility was put on my mum to educate us. I had already been socialised outside of my home to fear puberty, periods and that sort of thing. Sexual education was really bad in elementary school, to the point where all the girls were told not to talk about these things to anybody and to cover our bodies. We were all scared. They used to show us a video about girls on their periods in relation to boys starting to crush on girls and I could not relate. I thought all that was crap and just wanted to be free from it.

In an American context, femininity is directly related to whiteness, like the significance of having long hair and a fear of getting darker in the sun. Back when I was a gymnast, we had this male coach who lined us up and thought it was funny to point out who had the biggest butt. We were only 10 or 11 years old, some of us younger, but I was like, *Oh no, I'm black. I have a huge butt.* They picked my sister and me as having the biggest butts. We were the only black children. Looking back now, I can see that it was a racist experience. I felt so humiliated and as a result became obsessed with identifying my racial differences for the longest time. Like, why do we look the way we do? Why are our butts bigger?

Additionally, as a young black girl, I was often not listened to. Once, in day care, I brought my little stuffed animal for show-and-tell and stored it in my cubbyhole. By the time show-and-tell came, it was gone. I was distraught, then saw this white girl standing there, sucking her thumb and holding my stuffed animal. I went to her and said, 'That's mine, not yours' and she just started crying, claiming my toy was hers. I told a teacher but the teacher told me I was lying and went to comfort the other girl. I just sat there. I did not cry. I had believed that if I explained to the teacher, if I just told the truth, she was going to understand. That was how my parents were. They taught us not to lie and listened to us. But the teacher did not even give me two seconds before calling me a liar. There were more instances like that as a kid where I was not afforded the same attention and care as young white girls. If I broke down and cried, it did not mean anything.

When I was young, I never felt pressure from my parents to be a certain way gender-wise (although this is changing the older that I get). My dad, who is Nigerian, never commented on anything I wore or did. He did not try to enforce particular types of behaviour according to gender. He never said, like I have heard some parents say to their kids, 'Don't do that because you are a girl.' It was the same with my mum, who is Jamaican. The only thing I remember her telling me was, 'Close your legs. Don't sit like that.' Other than that, my mum is like a 'tomboy'. At home, it is she who fixes things, who paints things, who cuts things down, and she will be in her heels dressed for work when she is doing all these. I have always felt just as masculine as I am feminine, and I think my models were the women in my family and other female athletes.

So much of the mainstream LGBT movement in the US has pushed this argument that you are genetically born this way. That if you are gay or lesbian, you know by the time you are 14 or 15 years old. Many people can tell stories like, 'When I was 10', but I keep searching for those. I wonder if I had those moments, but all I remember is always being around girls and women and having intense friendships with them. I recall being friends with boys too, sometimes having crushes on them. When I was 5 years old, I developed my first legit crush on this white boy.

In high school, there would be all these jokes going around about gay people. But I was interested in female power and in empowering my friends. So I would say, about my close girlfriends, 'This person is so beautiful and has a great personality. I don't understand why guys don't like her.' I was the friend who was like, 'Girl you are worth so much and you don't even know it.' Those were moments where I recognised my friends' attractiveness, both emotionally and physically. With my closest relationships being platonic ones with girls, I felt, at times, that I never needed a romantic relationship, especially one with a boy.

After I left high school, I chose to go to an all-women's college. I believed that women were going to save the world and considered it a great university because it focused on women. There was an open, queer community on campus but it was very white. Surprisingly, with it being a women's college, and with people making jokes about our college being for lesbians, it was not that accepting. Initially I thought homosexuality was wrong because of my religious beliefs. But ultimately, I accepted the fact that people are people so why should that bother me? I kept asking myself, 'Why are there gay people?' I needed to figure it out. Eventually, through my own learning and personal relationships with other queer people, I began to desire dating women. It was a gradual liberation.

In college, I had a really good friend who I talked to about queerness. I always liked her as a person due to her energy, her vibe and her being. She was unique to me and I was drawn to her. I did not identify that feeling as something unusual. One day I was sitting down with her and we were talking about queerness. Then she was like, 'I should tell you because I feel like you're someone I can trust. I'm definitely gay.' I did not know what to do, but immediately after that conversation I realised I was attracted to her. I started identifying as bi after that and would have conversations with her about our sexuality.

She was a year above me in college. When she was graduating, she sent me a text that said something like, 'You said you are queer. What's your type?' I replied, 'What? I don't have a type.' Then she said, 'I just wish I was your type.' It was her way of telling me that she liked me. I did not tell her I liked her because I was not sure I wanted to pursue anything with her. After college, I visited her once or twice when she lived in New York. We had an intellectual connection. We would always have conversations but never address the feelings between us. I think she was dating somebody at that point.

At the same time this was going on, I began to build a friendship with the woman I would be with in my first long-term relationship. She was a friend of my sister's who was out in college. I met her when I was with my sister at this art exhibition and struck up a conversation with her. Afterwards, she offered to walk me home. I thought she was just being nice. After she graduated from our college, I bumped into her in Boston by chance and she invited me to have dinner at her place.

We were sitting on her couch and talking when the energy in the room shifted. At that moment, she started caressing my hand and my hair. I had never talked to her about being queer. I felt awkward and had to tell her I did not feel comfortable.

She felt so bad and apologised profusely. After that day, we talked and I told her that it was okay. She had not misread me. I just was not ready for that leap. It remained awkward with her for a while until I graduated from college and was looking for jobs in Boston. I ended up living with her before I was able to find an apartment. Eventually our friendship evolved into a romantic relationship.

Fast-forward several years. I came out to my mum so I could talk to her about how to get out of that relationship. It was not working. I am very close to my mum and value her opinion. I felt I needed to come out to her so that she, as someone I trust, could help me move forward. I expressed to her the state I was in. She told me she kind of knew, then asked me who. She moved from, 'Oh my God, did my daughter just tell me she was gay?' to, 'Let me tell you a story about finding someone who is truly compatible.' I was really grateful for that. She saw the pain I was in and gave advice. She showed concern for me being in a bad relationship rather than letting homophobic thoughts take over the conversation.

I am out to my sisters, one of whom is self-educated about LGBT issues and a pretty strong ally. I only came out to my brothers via text, years after bringing home the person I was seeing then, introducing her as my friend, not my girlfriend. My brothers sent me supportive text messages back. One of them was like, 'I knew it. As soon as I saw you with her, I could tell.'

I wanted to come out to my siblings first so that when I come out to my dad, they can support me. There already isn't an open culture in my house of talking about or bringing around the people you are dating. My dad perceives relationships as everybody being a friend until you are ready to marry them.

I am 29 years old and my siblings are also in their twenties, but there remains this fear of talking to Dad and being open about our relationships. I cry when I think about coming out to my dad. I fear that it may cut me off from a more intimate relationship with him and with my Igbo-ness.

Sometimes I feel like, in order to be queer, I have to be in a relationship. The world makes you feel there isn't a lot of affirmation of who you are otherwise. This puts a lot of stress on the queer communities I have been in. It feels lonely even though you have a community. I have seen really bad, dramatic dynamics play out in my relationships and among other queer people searching for healing and self-worth in relationships. I find people play out all the trauma they have gone through.

I have been in three relationships. I date both men and women. My first relationship was with a man and the other two were with women. I met my first boyfriend in Uganda. For three months, we were in a really intense relationship.

When I am in a relationship, I cannot focus on other people until it has ended and I have moved on. So much of my energy goes into it. It is only when I am out that I realise how exhausting it has been to maintain it. I have always imagined myself to be someone who is alone, someone who can be in relationships as long as those relationships are not co-dependent. Yet I have passionate relationships and intense friendships. I am struggling, trying to figure out how to create a balance. What I want is to feel peaceful in long-term relationships where there is growth, simplicity, and learning.

For me, a relationship should be free in terms of gender roles. I have not found this with the men and queer women I've been with. People have not worked through their own perceptions or a gender-free relationship isn't what they want. And maybe I haven't worked through my own, since this seems to be a pattern in my relationships. Everyone is on their own journey. Everyone has their own stuff to come to terms with. Everyone wants to be affirmed in different ways and sometimes in very gendered ways.

A lot of the people I have dated perceived me to be more feminine than them. Sometimes they've acted like 'the man' in the relationship. While some of these gender roles may be okay, some are not. Some of these things are not explicit and are hard to articulate, which puts a lot of pressure on both of us. This is not always the case in every interaction but it's been a point of contention in every relationship I've had so far. People who appear more masculine have said things that hurt and confound me. For example, asking me, 'Are you going to wear that?' I'm like, 'Are you really telling me what to wear?' It felt like they were telling me to be more stereo-typically feminine, which was offensive and presumptuous. I wear whatever I am comfortable in. These comments are damaging because they are heterosexist. If I have to be put in a box, I cannot really be my queer self.

I have been in my current relationship for a couple of years. There are stark differences in how we value the queer community where we met each other. My partner is genderqueer and being in spaces most visible for queer people is important. I tend to blend in on the surface. In mainstream spaces, people assume I'm a straight woman, which is frustrating. Or sometimes, other queer people don't recognise me because, aesthetically, I'm not sending off any signals. For me, whether or not a space is queer, I'll say, forget it, if that space isn't aligned with my values. I don't want a queer community for community's sake. I love other queer people, especially queer people of colour, and I'm looking to build a community filled with queer people of colour who I have a deeper connection with.

Currently, I do not have a lot of close queer friends whom I can talk to about issues in my relationship. When I talk to straight friends, I feel protective over my lovers. I can't really talk to my mum about it. She is helpful but terrified for me. My girlfriend and I broke up once. When I told my mum we had broken up, she just told me I would get over it. That was not what I needed to hear at that moment, even though I understood that she was just saying, 'This too shall pass.'

Some people believe that focusing on gay marriage is wrong because there are more important issues for the LGBT community. While I agree, I also feel that it is not so much whether gay marriage is the issue but whether or not we are asking the people in our community what they think. I think there is a diversity of opinions. I do not know how being in a long-term relationship with someone is not the same thing as being married. My dad would say that it is not, that what makes one married is the legality of it all.

I have mixed feelings watching people who are queer get married. On one level, it is cool that they can do what they want to because it is about love. On another level, a political one, I ask myself why they are doing that, other than because you get more taxes back filing as a married couple and other economic benefits. Some people in our community really do want marriage and some people do not care, while others do not care because they do not think marriage is a possibility for them. I'm more interested in the various perspectives within the queer community and how we honour that.

Me, I feel the government should have nothing to do with marriage. It shouldn't legalise gay or straight couples because of the economic privilege being married gives those who couple with their romantic partners. If you do not have a partner who you can build with financially, you have a harder time supporting yourself or finding support down the road because of the way society is structured. And there is no normalised culture that provides support for queer couples who decide to bring children into this world. We tend to focus on the broken family and all that bullshit, especially in black communities. People should be able to be individuals living their lives. Whether they have partners or not should not make or break their abilities to take care of themselves and to have and take care of their children.

It feels really odd that who you have sex with identifies you. Like I get that in a political sense, but does it really matter? Yes, I am queer. I am black. I am American. I come from a Nigerian–Jamaican heritage. I am Igbo. All those are main parts of my identity but I'm so much more complex than what those identity labels indicate. I claim certain identities depending on the audience – when I need to make visible, for good reason, certain experiences and perspectives or when I do not want to claim certain experiences and struggles that people assume.

I am not religious; I am spiritual. I went to a Catholic high school and as a kid I was super religious. I find religion interesting and value it. But now I do not believe in this idea of a god in the sky or heaven and hell. I approach religiosity through an intellectual frame. I love using religion as a historical process through which to understand the world, including sexuality. Recently, I learned a lot about emotions, pain, and rage from Buddhist teachings and black female writers and healers, some religious, some not.

Most of my professional experience has been in community organising and policy work. My areas have been healthcare, public health, education, criminal justice, and access to jobs. My interest has always been in black communities. I really like working with people. I am not just interested in providing services. I feel that, as a community organiser, on my best days, I have an entry point into the wider community and can do work that is truly people-centred. I can focus on true empowerment, which is not simply advocacy work.

At work, my sexuality rarely comes up. In California, people in professional spaces ask you if you have a partner, as opposed to whether you have a girlfriend or a boyfriend, because they are sensitive to the fact that people may be in same-sex relationships. Although I don't like being asked if I'm coupled, period, it's kind of nice. That hasn't happened to me in other places.

I have a mentor who passed away recently. She was 87 years old. She was born in Jamaica and travelled and lived all over the world. She came into a lot of money at a young age and travelled all over Europe before ending up in Ghana. I met her in Boston where she approached me and the person I was dating at the time. She just started talking to us, saying all sorts of interesting things about Maroon communities.

She decided that she was going to help and teach us. She could be a hard person to be around, but I loved her because she was against conventional thinking and helped me see the importance of deeper critical thinking as healing. She also helped me see the importance of focusing on joy and being playful. She taught me a lot about boundaries because she was crossing mine all the time. I am saying all this because the best advice I got in life came from her. It was not because she said anything in particular but because she was so authentic and unafraid. It is because of her that my sexuality, politics and purpose have evolved to fit who I am more accurately. She steered me away from responding neurotically to pain, hurt and oppression. In all that you do, do not lose the practice of experiencing joy and creating it.

– *NS, age 29, Imo State / Chicago, USA*

My Sexuality Is Just The Icing On The Cake

'She asks, "You are the dude, right?" I reply, "No, there is no dude. I'm the girl and she's the girl."'

Content Note: Child Sexual Abuse

I grew up in a family where I got whatever I wanted as long as I behaved, so childhood was fun. I have a large family – three aunties and three uncles on my dad's side and the same on my mum's side, so it's six-six. I have two brothers (one is an engineer and the other is a medical doctor) and I am the only female child. My mum and dad are very religious. My dad is a pastor and my mum is an evangelist.

I have a lot of fun childhood memories. It was mostly hanging out with my friends and my brothers' friends. My favourite part was getting in trouble with my brothers and my brothers getting punished for me. I would be left out of the punishment because I was the only girl and my father's favourite, even though I might actually have been the one to cause the trouble.

I remember one particular time. We were not supposed to go to a neighbour's place – you know the Nigerian thinking: Don't eat at the neighbour's place – but we went over. We ate there and my mum came home. I immediately went to sleep, pretend sleep. My brothers started explaining. They got their asses whooped and, because I was sleeping, left me out of it.

I liked school. It was fun. I'm from this family that is so much into education. My dad is a doctor, not a medical doctor but a doctor, so he's keen about you getting educated and having a culture of reading. That's the kind of family I come from. Whether I liked school or not, it was compulsory in my family. So, I decided to like school. So far, it has been good. I'm a deep thinker so that helps me a lot.

Primary school days, I hated girls. Seriously. Girls talk a lot. They cause trouble. I'm surprised I'm actually gay now given how much I hated them. I just liked hanging out with boys. That changed in secondary school. My first real attraction came when I was in SS2[1] and this particular girl transferred from another school. She was the hottest girl in school. Guys drooled over her and girls hated her but I liked her. She sat next to me, so we started talking and got close. I went to a mixed school but luckily for me, she came from a girls' school. Girls who attend girls-only schools are more open to homosexuality, unlike girls who don't, because it is considered a norm in some schools.

I was really attracted to her. I cannot even construct one line now, but back then I wrote poems on love. I would send her poems and letters and call her – and we kissed. We'd usually hang out in the school library and make out. My friends really hated on the girl because I stopped hanging out with them. We would just go to the school library and make out. I wasn't experienced then, so it was just kissing. It lasted one and a half years until we wrote WAEC[2]. She decided she didn't want to date a girl any more, so I just let it go. I've seen her a couple of times since then but she's not the type of person I would date now. I'm sorry to say it, but I'm out of her league.

The whole time, my friends knew what was happening but they did not tell me. It was only when we went to university that I came out to them: Seriously guys, I like girls. They were like, *Oh please, we know. You and that girl ...* I had some other really close friends at that time who were much older than me. When I was in SS3, they were in 200-level[3] or 300-level at university. I told them, 'See, I like girls. I'm attracted to girls.' They didn't say anything. They were cool with it.

So, I had fun growing up, but I was also disturbed. A woman and a man both molested me when I was younger.

The woman was my neighbour. She would take me to a place, do stuff and ask me to do stuff to her. I didn't know what it was. It was only when I grew up, when I actually understood the way stuff works, that I realised what she had been doing to me back then.

But my uncle's abuse I can remember very well. He was my father's youngest brother. He started when I was 3. I would be sitting on his lap, with him pressing his body against me; you know, that whole thing. Then we moved to this new place and he stayed with us. The whole thing went on until I was around 11. It got so bad that he would come over to my room in the middle of the night when everybody was asleep – and my parents' room was directly opposite.

One particular time, my grandmother came over to our house and slept in my room. He came over to my room, even though his mum was there. I think that was the straw that broke my camel's back. I couldn't handle it any more. I came out with my robes and was like, 'He's threatening me.' That's the word I used. I can still remember in my head: 'This guy is threatening me', and that was it.

After that, I was taken to a medical doctor to check if I was 'still a virgin', as they put it and the shit came crashing down. My father blamed my mum, said she was probably not looking after me enough and that was why it happened. Later, my dad blamed me, saying he was probably giving me money, which was why I consented to it. He used some seriously derogatory statements against me that were quite hurtful.

I don't know if they ever blamed my uncle. We stopped talking with him for a while but now everybody is back together. I see him a lot at family events. Hey, it happens – which is fucked up.

Anyway, that was the bad side of my childhood. Each time I remember it, it doesn't exactly make me happy. I'm over it but, looking back now, I figure I was really disturbed by that. There are times I like being in my own space, not talking to people, not even mixing with anybody. Sometimes I hate everybody and sometimes I go with the flow. In a way, I feel it messed me up in terms of relationships. I can't have a key relationship with anybody. It's difficult. I get tired of people easily. If I met somebody, I might like them for two weeks and then I'm over them. That's how far I go.

The first relationship I had was in 100-level. She was in my church. We would usually hang out, do stuff and talk all the time. There was nobody asking anybody out. We were just having a relationship. We were dating and that was it. We did stuff, not the main sex thing, but we fooled around. Then the thing ended. I think I just got tired and we stopped talking. I guess she is actually straight and was just having her fun. I think she was around 30 and I was around 17. Don't worry; it was not sex with a minor. I consented to it. It was not sexual whatsoever.

Further down the line, I dated this bi woman. She was twelve years older than me – I like dating older women. It was really fun and going well. I loved her. Then the guy she was dating found out – she was about to get married – and she had to call us off. I was heartbroken. I really liked her. The sex was awesome. I knew she was with this guy but we never talked about it. She's bi so I should have known it was going to happen. Sincerely, the Nigerian definition of being bisexual, as far as I am concerned, is: I am bisexual, I have a boyfriend and I have a girlfriend, I'm with two people. That is their definition. I had another bi girlfriend when I was serving in Edo State. I think I have a thing for bi women! It was fun but she told me that she wanted to get married to a guy. I later found out she went back to her ex-girlfriend. That was when I decided, *Fuck this, I'm never ever dating any bi woman again*. That was it and I started dating women who were actually lesbians.

Then I had another girlfriend. We were together for a while. What really rocked the whole boat and screwed everything up was that she was sleeping with men for money. She told me. I tried to understand, but I just couldn't. I believe in being with one girl at a time. I'm very health-conscious. I don't have an STD check before I have sex but I do ask them. That's selfish, I know, because the only time it happens for me is if I have to go to the hospital when I'm actually ill. I do ask though – I don't want any kind of sexually transmitted infection. So, with her, it got to a point where I couldn't take it. We said a lot of things to each other we didn't mean and it ended.

I'm in a relationship at the moment. We have been dating

for more than a year but it's not going well. I'm trying and she's trying but I'm tired of the whole thing. We were friends for three years before we got together. She wasn't in any relationship and she asked me to hook her up with someone. Jokingly, I asked her, 'What about me? Like seriously, are you going to see me and go out there and be searching for someone?' And she said, 'Seriously? Are you serious? I've had feelings for you all the while.' That was how the whole thing came crashing down. I was just joking and she took it all serious, and I was like, *What the hell man?* So I thought, *Let's try.*

Along the way, I could say I developed feelings for her. It was really good, because she's a very good person. She is fucking awesome. But it is not working. First of all, I don't want kids and she does. That is a deal-breaker any day, any time. And secondly, in physical features, she's not the type of woman I want. She's very skinny. And then there's sex. Sex, to me, is the most important thing in a relationship but it boils down to whom you are having it with. Currently, I'm not feeling that connection. I'm her second girlfriend ever since she found out she's gay. She's still a little bit ... let me use the term 'stuck up'. She's not that open. Her first girlfriend, they never even had penetration. There are a lot of things she didn't do with her so it fell to me. I assured her that it was okay. We took it easy. We took it step by step.

Obviously, she doesn't have any experience, and I'm not too patient to teach anybody. I try to avoid sex with her every way I can. I mostly lie that I'm tired. But it's something I enjoy having, especially when it's with someone who is experienced and knows what she's doing. The best sex I had was with an ex. We would play roles, get really high and have sex, try new things. I'm quite sexually adventurous – as long as you are not penetrating me. I'm fine with penetrating another woman but not the other way around. I don't know. I don't want to say it has any relation to my past, to the ugly story I told you, but I just don't get any enjoyment from being penetrated. I have tried, but it doesn't feel good to me.

For me, friendship is very important. You have to have that kind of connection where you can talk about everything and anything. But the sexual connection also has to be there. Seriously, I can't marry her and I'm not the kind of person who dates someone I can't marry. I tried breaking things off, but she's insanely in love with me. She cried. She screamed. So I had to take it all back.

I like having relationships but the problem is everybody I have dated really doesn't understand the fact that I'm not the kind of person who likes you to be with me all the time. I understand if you don't want to see me for a week, you don't want to see me for two weeks. I like that. I like having my own space. I like solitude. It gives me time to think and clear my head. A lot of people don't understand that.

I've been told several times that I'm very sweet in relationships. I will do anything for who I am with, and let me just say that a lot of people I have been with have taken advantage of me. There are some people who, when they know you love them, will do anything to you just because they know you will come begging. That has happened a lot – probably because femmes like douchebags. They like studs who are actually arseholes. So, they think of me as a stud and it boils down to me being initially nice then getting taken advantage of. So I just figured, hey, being a jerk kind of helps.

I'm not particularly keen on labels. For me, it's about

being there for your woman and taking care of her. I dress the way I dress because that's what I'm comfortable wearing. I'm attracted to girls who dress very feminine, wear heels, have long hair and paint their faces. Yeah, I get what that means but it doesn't mean anything to me.

The issue of gender roles is a problem. I have been with women who think, because I'm a stud, I have to assume the male role so I have to pay the bills and do all the manly things, which is not my thing. I am not a man. The way I dress doesn't mean I'm a man. You can't tell me to assume the male role.

I think every relationship has the controlling person and the other person who is the submissive type. That's where it comes from with a stud and femme kind of relationship. The stud is supposed to be doing the domineering part and the femme is the submissive one. It doesn't mean anything to me. I have dated women who have been domineering while I have been submissive, although not sexually – I'm never submissive sexually.

Having two women in a relationship and one being 'the man' and the other 'the woman' means we are actually bringing the whole heterosexual concept into homosexuality. It is in a heterosexual relationship where you see a man and a woman, and gender roles are the whole problem in society. Women are not supposed to be this way and men are not supposed to be this way.

I like to be free of gender. In the homosexual context, you see man and man and woman and woman. It shouldn't be that you assume gender roles, but people have misguided opinions. Even now, whenever my aunt, who knows I'm gay, asks me about who I'm dating, she asks, 'You are the dude, right?' I reply, 'No, there is no dude. I'm the girl and she's the girl.' I like us to be two girls having a relationship – split the bills and do the chores together. That is what I like.

All my friends know I'm gay. All of them. I have a friend who I met when I moved into this building. The first or second day, we were chilling and she asked me if I was gay and I said yes. With my friends, I'm free. I'm myself. None of them have any problem with it. The worst is that they will tell me, 'I don't like your sexuality but you're my friend and I love you.' So that's just it.

It's different with my family. My immediate brother found out sometime back. He used to ask if I had a boyfriend and I would say no. I think he figured it out for himself and asked, 'Are you into girls?' He preached to me. He's very homophobic but hey, I'm his sister. Since then, we've never talked about it. It's like a don't ask, don't tell kind of thing that we have. He knows that I am, but he has never asked me about it.

It's affected our relationship. I'm not as close to him as I want to be. I would want to tell him everything about me if we were close but there are lots of things I can't tell him. I'm close with my eldest brother but we never talk about it either. I did not tell her, but I'm sure his wife knows. She was on my BBM and I talk about girls. Once, she actually put up a girl on her DP and was like, 'The girl is very fine, but sorry, I'm straight.' So obviously she knows what it means. She understands. My aunt knows too. I told her and she was like, *Okay, no problem.* She's a liberal person. I have another cousin who I told and he too was okay.

I could never tell my parents. They don't even talk about it in my family. It's taboo. A few years ago, I was working in an NGO and really liked my job. Someone, I don't know who, but

I'm sure that person is in my family, sent a mail to my father telling him that I'm a lesbian, outing me to them.

My father summoned me back home. He told me to quit my job, pack my things and leave. He is very controlling, so whatever he says, you do. I'm 25 but I'm still under him so I had to quit my job and go back home.

He didn't talk to me the whole day I arrived. The next day, he called me and showed me the mail. He couldn't even read it out: 'Your daughter is a lesbian.' I didn't know what to say. My brother had already given me a clue of what the mail was all about so I told him, 'Ah, it's not possible. It's a lie.' The mail had some names so I quickly read them and said, 'It's this guy who has been asking me out and it's probably because I refused him, that's why he's writing all these things about me.'

I had to stay home for six to eight months. I had already quit my job so I didn't have any other option. I would wake up, run errands for them and sleep until school came through. School was my saving grace and I moved away to do my Masters.

My family is very religious – my father is a pastor and my mother is an evangelist after all. There is a lot of preaching against homosexuality in the churches. It affected me growing up, but I've not had any conflicts since I've been exposed. Whenever they talk about it, I just zone it out unconsciously. It makes me feel like they are preaching hate. They are speaking on God's behalf, but you cannot tell me this is what God is saying when you're not God.

I'm spiritual rather than religious. I studied philosophy as my first degree so I think a lot. For me, religion causes the problems we have in the world right now – the killings and everything else. I'm not religious in the sense that I don't believe most of these things. I don't believe there's a type of way to approach God. I don't believe there's a type of way you have to behave to be religious. My spirituality involves me communicating directly with God. There are times when I study the Bible and I figure, seriously, all these things are ancient laws. It doesn't apply now. The main law that applies now is, love your God and love your neighbour as yourself. So how can loving someone be wrong? Most of the things they preach I don't believe because it's against my own belief. My main thing is, as long as whatever you are doing is not causing harm to you, to me and to people around us, emotionally or physically, then you are free to do whatever you want.

I think people are getting more enlightened now through reading and meeting people. The problem is when you are not being exposed. Say I've been in Ibadan for fifty years. I don't know what is happening in any other place in the country or outside the country. My beliefs would be based on what is happening in Ibadan. I think people are getting more exposed through meeting people, going out there, reading and seeing things. I think it's a little bit better, at least for the educated people.

It's not an issue for a lot of people. It is not. There's also a generational difference. My grandmother, when she watches *The Ellen DeGeneres Show*, will say, 'Oh she's married to a woman. I like her.' If it were my mother, I am sure it would have been another statement. I think older people, not fifties or sixties but seventies and above, are more tolerant because it was normal in the culture back then – female–female and husbands having lots of wives and stuff going on between the wives.

There was this spirit where, if you are in my community,

we are brothers and sisters. That is what it means when I can have a friend and my husband would marry this woman just for us to continue. There is this story I read. It's a book that was written in 1871 called History of the Yorubas. It tells of a woman whose very close friend was enslaved. The woman looked for her for almost a year, went to the palace and found out she was married to the king. The king said, 'You have courage to look for your friend,' and brought her to the palace so she and her friend could live together. The king made them the rulers of one state and sent them away with lots of maidens. The two women became the most powerful people in that state. They had a lot of maidens; seriously, what could that be? So it wasn't seen as a big deal in the past.

It is really important to know about this, and that there are others out there. It took a while for me. When I was in school, say in my undergraduate days, I didn't know. It was only afterwards that I understood there was a community and started making friends. Now, 80 per cent of my friends are gay, bi or lesbian. It means you can build yourself with people other than your family. It has helped a lot to have people I can relate to. Now, I have people to talk to when I'm feeling down, who understand. I can't talk about these things in my family house, so it has really helped emotionally.

We need to keep pushing on and not give up. The most important thing is to do something with your life. There are so many attacks on homosexual societies because a lot of us are jobless and don't have stuff going on with our lives. My family would come and bug me about getting married to a man and if I didn't have my own life going for me, then they would be able to say, 'Maybe because you are gay, you don't have a job. You are gay because your life is not going well.'

The moment you do something with your life, nobody cares about your sexuality.

I tell people that my sexuality is just the icing on the cake. First of all, I'm human. Secondly, I'm a philosopher. Thirdly, I'm a librarian. My sexuality doesn't define who I am.

– OW, age 25, Ondo

---

1   SS2 = Senior Secondary 2

2   WAEC = West African Examinations Council

3   200-level = Second year at university

I Am A Proud Lesbian

'People have talked about me, seriously, but I am not the kind of person who listens to them.'

Content Note: Sexual Harassment

Growing up, I was a quiet person. I still am. You'll only see my noisy side when I am with friends. I have to be very close to someone for them to know that I can talk. That part of me really gets to some people and they don't like it. Half the things I do, they don't get cos I don't talk a lot.

My time at primary school was not particularly interesting, but I played football. It has always been my favourite sport. I was the only girl who played with boys in primary school. My parents were okay with me playing football though, and when I got to my junior secondary school, I was still the best footballer. In my senior secondary too. I never had to beg the boys to play. I was just another person who could play. My teachers would punish me for that so I left. I was like, *Are they not human beings? What are they protecting me from?*

I was brought up Christian. I believe in Christianity but I am not the kind of person who goes to church or prays every time. I go to church only on Sundays and I pray when I remember to pray.

We grew up in Jos. Plateau State has the best weather I have ever come across. Heat really gets to me so the weather in Jos is perfect. If I am to settle anywhere in Nigeria, it would be Jos.

I grew up with six siblings. I am the middle child, fourth out of seven. Sometimes I think growing up with so many siblings was not good. Sometimes I think it was good and other times I would like to have been the firstborn. My brother is the first and my parents don't doubt anything he says. They just believe him.

My brothers and I, we talk. We don't fight. We are cool, but not to the extent of knowing I am gay. That is my biggest secret, so I have to know who to share it with. I have discussed being gay with my cousins but not with my immediate family. They have never raised the subject with me. I think all my sisters and brothers are straight. I am sure. Even though they might suspect I am gay, I have not even thought about telling one person in my immediate family if it is true or not. If I had to talk to anyone, maybe it would be my elder sister or my immediate brother. I know that if I tell them, they might have no problem. Maybe they will try to talk me out of it, which is the normal thing.

My cousins have talked to me about it, but now they realise that this is me, this is what I want. Only one of them is older than me but they give me advice on relationships. They give me advice in situations where I tell them, 'See this girl, o, I like this girl.' They might talk to me about her. They see it as a normal thing now. I told my cousin's sisters, and I actually had a tiny crush on them. That is why I opened up to them. My wanting to do something with them would have told them what kind of person I was, so there was no point keeping it from them.

I did not really like school. I went because I had to. There was nothing interesting or important about it. But now I am studying psychology at ___ University. It is fun. I have always loved psychology and I have always wanted to be a psychologist. It is a very interesting course because whatever they teach you, it happens. What you learn theoretically is easy to put into practice. I like economics too but I don't like maths at all. Maths is hard.

But university is fun, seriously, and I get to see my friends. After lectures, there is a place we normally meet. Then if we have money to go hang out, we do. If we don't, we will stay and gist, and look around and see people passing. School is so good but I don't really like the endless strikes. Sitting like this, staying at home, makes me feel sick. I am not the kind of person who will stay, wake up in the morning, sweep the house, sleep, wake up. That is no life for me. It is only sick or lazy people who do that.

My friends are very important to me. I like having people around me. I cannot just be there. I have to have somebody to talk to. I have three people who are very close. The four of us attend ___ University but I always hang out with just one. The other two do not really like hanging out like that.

Growing up, I only used to talk about girls with my gay friends. I did not have any business with guys. Although most of my friends now are into guys, some of them are lesbians and I have bisexual friends too. I am only able to talk about girls and everything to my gay friends cos they know about me.

I didn't know anybody else like me when I was at school. The first person I knew was the first girl I dated, my first love, M___. The first kiss we had was special. It was as if I was in heaven. If I recall it now, it was ... *Wow.* M__ was the first person I was attracted to. I really liked her. She freaked out and became very shy. The day after we kissed she didn't talk to me. I was scared but I picked up the courage to talk to her.

I can't quite remember how everything started, cos when we broke up, I decided to forget everything about her. But whenever I saw her, my heart ...! It got to a point where she would be sitting down in front of me in class and I wouldn't be able to concentrate on the teacher. I would look at her all the time. Eventually I had to sit in front of her because of the distraction. It was really fun and then we started dating. For me, love grows with time. Love at first sight has never happened to me so I can't say if it exists, but I think people say they fell in love at first sight to get what they want.

The second person I dated was in SS1. R__ was my friend from school and I really, really loved her. We used to visit each other's dormitory rooms. One day, on her way back from my dormitory, I just kissed her. I don't know how it happened. That was how everything started. But we broke up in SS2 because they found out about us and she wanted to please her friends.

When our friends found out, they spoke to her and then to me. They said we should stop this thing, that it was demonic, devilish, what, what, what. I said okay to whatever they said, just to make them to stop talking. I told them I'd heard. They started talking about change, change, change, as if they were perfect. Trust me, I cannot change for anybody. This is just me. This is the life I chose to live.

It was a mixed school and I know the gist really spread. People heard we had dated but only my friends had the courage to talk to me. Others might have talked behind me,

I don't know. But it wasn't really a problem. Being this way was always normal to me. We were just being ourselves.

I do think of my ex and previous lovers. I talk to most of them. We just talk normally: How are you? How have you been? How was your day? How is your family? You need to ask those kinds of questions. Right now, my best friend is the most important person in my life. Whenever I need her, she is there. Actually, we dated, but we broke up and now she is my best friend. She always knows the right things to say, always knows the right thing to do. She is just perfect. She does a lot for me. She is a very good friend. If there is anything I do not want to lose in this life, it is her.

Even though I have never dated a man, being a lesbian doesn't affect my life. People don't know about it, so I live like a normal girl on the streets. Though they suspect and talk about it, I don't care. They see me mostly with girls but I have friends who are boys. Maybe it is my dressing and all that. People have talked about me, seriously, but I am not the kind of person who listens to them. They say, 'She is a lesbian, she dates girls, she brings different girls to her house ...' Neighbours, everywhere I go, like to talk about it. They see it as something demonic, something devilish. I don't have any business with whatever they say. If I listened to them, I wouldn't be alive. I would have killed myself. Everybody has his or her own way of living. That is what they don't understand.

I don't double-date. If it is you, it is you, that is my life. Sex is really, really important cos I am a human being. I have needs. When I am in the mood to do something, and you are not there, I am sometimes able to control it, but at other times I will not be able to control it. Seriously. In a relationship, sex makes you get closer to each other. I have never, ever cheated.

Never. And I have never gone a year without sex. The longest I went without is six months and I got used to it. When I start, I can have sex every day. Every blessed day. Along the way, I met someone who wasn't that way and I had to just take it. To cope, I got used to having less sex, so now it is not addictive for me. I can control myself – except when I am high, so I try to avoid girls at that time.

I don't think much about gender roles. The way I am is just it. Whatever a man does, I would like to do. That is what I have always done. I have always been the one paying the bills and all that. I don't like anything girly. I don't wear make-up or anything and I have never dated someone who is too much into make-up. I don't see the point. I have dated a really feminine person but the make-up shouldn't be too much. When you look at the person, you should still see them. A girl who dresses very well, decent, that is my kind of person, not those ones who use long nails, long eyelashes, eye shadow everywhere … I can't even get attracted to that kind of person. If I see them, nothing in this life could make me picture us building a life together.

The lesbian community in Jos is huge. I know one when I see one. I know by the way you talk, the way you behave, except if you are someone who doesn't really talk much or you are too secretive; if you are trying to hide that this is who you are and you never talk about it. It is hard to find them but they are everywhere. Finding them means knowing how to say the right things, how to move with people. You need to use psychology to know. If not, you will goof. I mostly meet people in school. Everybody meets in school. Also through sports, but I don't really train any more.

Football was everything when I was younger. I probably

would have ended up being a professional footballer. We have many queer people in football, but most of them are bi. I cannot have anything to do with them because of the lifestyle: everybody wants to sleep with you before they give you a chance to play. I cannot sleep with guys. Most coaches want to do something with you. Male coaches, yes, but there are female coaches too.

It is really hard to make it in football o, unless you get someone to sponsor you. Someone with connections. That is how it works. But now I accept that football is not everything. When something doesn't work, you have to let it go. Maybe it wasn't my field. It wasn't what I was supposed to become.

I started up a business recently, so I have people working with me. I am also quiet at work. It's not like I do not talk to my workers; I do, but there is a limit, or there should be a limit, so they know you are their boss. I don't just talk to them anyhow, no matter who. That's what everybody wants to be – their own boss. I have always dreamt of that sha.

I am really, really trying to work hard so that at least if I don't get married, nobody will disturb me. I don't see myself getting married – ever – to a guy. It cannot be. I cannot love somebody out of pity. Or tell you I love you when I don't. If I don't love you, I don't love you. So if I get married, it will be because my parents were pressuring me. But still I cannot. I have not experienced the kind of pressure that makes me do what I do not want to do. But marriage to a girl? I am not sure, not yet.

Living my life makes me feel very good. Most people lie. Me, I am just open. It is not hard to know the kind of person I am if you are close to me. I am a lesbian and I am proud of that. I don't hide it. If you know about it or ask me about lesbians, I can't hide myself from it. I think everybody should just live the life he or she chooses, the way they feel free, the way they feel okay. Just be you. Don't try to be something people want you to be or do things to impress somebody by being fake.

When I look at the future, maybe when I am 40, I know I would have made a lot of money. I would like to be remembered as someone who really helped people. I have always had a mind to make money, not just for myself but for people who really need it. I do not see myself living at home. I won't be in this country. I imagine myself in my house, with kids, with somebody, living a perfect life. I imagine she'll be older than me but not too old. She will have a responsible job that will bring her home at a good hour, not keep her out from morning till night. A job where she will be a boss. I will be a boss too.

But I recently broke up with my girlfriend. We met through a common friend. We were together less than a year and it was a mutual break-up. We were fine until she told me about her boyfriend, whom she had never mentioned before. She said that I was her first and that she was not a lesbian. She didn't do it because she wanted to be a lesbian but to get close to me and make me stop being a lesbian. She told me that she needed to bring me out of this. She actually wanted to marry the guy so I had to break up with her cos I am not into guys at all. This is how I want to be. She can be what she wants to be.

My biggest lesson has been to not give my heart and fall in love with one person. If anything should happen, it will affect you deeply. After this break-up, I do not think I want to be serious with anybody again. I have locked away that part of me that loves, for now. I don't know how long it is going to take because I am tired of being heartbroken and I am not ready for it again. That feeling is not sweet at all. Maybe I will just live life, have fun with it, tell girls I love them when I don't. That is what they want, isn't it? When I was being good, they just played with me. So I am not ready to be good to someone who will not even appreciate it.

– *LN, age 22, Plateau*

If You Want Lesbian, Go To Room 24

'Then at some point I said to myself, "We all die one day. Let's just die if we have to die."'

I come from ___ State, from a family of four children. We lost one of my brothers in 2014, so we are now two boys and a girl. I studied in ___ University, served in Lagos, worked there for a bit. Now I am with an NGO in Abuja. I am a paralegal. I relocated to Abuja a year ago. It's great. I can't compare it to Lagos cos of the fun in Lagos, but for every other thing Abuja is great. Cool, quiet – and expensive, which is not great.

I am very close to my family. I am the middle child and, as the only girl, my relationship with my brothers is amazing. I call my 24-year-old brother my boyfriend because of how close we are, and my relationship with my immediate older brother is great too. Sometimes, I think my mum, dad and siblings are all children. There is no mother, father, older or younger. Everyone is equal, to an extent.

I was a regular kid growing up. A bit noisy but not always. Sometimes the indoor kid, but pretty much fun. I used to get very upset when everyone was playing computer games, because I didn't know how to play any game. I would sit in a corner, until I learned how to play *Mortal Combat*, which is still the only video game I think I can play. I am good at Ludo, Snakes and Ladders, Scrabble, Monopoly and draughts, and

I am still learning chess. I played a bit of football. But I had to be the keeper cos I didn't want to run up and down.

I was never the person reporting issues. Instead, I was the person everyone was reporting. At one point, I kept getting on everybody's nerves so my dad was like, 'Nobody touches her. I do not want to come back one day to find that you have killed this girl. If she does anything, wait till I come back and report to me, and I will be the one to beat her.' But before Popsie came back, I would bribe, beg and tell you that my ice cream and chocolate, or anything he brought for me was yours. I kept doing the same shit and bribing my way out. I had a strong hold on them because any time they wanted something and wanted it fast, they had to go through me. I was the one who begged my dad with a crying face. If they really wanted anything they would be like, 'Tell daddy.'

As a kid I was in-between. I used to wear my brother's clothes, all these baggy knickers, and shirts and bounce with them to the filling station, yoppying up. Later on, I got really girly. If you ask me about my sexuality, I say I am a lesbian. But I have my moments where I dress how I feel ... and it is seasonal. Now I sometimes say I am genderfuck. Sometimes I am very girly and sometimes I dress masculine. And then other times I am very tomboyish with a touch of femme. And people will be like, 'What's up, which one are you?' I have a picture on Instagram where I said, 'Stop trying to figure me out. You are putting me in a box, and I can't fit cos I am too big for that box. This is me. Take me as I am. If I wear this, take it as that. In fact, I can choose to go naked on the street one day and you won't ask me what gender I identify as.' In the picture, I am wearing a shirt, jeans, no make-up, a cap and a masculine posture. And it got a lot of likes. I don't know if they like the feminine or masculine part of me but I like both.

I live a very ordinary life. Apart from work, when I have free time, I play with social media. I love Snapchat, Instagram, Facebook, sometimes BBM and Tumblr, but I don't frequent Twitter that much. I play music almost all the time, dance or have sex when I need to exercise. I have a lot of books on my Kindle. Right now, I am reading *Craving You* by Liv Nilsson. I am also really into the song *Nobody Has to Know* by Kranium and obsessed with the TV series *Empire!* I love, love, love Cookie and I see myself in her. I like lesbian films such as *Elena Undone* and *Anyone but Me* ... There are too many to name, but my favourite movies any day, any time are *Rush Hour* (1, 2 and 3) and *Step Up Revolution*. I scratched the DVD so bad I had to get a new one.

I am not religious or spiritual. I was born into a Christian family but the last time I was in church was 2008. I believe in God and His existence, I just don't have to be in church to worship Him. I pray in my own quiet time if I feel like it. I can talk to you while praying in my mind. I have my own personal relationship with God.

I wasn't born with a silver spoon per se, but we were comfortable and okay. Then things got shaky and I said, 'You know what? I am going to take care of myself.' So I upped and left. I travelled after secondary school when I was about 17 or 18. I had a little issue with my dad because they found out I was seeing a guy, F___. Immediately after I met him and decided to date him, I told Mumsie about it and she was like, 'Oh nice.' He was a year older than me. They had never heard of any boy around me throughout secondary school so Mumsie was like, 'Okay, be careful.'

I didn't have a phone then. Well, nobody did. So F___

would call my mum's phone and we would talk. My mum is very open but my dad found out and went whoosh! My aunts told him about it and it was terrible. Maybe they thought I was gonna get pregnant – the usual things in Nigeria. It was so serious. He beat me up. I was supposed to sit for JAMB[1] and my dad was like, 'No. No exam for you.' That was my punishment. I didn't sit for the exam so I was upset. And I harboured that anger for a long time.

Before the next JAMB, I planned. Any money I got, I saved. When I'd saved enough, I travelled on my own without anybody knowing. One Saturday, while Mumsie was sleeping, I took off on my road trip to the east. For two days, they looked for me. But then my aunt called her to say I was fine, I was safe, that I'd gone to her place and they shouldn't worry because I told her everything and she knew how my dad got when he was upset.

I didn't go back to Lagos that year. I started hustling. I would go to my aunt's shop and sell things. I also started travelling to Lagos to buy stuff and bring it back to sell. Like that I got money. When a year had passed, I said, *Okay, it is time for school.*

I wrote JAMB and passed. I paid, did everything on my own and gained admission. When I got the admission and saw my name on the board, I picked up the phone and called home. I said I got admitted to ___University. My mum was like, 'God, what kind of girl is this?' She was really excited.

But Popsie – we hadn't spoken. I hadn't heard from him for a long time and I wasn't planning on calling him. At this time, he wasn't angry but he was still worried cos my mum refused to tell him that they had heard from me. She later told me that she had told my father to provide for her daughter, so he was still trying to find me by himself. My siblings and everybody knew but nobody spoke to him about me even when they saw him eaten up.

He came to the east during my second year. I learned he was around. I was in my aunty's house cos it was a weekend. When he came, I heard his voice from outside so I came out from the room and greeted him. He was in shock. His eyes were red. I could see the tears. He was like, 'Okay, how are you? So where have you been?'

I told him I had been living with my friend's family after leaving Lagos and that I was in school. He said, 'What school?' I said I was at ___ University, that I'd sat for JAMB, got admission and was in my second year. He was so shocked. He was sizing me up, seeing that I was a lot different. It was good, though somehow painful. I had done it and I was proud.

He collected my number and said that if I needed anything I should call him. School fees, pocket money, anything – just call him … I said, 'Sure.' But one thing I'd told myself from day one was that I wasn't going to ask for any payment from anyone till I graduated. That is what I did. Till I finished, I didn't ask for money. And they couldn't even come looking for me when they couldn't contact me.

It was pretty tough but I pulled through because I was selling stuff while schooling. I knew the Lagos market very well. When I went to Lagos I would buy jeans for N800, go back and sell them for N3,500 or so. The shirts I got for N1,200, I sold for N6,500. Where I was, they spent a lot of money on clothes and they liked good stuff. I did that for a long time. I was even going to Abuja. My biggest customers at some point were bankers, cos I started selling suits. And I got them for N4,500 and sold them for N16,000. Some cost N8,000 and I sold them for N24,000. When it is well packaged and everything, they think it is foreign, so I made money. And

I saved. I had an account for business. I never touched it. I never even had an ATM card.

It was hard because ___ University is not the best school. I am sorry to say that, but it is a fact. After studying, you still have to pay your way there. Lecturers are horrible. They want to sleep with you before they give you your grade. It was really crazy. And when you are in class they don't even notice you so I wasn't always in class. But anytime they had a test or whatever, and I couldn't go, I got someone to sit for me. I did what I had to do. I didn't graduate with a good grade but the fact that I finished is what I am proud of. I know the cost of education.

The first person I felt an attraction to was one cute young girl back in secondary school. She had this chubby face. I can't even remember her full name, but I know she was Hausa, average height and hairy. I had a thing for her and she had a thing for me too. I think I was in JSS1 then and we were in different hostels. We were friends, yes, but not so close. Any time she tried to come around for us to spend time, they didn't allow it. You know boarding schools.

But one night we managed to sneak in, covered up. We were gisting, then we kissed and slept. I don't know if I kissed her or she kissed me; maybe we both did. I sha can't remember but we kissed, then she went back to her bed. The next morning, we didn't talk. We pretended nothing had happened. I walked past her and she passed me. We never spoke about it again. We never even talked again until she left the school in JSS3. We would stare at each other from afar, but before one made a move, the other walked off. Now, every time I remember it I am like, *What the fuck?* I don't want to see her but sometimes I wonder where she could be. Is she still alive?

My first relationship was with a guy. We met, started dating and broke up. I loved him. I do not want to say it wasn't love. It was. He was the guy my dad tried to break me up with, but it didn't work. At some point, something about me kept going off. I felt myself disconnecting from him. I didn't know why and I couldn't figure it out. I didn't think it was something about women until I met this amazing girl, P___, long after I broke up with him.

P___ came to my school from the University of ___ to visit E___, a friend she was in a relationship with. P___ and E___ came to the lodge where I lived to visit a friend, and when I saw P___ from the balcony, I contemplated, *Is this a guy or a girl?* She looked so much like a guy, with nothing on her chest. I was like, *This person is too cute to be a guy*, so I came downstairs. I went down to the person they came to see and asked if her friend was a girl or a guy. She laughed and said she was tired of answering that question but said P___ was a girl. I was like, *Wow*, then I went back upstairs. Shortly after, we kind of got to know each other in the compound. Both P___ and E___ were hitting on me but neither of them knew about the other.

During that visit, P___ had issues with E___. After P___ travelled, E___'s phone was bad so she asked to use my phone to call her. I was like, 'Sure, call her to make sure she arrived safe.' After E___ called her, P___ saved my number and called the next day to talk to E___. I said, 'No. She is gone. She didn't sleep here.' Later, P___ called and said, 'Thanks for checking up on me.' I was like, 'I did not check up on you. E___ used my phone.' She was like, 'Okay, can I call you from time to time?' I was like, 'Okay, as long as it's normal.' She then asked if I would be around and said she was coming into town the next day. I was like, 'No, I am travelling cos it is the weekend.' She asked me to please stay but I didn't think anything of it so

I told her I would see her after I returned. I didn't know she was trying to flirt with me. I did not come back that week and she kept on calling.

The calls got too much and I didn't reason anything until one evening she called and said, 'You have been saying you will come back but I still haven't seen you and you haven't returned my calls.' I was like, 'When I come back, I will call you,' then I dropped the call.

Then I sat down and sparked. Why was this person even calling me like this? I called her and said, 'Why are you calling me like this? You have been calling me for how long. I don't understand. What is this thing? You want to see me, why?' She listened to me rant then said, 'I just wanted to see you. I will come in tomorrow.' I said okay and dropped the phone.

The next morning at 7am, I packed my things and headed off to school. She kept calling, saying, 'What will you do when you see me?' The conversation got there just like that. I was like, 'I do not know, probably hug you.' And she said, 'Only hug?' I was like, 'What more are you asking for?' Cos already I felt that there was something.

I got home. While cleaning up my dusty room, I left the door open. She came and kept knocking. I told her to come in but she wouldn't and just kept on knocking. She wanted me to come to the door and open it so I did and gave her a hug. She came in and dropped her laptop. We played music and gisted.

After a while, I played this Beyoncé and Rihanna combo CD that I owned and *Slow Love* came on. Interesting song. She said I should dance for her. I was like, 'I am a very good dancer. Don't let me tempt you.' She said, 'Let's dance.'

And I rocked the song, slow winding and all that. It was crazy and fun. But then we were rocking seriously and I was like, 'Okay, that's it. Cut, cut, cut, it is getting out of hand.' We sat down and started talking. Till like, 9pm. This was really late and I said, 'You are not going?' She said she would stay till tomorrow. The next day she stayed. The third day she stayed ... E___ was already calling but she wasn't picking her calls. I didn't know they were having issues and I was like her getaway.

We kept spending time together, gisting, and on the third day she was like, 'I think I have fallen in love with you.' I was like, *Ahem*, 'What? Just like that?' She said yes, she thought so. We hadn't had sex or even kissed. Nothing.

And all of a sudden, it just felt like I knew it all. No more questions. It was just normal. I just knew about her and E___ and everything. So I was like, 'But you are in a relationship.' She said yes, but they were having issues and that had been going on for a long time. I said, 'Wow, well you can't be with me and someone else; it is that straight.' And she said she'd known I would say that so she was going to talk to E___. I was like, 'Cool. You know you need to go home right?'

So she left my place and went home. I travelled the next day too, cos I was supposed to pick up some of my goods in Onitsha. I was on my way when I got a call saying that P___ went to E___'s house with two of my friends to pack her stuff and E___ went crazy and started fighting with her. They grabbed what things they could and went back to my place, but E___ followed them and found out that I was the person P___ was spending time with. They told me she came to my place with two guys and banged on the door, telling them to open it. And my house is hard to enter. I had two protectors. So when I got the call, I was like, 'E___'s going crazy in my house with men? Don't worry. I am coming.' When I got to Onitsha, I took the next bus back without getting my goods.

When I came back to town, E___ was gone. She wasn't in my house. Meanwhile, I had called the bike guy who ran errands for me and told him to wait downstairs. I told my friends and P___ to climb the okada bikes outside and we went to E___'s house. When we got there, I called her: 'Babe, please, I do not understand. Why did you come to my house with some guys?'

She got all mushy because she didn't see the guys who'd come with me, and said it wasn't like that, that she was just really surprised, and how could I do this to her? I was like, 'No this is insane. You can't come to my house and threaten my security; who does that?' She said she was sorry and hadn't come for a fight, just wanted to figure out ... But then my friends came out from the corner and she started screaming and cursing. I was like, 'Don't try it. You really do not want to get in a fight with me.' I told P___, 'Pick up your stuff.' And she packed all her things and mounted the bike.

E___ started cursing: 'You are mad. You are crazy, bitch.' On the street! I didn't know what to say, because I am not good at all this so I went to the bike and I told P___ to come down. And while E was looking at us and cursing, I grabbed P___ and kissed her. Right there on the street. My two friends were in shock but they screamed and jumped. It was a semi-busy street. There were small shops there, a bar, people passing by.

Then my friends were like, 'We need to get out of here before somebody stones us to death.' E___ was just deflated. When we got back to the house, P___ asked, 'What was that?' I said, 'I don't know what happened. I was upset and I wanted to get back at E___.' But it turned out well. We were laughing. I didn't see E___ again and we moved on.

We were together for a while before she went back to school.

She had issues at school but she hadn't told her parents that she was having issues before coming to my school. I insisted she tell her parents so they could try to fix it because they had not heard from her for about three weeks. She called her mum, told her everything, even told her that I was the person who made her call. Her mum spoke to me, thanked me, and asked if I could please get her to come home? I said sure, and two days later she was on her way home. She said her father almost killed a chicken when she got home!

From then, her mum kept asking me when I was going to come around. I visited for her sister's child's dedication. At first I was scared her family would say this lesbian had kidnapped their daughter, because they knew that she was gay. She was so out there. She never hid it. She has been like that since and she just told them when she was a kid. Sha, I went there for a couple of days, and it was fun. The hospitality at the reception was amazing!

Because she was not in school, she spent a lot of time with me. For a year, we were practically living together. Then one day we had a little issue. I took a short journey and I told her I would be back, but she left with my friends to Port Harcourt. I was so upset when I came back! I blanked her, so we were off for like two months.

She tried to get in touch all the while, but finally a friend of mine called and said, 'Do you know your girlfriend is dating someone already?' Apparently, P___ had been telling them not to tell me. Her plan was that if we got back together, she would break up with the girl and come back to me. When she called the next time and was like, 'Oh baby,' I said, 'No, don't worry. I know about your girlfriend. You have moved on. Just be gone.' That was it. We were together just over a year before that happened and we broke up. It was interesting, amazing;

at the end of the day it was whoosh. But at least she helped me realise myself and that part of me.

My first sex with a girl was very awkward. In 2007 I had this friend who was pretty into me but I didn't know what to do with her. I liked her as a friend – I still do – but nothing else. I visited her one day and she was all over me and tried to get all mushy. I didn't know what to do with her. I didn't know whether to touch her or not. I was very nervous. I didn't feel what she was doing but she got really down and we had sex. She did all the touching and I was just a pillow queen. When she climaxed she lay down and I thought, *Thank God this is over, so what next?* But all that was before P___.

With P___, it was just wow. There was no definition. It was deep. Deeper than deep. The connection was amazing. We didn't have to talk about where to touch, how you like it, what you want to do – we just kept doing everything right. I don't know how. It was amazing. We are still in touch today. We still talk once in a while. I advise her and stuff. She is seeing a girl in Lagos. They are living together and it is good for them. I think the law doesn't even affect anything cos people are still living together and doing their thing.

I have had four relationships – one man and three women. What I consider a relationship is when I meet someone I really love and we share a connection. We have that understanding, that agreement that this is what we want to do and this is how we are doing it. It has to be an agreement between both of us, not just an assumption that we are dating because we've shagged. You have a date, and there has to be an agreement before you can say you're in a relationship with this person and this person is in a relationship with you too.

A relationship is one thing but sex is different. I think people just want to have sex all the time. They don't talk about what they are doing, they just do it. I do not know how easy it is for others, but I have to know you before I get down with you. I meet people who just say they want to get down with you. I do not know about the rest of the community but sex is so easy at times and so hard at others. The community is big. There are lots of people but they are hiding. All you have to do is reach out. The circle of people who are out is so small.

I have met a lot of people online. A lot of people try to contact me on Facebook, because online I am very open, so when they see that rainbow flag, they try to add me. I always go through their profile first. I have to be careful. I have to check who you are friends with, the connection, if there is someone who I know, before I add you or not. But I try to chat with ladies when they add me. I try to have a conversation, no strings attached, but I try to be careful about what I say and how the conversation goes. Most times I meet people and it turns out that someone from the community already knows them, so that is good. I try not to get personal, but when I get to know you, I try to bring you to the community centre and everything. I have even invited two people from Owerri to Abuja for events and stuff at the community centre.

Meeting other people is not hard, nor is it easy. I do not know if people believe in this 'gaydar' thing, but I do. I have very strong gaydar so that if you are family, I know. The thing also is not knowing but approaching, and I don't do much of the talking or approaching. Most of the people I have been with came to me. Not that I do not admire people and want to go to them; sometimes I just think, *Let me give it a rest.*

After school, I was even more out. University life followed me to Lagos because even in NYSC camp, people knew – maybe because I told a couple of guys that I was not interested in them and then they saw me happy with girls all the time.

When I started working, even my bosses knew. My first boss asked me out and when I turned him down, he figured it out. At my second place of work, my boss knew and he was so cool with it. He even tried hooking me up with a girl one time. And I didn't hide. I didn't pretend in public. I was just me. People in school knew. Everybody knew at some point.

One time, we went to Port Harcourt for a gay party. While we were away, someone posted a sign on my gate: 'If you want lesbian, go to Room 24 and Room 18.' My room is 24 and Room 18 is where P___ and E___ came to see me the first time. But before I got back, my friends took the sign off. I was like, 'Ahhhhh, why did you take it off? Those people are bringing me customers and you are fucking me up. Post it; go and put it back!'

Till today I do not know who did it but I heard rumours that some other lesbian group that was reigning at the time were the ones. I still don't understand why but I had graduated at that time. The guys, on the other hand, would beef a little that all the pretty girls liked coming to our place to hang out, but because they liked me, they didn't do anything. The people they beefed more were P___ and the other tomboys. I never experienced any violence or threats, even though I was out there.

I am not concerned about my security. I feel like being at the right place at the right time helps. I do not wait till late to go home. I do not work late nights. There are certain things I avoid. I go out a lot but you can hardly find me alone cos I know that with eyes on me, I am safe. I've always made an effort to have a good relationship with my neighbours. A friend of mine from secondary school once contacted me on Facebook. She was like, 'Long time, no see.'

After the whole catching up, the conversation went like this:

'Are you married?'

I said, 'No.'

'Are you seeing somebody?'

'No.'

'So what is going on with you? When are you planning to get married?'

I said I wasn't planning to, so she was curious as to why. I said, 'Because I am gay.'

'Gay? How? I do not understand.'

'I don't know what else you want me to say or how to break it down? I am a lesbian. I am not planning on getting married to anyone.'

'Oh my God, who has done this to my friend? What kind of thing is this?'

I was like, 'Done what to who? What do you mean who has done what, and what do you think they are doing? This is me.'

'No, this is not my friend, that I know.'

I said, 'People change. This is me, but when we were in school I had not realised my sexuality and you didn't know. But now you know.'

She felt it was an abomination. A curse. Someone must have done something to me. I cut off contact. I am no longer in touch with her. We are not friends. That is it. She can't ask me stupid questions to get me questioning my own self. That can't happen.

Also, have you ever heard how straight people talk about gay people? Can you imagine how terrible that conversation would be? Why do these people exist, Sodom and Gomorrah, the world is coming to an end. They make it look like we are the reason the world is coming to an end. The reason God is going to send floods to flush the world. He is even going to send fire and brimstone. Sometimes when they talk, I am like, *So if I just open my mouth to say I am gay, I am dead?* And then some people are like, 'Maybe it is a curse. Maybe it is from the village. Maybe it is a mental disorder ...'. There is always something terrible attached to it. And some people are like, 'If I ever know anyone, even suspect: straight to police.'

In fact, I once got into a fight with a straight guy in Lagos. I went out with a friend who invited me for a drink, and they didn't know I was gay. She was always like, 'Let's hang out with my friends, lets hang out with my friends,' and that day I said okay.

When we were drinking and talking, the conversation at the table somehow diverted. A lady sat down with another lady at the bar and they had a drink. They were so engrossed in the conversation and you could see, not only the connection, but the interest. They had so much focus on one another and it was really serious, like they were trying to sort something out or get something straight.

Our table started talking about them. They were like, 'Maybe they are having issues, relationship matters, or maybe there is more to it.' For about an hour, the conversation was just about them. And the more they talked – you know how nasty they get with words – the more it kept eating me up.

At some point, I was like, 'So what if they are gay? If they are trying to sort out something, let them sort it out. Why are we here talking about some people when we are supposed to be having fun? We are not even saying anything interesting.' This had been boiling and I was thinking, *Beat me up if you have to.* I was like, 'I don't even know why I came out here; babe wassup? How do you even invite me to hang out with this set of people who are not thinking in the right direction? Everybody is thinking aggressive. Everybody is being negative.

Everybody is trying to be a "man" ... You know what? I am out of here.'

And one of them was like, 'What did you say? Do you want to stand up?'

I said, 'So if I stand up, you will beat me up or what will happen?'

He said, 'Do you know I can pick this drink and pour it on you?' I looked at the girl who invited me; she was giving me the sign not to make trouble. I shook my head, took my bag. He picked the glass and wanted to pour it on me but one of his friends hit his hand and blocked him so I felt only a little splash.

I turned and said, 'If not for the fact that we lesbians know how to respect ourselves in public and not embarrass ourselves like mad men, I would have done exactly what you did and nothing would have happened. But we are not the same, as you all can see, so I am out of here.' I left the place, deleted her number immediately and erased her from my memory.

Those people were her friends but she did not stand up for me. She didn't say, 'This is my guest and you have no business pouring drinks on her.' She was just quiet and trying to say, Why are you behaving like this? I felt she was supposed to say something on my behalf. She didn't say anything until the day after. That is not friendship. When she tried to get in touch to talk about it, I was like, 'Look girl, I understand. It's okay, but we can't be friends.'

I am out to everyone at home. Hiding is not the thing for me. I mean, I am out there. Even if I try to hide, you would see me and go, *Hmm, there is something about this one*. It was there so I didn't hide.

Well, I am out to everyone except my dad. I haven't had

a one-on-one conversation about it with him, but he knows. After my last break-up, he was like, 'I learned that you and your friend in ___, you don't go there any more. I hope you have stopped keeping carnal friends.' I laughed and wondered, *What is carnal about the friendship?* He was trying to say that maybe I got over it. Maybe it is a phase I have passed through. But my mum knows. We talked about it, cleared the air. Right from time, my mum knew but we didn't talk about it.

There are certain things she does and I go, *Are you sure this woman is not gay herself?* My first girlfriend, P___, used to come to the house, and my mum loved her. If she didn't see her for a week or two, she would call and ask, 'What happened? Have you started fighting?' And then sometimes she was like, 'How is your wife?' As in, those are the terms she uses, and even when we fought or I had issues with P___, she would be like, 'All this husband and wife fight – don't worry, it will pass, you people will settle.' Weird stuff like that.

And the way she took it when I came out to her – it wasn't a surprise. I was 28 at the time. It was kind of a bad time for me, because I was going through the break-up with my ex N___. I went home to Lagos two days later for my brother's memorial service.

When I came to Lagos, I went to the house and I kept receiving calls. She kept wondering cos I had the phone 24/7. I would have these long conversations then come back with red eyes and a swollen face. When she asked what was going on I just told her. I said, 'Look, you know N___, who you have been talking to once in a while over the phone? And you know I visit her constantly? We broke up. She was my girlfriend. We were actually in a relationship but now we are not any more. We had a fight, and that is it. We broke up. And I have been trying to get her to understand that what she heard about whatever is going on is not true, but she says no, she doesn't want, and I love her so much ...'

I didn't want to say, 'Oh I am gay' but I kept using words that were questionable. She just hmm'ed. She kept studying me. She saw the pain, and she was like, 'Do you want me to call her? Do you want me to try to talk to her for you?' I thought about it. I was surprised at first. But I was like, 'No, it's okay. If she doesn't come around, if she doesn't believe me, then there is no trust and she doesn't know me by now even though we have been together for two years. She shouldn't worry. I will be fine.' Mumsie started lecturing me, telling me that I would be fine, I should give N___ time, she would get over it, and would come around if truly she wanted to be with me. That if she didn't, that I should move on, you know, try to be strong, take it like it is one of those things. And I just looked at this woman like ...!

After that conversation, I felt a lot better and was like, break-up or no break-up, I gained something. My mindset was, I am going through this, I am really devastated, if this is it, let it be it. So let me just use this opportunity to tell my mum. If she wants to get upset, if she wants to disown me, anything that wants to happen should happen. I was ready for the worst.

I couldn't believe her reaction. I had to put on the recorder on my phone and when she saw the light, she asked if I was recording her. I said it was pings coming in. I just couldn't believe it. Later, I played it over and over. When I left Lagos, I had to play it for my friends. I felt that if I told people, they would say it wasn't true, that it couldn't be coming from an Igbo woman. Mind you, I speak to her in Igbo and in English, and this conversation happened in both languages.

I had this conversation again with my mum, about six

months ago. I was at the office when she called, talking about some guy being interested in me. She was like, 'What about your friend F___, is he serious? People are coming o!' So I went downstairs at work, balanced very well and started the conversation again. I said, 'Mum, I think I need to tell you because you have to know at some point. I am not getting married to any guy. I am not planning to, not F___ or anyone after him. I don't plan on marrying a guy. I am a lesbian. I love women. You know this D___ person you have been talking to over the phone? She is my girlfriend and I have made up my mind that if it works out, we will get married. But because the country doesn't permit it, I am going to relocate and get married.'

I told her I would give her kids; that is not a problem. She said I'd answered the question she wanted to ask. Since I said it wouldn't be problem, she was okay. I explained to her how I was going to go about it. She said fine, as long as I am happy. That's is how she loved my girlfriend D___ all the more. She saved D___'s number and calls her from time to time. Sometimes I am like, 'Hey babe, why is my mother calling you and not me?' She will say, 'Please don't pick my call. That is my call.'

After that I came out to my older brother. We were talking over the phone and I told him. Just like I did with my mother, I didn't say I was gay. He asked me about my ex F___, the first guy I had been in a relationship with, because he knew we were in touch. I said, 'Ah please, that is history,' and gave him the gist from day one of how I started dating girls. He listened and and was like, 'Yeah, that makes sense.' I kept talking and he was like, 'That's okay as long as you are happy.'

As long as you are happy ... That is what they all said. I wonder why they are not worried, cos I am the only girl. But at the same time, I am grateful. I haven't come out to my little brother, my boyfriend yet. Well, not in detail. I haven't told him that I am seeing a girl and my plan is to settle with a woman, but I told him I have a girlfriend. And the term girlfriend is open – it can be just a friend, it can be anything. I trust him not to have a problem with me dating a girl.

I think the people in my extended family know. At least two of my cousins are gay. I do not know about the men but a few I know are bi. In fact, there is this girl, my cousin's friend, who has a huge crush on me. They kept telling me, 'This girl likes you, she really has a crush on you.' It is not so much of a big deal. So, a lot of my family and family friends know, my close cousins, everyone that matters to me knows. The ones who don't know do not matter. No matter how down I feel, no matter the situation I find myself in, when I remember the fact that my family accepts me the way I am, I get a flush of joy. I know it is not so bad after all and I move on.

About same-sex marriage in Igboland: it is not like you will just get up and say you want to get married to a woman. You can be married to a man and if you don't have kids, then you can marry a woman to come and have kids for your husband. That person is your wife. Not his wife. *Your* wife. Choosing not to go through a guy should not make me a criminal. Cos that is not a curse. That is not wrong. Not an abomination. It is not illegal. I think picking a wife just so she can have your kids even though there is no man in the picture might also be allowed. There is also something like you marrying a wife because of your family name, in a case where your father has only girls or you are an only child.

Right now, I am very happy. I wake up so happy. People look at me and wonder if I won a jackpot. I am very active and sometimes I wake up on the bad side of the bed but

I find a way out with things like music, dancing, cooking, chatting with people, hanging out, gisting, the thought of my relationship and my love life …

I know that the country is not safe so I try to keep it cool. I was a little bothered when they tried to pass the law, considering the fact that quite a number of people know I am gay and I didn't know how it was gonna connect to me. I wasn't really bothered about getting arrested. My concern was, how much worse can it get? Fourteen years is scary but what comes after the law? Then at some point I said to myself, 'We all die one day. Let's just die if we have to die.' It was a bit threatening at first but now we laugh about it. According to a friend of mine, they will put you in a women's prison so when they put you in a cell, make sure they put you in with a lesbian. Just continue with a new relationship. Life goes on. And these days it doesn't really bother me so much. I do not even remember that the law exists.

– *RD, age 31, Abuja*

---

1   JAMB = Joint Admissions and Matriculation Board

Living A Double Life

'I don't see a future as long as people's perceptions stay this way.'

Content note: Rape, Sexual Violence, Abortion, Threatening Behaviour

I'm human, just like everybody else. I understand there are challenges for people who are not gay, but for us there is a very complex situation here in Nigeria. Right now, it's hard to find people who you can actually talk to about how you feel. Even with close people you are not able to tell how they will react sometimes. I have older sisters and brothers. They identify with this odd person I choose to be with them. None of them know about me but I believe they suspect. So, we are close but not close because there are certain things I can't tell them, things I only feel comfortable sharing with a friend who knows about my sexuality.

It has become so much worse lately. It was personally depressing for me when the law came into being. I already felt unsafe, and then somebody came and said, 'Oh, you're a criminal.'

How do you begin to process that? That did it for me. The law has renewed a lot of anger against us. Recently, I got talking with a friend. He said, 'LGBT people are going to hell. They are the Antichrist.' I asked him, 'Is there any reason, apart from what society tells you? Is there any particular experience you have had with an LGBT person who has given you this kind of notion about them?' He wasn't able to say anything – which I expected.

People think, 'How dare anybody come up with the notion that people can have same-sex relationships or even consider it?' I don't know what they're not happy about. Why is it such a problem? I don't see a future as long as people's perceptions stay this way. Look at my family. If anybody is going to support you, it should be your family. You shouldn't have problems with them. But they are disgusted by even the thought of homosexuality.

I find myself living a double life. I'm not able to express myself in certain ways. I'm extremely cautious in everyday things that everybody should find easy. When I'm walking on the road, I'm conscious of how I look, the way I walk, what I put on. It's constant. I find myself not thinking about other things I'm supposed to be thinking about. My thoughts are centred around my sexuality. Every decision I have to make, I'm thinking about what somebody else might be thinking, what somebody else might imply.

Life has been tough. I'm grateful now because I don't have to be at home with my parents. I'm so thankful that I've experienced a bit of independence, that I had an opportunity to get an education. Of course, nobody can be an island. You have to relate at some point or the other. But it makes me happy not to be totally dependent. That's something I regard as a privilege.

My family has been quite supportive financially. My childhood was okay. There wasn't any kind of problem or dysfunction at all. We were not rich but my parents were working. They could afford to care for us and pay school fees – and beat you when you were naughty. It was normal. I have pictures of me as a child in which you can see that I was a bit of a ruffian. I was an independent child. A curious child. The first experiences I had with working with my hands was fixing stuff. I was always climbing trees and fixing doors. I would open up the TV because I wanted to know how it worked. If I was able to fix anything, I would fix it. It was fun. I still find myself enjoying the fact that I can fix things with my hands.

Where my family haven't been supportive is the way I choose to express myself. My dad is a laid-back kind of person. Perhaps he thinks about these things, but he has never expressed them. I think he's cool but I'm not sure he knows about my sexuality. My mother though! I have had my mum complain about the way I dress. When I moved out, she was all up on my case that I should not go and live alone. I can't help it. I wear what I'm comfortable in. I had to leave, otherwise I would have run mad, or something would have happened to me.

Recently, my parents confronted me about my sexuality. I don't know if they had their ideas before that, but I had a woman move in with me and that got them questioning. They called me and asked me to come to the house. My mum had this face like, *Oh, you've done something terrible.* They asked me to sit down and then said they'd heard that I was living with a woman – like a husband and wife do. They confronted me with questions: 'Are you like a couple?' I don't know where they got that. I've tried very hard to keep things balanced, so it was shocking. I was terrified. As much as I would like to be independent, in this part of the world it seems to be bad news for one's parents to discover that they might have a gay child on their hands. I wouldn't want to break their hearts.

So, when they asked me, I denied it. That seemed to be the proper thing to do at the time. I told them, 'I'm not what you think I am. Even if there are people like that, there's no point discriminating against them. It's just who they are.' I don't know how they took that. I suspect they knew that I might have homosexual tendencies already but I wasn't going to say or admit to anything. I know it's going to be revisited. Just before I left home, there was all this pressure about marriage. It's been there for years but it's really increasing now because of my age, I think, and because I've not been bringing any guys home. I told my mum that I wasn't too interested in marriage but would like to have a kid or two. Her response to that was, 'Well, why not?' But my mum, with who she is, that might not be the end of it.

For me, it came so naturally. I can't remember the first time I liked a girl. If I looked at a boy, I thought *I like his dressing*; things like that. I may think, *He's a cute guy*, but not because I want to be hitting it with him. Instead, I've always imagined and fantasised about doing it with the female gender. It's always been there. I liked girls from when I was young. If we went to a birthday party, I would be checking out all the girls. I'm kind of a shy person so there was no telling anyone that I liked her. I wouldn't say anything but I'd think she was cute.

There was this girl I really liked in secondary school. I was 12. We went to church. We would meet. We would talk. I realised I liked her. I was not going to church the next week so I wrote her a letter. After that, we exchanged a number of letters. They would be full of the normal things you tell a girl you like – not that I wrote that I liked her, but it was full of the usual: How was school? How are your brothers? I never did tell her I liked her but we spent a lot of time together. My mum actually ended up reading one of our letters. She was supposed to deliver it as she was going to church while I was staying behind. She opened it. I saw her read it. I was very uncomfortable with her reading it. It was personal. I stopped talking to the girl. We just stopped seeing each other.

I didn't know anyone like me when I was younger. If girls I knew liked other girls, I wasn't talking to them. I was always on my own because I wasn't comfortable around people. It felt strange. University was terrible. Just me, fantasising about all these girls. When I was in university, it wasn't that there wasn't a law in place, but I wasn't aware of it. Nobody talked about the law at all. On occasion, people would say how unnatural and disgusting these kinds of relationships were and there was a lot of preaching against it, but much less than there is now. It wasn't that there was a law people talked about but that the mere fact that you were thinking that way was shameful. Because of that, I wasn't easily the make-friends kind of person. I had a lot of people telling me how I should change and stop looking and dressing a particular way, so I would much rather stay on my own. I got this so much. Even the few friends I had would say this.

The first time I had the courage to tell a girl I liked her was when I started working. I was about 27. She was in my workplace but we were in different branches. I used to call her, go to her place, follow her around and it was nice. She had a boyfriend but I thought that perhaps she was bisexual. She didn't have a problem with me hanging around so I thought, *Maybe?* She saw me off one of those times I had gone to her house and I summoned the courage. I did it. I told her.

She just thought it was weird. We were still friends afterwards but she was a bit uncomfortable around me. I was staying alone then but I was always going to her place. I think it was a problem for her to visit me. When she did finally come over, we had some big fight about some irrelevance she picked up. I got tired. We were still friends afterwards but when she got married, that was it.

It's painful to tell someone you like them when they don't like you back, but that experience itself was nice. I've suffered from not being able to express that part of myself for so long. I've struggled with self-esteem, so it felt good. You should be able to tell someone you like them. Now, I can tell them – more or less.

I have tried with men though. My first kiss was with a boy. I can't quite remember who – I've locked some things away. I do remember one guy who grabbed and kissed me. He had come to the hostel to see some friend of his. I don't know how it came about but I was the one seeing him off. We got to the corner of the hall and it happened. I was in shock. It felt weird. It felt yucky, actually. I didn't think it was right. I felt as though he took advantage – but I couldn't say that to him.

I felt like I couldn't do anything about it, couldn't complain. It would have looked and sounded strange – or so I thought at the time. After all, it's supposed to be normal when a guy kisses you, right? Nobody freaks out when a guy kisses them. In a way, I thought, *Fine, it was acceptable, it's no big deal.* But, of course, it was. I know that now.

I've found myself in many situations like that over the years, even when I was much older. In my twenties and thirties I was uncomfortable many times. There were many times over the years when I had to pretend things were cool when they were not.

Once, I was alone at a bar at a time when I was seriously considering just getting married and getting this pressure off my neck. I met this guy and we fixed a date for another day. I told him I wasn't into guys. We ended up at mine. The experience was uncomfortable from the start.

I remember three situations like that when I was thinking about marriage. It didn't feel right but you felt you had to go ahead with it. Most of them would want to have sex with you and you couldn't say anything about it. I always ended up alone with them. I thought, *Let me just do that.* Maybe, I felt, if we do what we have to do, they will go. Even if you tell them you're not straight, it makes them want to have sex with you more. We would end up doing stuff I hadn't planned to do.

Most of the time, it was under the influence of alcohol. I wouldn't be totally gone – I would still be conscious – but I would have been drinking. There was this one time when I was at the bar alone, drinking and smoking. Some guy came around, and you know the usual way guys think they can push people around. I said, 'Okay, whatever.' I was drunk, so I followed him back to the hotel room even though I had to be home that night. I was still staying with my parents so I was determined not to sleep over. I did things I didn't want to do. I told him about my sexuality. That doesn't stop everyone. They just want to sleep with you or they want you to do stuff with them.

That's happened many times. I've been with guys and they've been the ones forcing me. And I haven't been able to say no. One time was quite extreme. There was quite a bit of force from his part but I thought, *I know him. No big deal. It's alright.* I had never had penetrative sex before.

I had just had my period so I thought nothing could go wrong. I was a bit naïve. I got pregnant. I was so devastated the night I discovered I was a couple of weeks gone. I had been suspecting because I hadn't seen my period. I went to the hospital and the test was positive. I felt it was my fault. I should have been more careful. I was coming from a place where I believed you had to be married to have children. I see this is totally wrong now but it's what I thought at the time.

I told him about it. I thought it was right to inform him. I think I made it easy for him. I told him that I knew he might not be ready and that I had made the decision that I was not going to keep it but I wanted to hear what he had to say. He told me he wasn't ready and that it wasn't a big deal – why was I being such a child?

I had to deal with it by myself. I had to get rid of it and try to forget. I was seeing a girl at the time. She helped me. She gave me some pills – which didn't work. We went to some shack place and it was done. It was some kind of suction thing – very painful. I felt so strange and alone but she helped me. I knew that nobody could know and I just needed to let the pain happen. I went with that strength. It was a terrible ordeal. It was painful. I cried throughout but I knew that once this was done, I was done for good.

A long time afterwards, he called me. I had cut all communication with him – I didn't want to remember him. I didn't want to remember anything that had happened at that time. He wanted us to be friends. I told him, 'There is nothing connecting us any more. I had a terrible experience with you. You didn't even call me after I had the abortion. You told me that little schoolgirls do this thing, stop being such a baby.' I was really shouting at him. He never called me again.

After that, it was just once again that something like that happened. I told that idiot that I didn't want penetration – and he did it anyway. It happened in the back of my car. A total stranger. I think I was depressed. But that was the last time and it's going to stay the last.

I've been thinking about those times and feeling I shouldn't have gone down that path. I don't know what happened to me. But I had pressure from home. I was trying to please my parents. I thought maybe I should get married and get everybody off my back. I must have been thinking that since I can't have a child out of wedlock, I need to be with a guy, and maybe if I tell them about my sexuality, they will still want to go ahead and get married. I was thinking a lot about the importance of marriage and children. It's only now that I'm able to understand that I have choices. I can choose. It's normal. I've attended programmes for LGBT people. I made friends who know about my sexuality. That is what has made the difference.

It's difficult though, especially if you want a relationship. I think relationships are important. I strongly believe in sex with consent. I don't think it should be abused. I had a girlfriend who I didn't even try to kiss until I felt she was comfortable. Sometimes you get the urge, but you need to control yourself. I have been able to control myself for a long time. It's not do or die.

I've had sex with girls who have just come to the house but, for me, it's important that we build a relationship. No matter how short it is, at least let's establish something. I've been monogamous so far. Even though I've thought about being with different people at the same time, I don't think it's right. I can be, but when I think about it, I think it's going to hurt the other person. Everybody needs a healthy relationship, room where both of you can share ideas, uplift each other and help each other. You are like best friends but having sex as well. You need to understand that I'm not perfect. We can fight but we are still there for each other. When I'm down, you can lift me up. When you're down, I can lift you up. We gist. We laugh. Two people being together, enjoying themselves naturally.

That's the ideal, but with relationships, particularly same-sex relationships, you make-do with what's available. It's limited because few people openly identify as gay. That also affected me. There are girls I have been attracted to. You want to get intimate with them, you want to kiss them, you have fantasies about them – but you can't do that. You don't want to say anything. You don't want anybody to know your secret. I've been introduced to all my girlfriends by our friends. I wouldn't go out and talk to anybody. Even if I like you, I'm very careful, constantly conscious and watching.

I can't remember the first time I kissed a woman, but I do remember the first time I had sex. I was twenty-nine. It was fun. I had only kissed one girl once before so I hadn't had much experience with women. I had started work and had my own apartment – in the boys' quarters – so I had some kind of freedom. In the house I was staying in, the woman was okay with people who had other sexual preferences. She was an active lesbian even though she had kids. She would even bring girls into the house. I wanted a girlfriend. I wanted to be close to somebody. She introduced me to one of her friends. It was the very first time that I had sex. It felt good. It felt normal. Maybe it's because it was the first time but I can't forget it. I wanted a relationship with her. I tried to be friends with her but she was one of those girls who was just experimenting.

A few years ago, I was introduced to a girl whom I eventually ended up dating for about two years. This was the girl who was with me when I got pregnant. Looking back now, I think she lied a lot. I knew she had had boyfriends but she didn't tell me she was with any man. At the end of the day, I found out she was sleeping with guys. I was going to work a lot, leaving early in the morning. There was a particular day that she was talking to a guy. Looking back now, I think something happened between them. This happens a lot – suspecting that girls I've been with are bisexual. They have a boyfriend as well as you.

Anyway, at one point, she came up with this story about her pastor saying she should not do that kind of stuff again. Her boyfriend, the guy who was going to marry her, threatened me. That was after we had stopped seeing each other. He told me he knew about me and he was going to tell the police. We were very far apart and he was only working based on the information he had from her. He had both my numbers but when I thought about it, I realised that this guy couldn't really get to me. It was scary though. I was so worried, coming from a background where I had hidden so much. Of course, I parted ways with the girl. After a long time, like almost two years, she came to preach to me about my sexuality. It was a shock. I told her I didn't need her pastor to pray for me and that now that she's born-again, we should go our separate ways. I stopped speaking to her. I hate hearing things like that.

I used to be active in church. If I didn't go for a service, I felt that was not good enough. I don't go to church any more. It was a decision I made because of things I heard. First, my mode of dressing was a problem. I'm a gender nonconformist, meaning I usually wear my jeans and a shirt – what they call 'boy' clothes. I tried every Sunday though. I tried for the sake of church. It was a lot of pressure, a lot of stress and struggle. When I started working and was independent, I picked a church where I could at least wear trousers. I started going there and it was fine.

Then there was a particular day when the pastor started talking about homosexuality. He said he knew they don't exist. My response was, *Is this guy for real?* I was a serious Christian but I thought, *I'm done with this shit, I'm not going to church any more.* I was struggling. I was moving from one church to another. I realised I couldn't continue like this. That sermon was the last day I stepped into a church.

I'm more comfortable with not going to church. The kind of church I used to believe in doesn't work with what I believe in now. I believe in God but I won't practice religion that way. I don't have to go to church to believe in God. I can do it on my own. I remember one thing in the Bible – 'Treat your neighbour as you want to be treated' – and stick to that.

Apart from girlfriends also dating men, another problem I've had in relationships is the issue of roles. I don't know if it's right or wrong but I've always seen myself as the guy. There's this societal expectation and label of who the guy is. I'm the one in the shirt. I could never wear a skirt. If society advises that it's a girl who wears the skirt, maybe I'm the guy.

I've been exposed to various views and lectures about roles, how they are problematic and what feminism means. Despite all of these, I've always seen myself as the one to provide and fulfil the sexual roles. When it comes to the activities in bed, I do not ever like to be under. I think it's the way I'm wired but it can to be a problem in relationships with them asking, *Why must it be like that?* I just decided that I'm going to be myself. If that's not good enough, that's fine.

I absolutely don't believe it's about power. It's silly to say I have more power. Sometimes I feel so powerless. I'm not even sure I can protect myself. Whenever I go out, there's the fear factor. Before I go out, I think of where I'm going, how safe it is, who I am with. I'd rather not go out at all. I don't feel safe. How can somebody who is feeling that way have the capacity to protect somebody else?

Look at me. I walk on the street. Everybody is looking at you. They're not even sure if you're a girl. It's better now because I've had my hair cut. I've always wanted my hair cut but I had to plait my hair because of pressure. When I was plaiting it, the stares were serious. It's one thing to look at somebody because they catch your attention, and then look away. It is another thing to stare and wonder, *What are you?* It's better now. They'll say, *Oh, she's just a girl that looks like a boy.* There aren't many people who dress like I do in this area. For that reason, I don't feel safe because somebody might be so curious that they would actually try to do something. Nothing has happened yet, but even the stares are enough – and of course, you sometimes have words thrown at you. I don't say anything but it's enough.

Apart from that, right now, life is okay. I'm doing a project in ___, which I spend my days working on but I try to get it out of the way so I can focus on my passion, which is painting. I've been painting for a while. I went to some training school as I needed more information about how the business of art was run but I'm mostly self-taught through reading books. I was particularly fascinated by oil painting, which is currently my strongest technique, although I've also done pieces in pastels, watercolours and other materials. I've been doing this for a while. I always liked to draw right from when I was small and just developed it. It feels like a job that I can do that I'm passionate about. It feels like an achievement for me to see something beautiful that I've created at the end of the day. Since I've taught myself, it's much easier to promote myself too. It's a job I can do on my own. I don't have to wait for employment to do it.

I'm an artist now but I used to work with a bank. I had to dress in a certain way, have a certain type of hair and do the whole girly thing. I tried to conform to that. It was difficult. We had certain dress codes because you can't look a certain way in a formal setting like that. I hardly wore make-up but I had to do my hair. I particularly hated extensions. I was fine wearing trouser suits, but it had be a feminine cut, which I didn't like.

The work was tedious. It drained you. You had so much time invested in there and little time for yourself. I enjoyed getting a regular income. That was enough for me, so much so that I was able to build my own house. That achievement, until tomorrow I'm grateful for. If it wasn't for that, I wouldn't have a place to stay and it would have been quite difficult now because of my situation.

They didn't treat me well. I was dismissed eventually. I had been working with them for five years. I had it good for a while. I was transferred here by the influence of some big boss because he really wanted to get close. What do you think about a man who says, 'Call me any time. Tell me about anything'? Maybe he was just being nice – but I doubt it. During that time, I refused to sleep with anybody. I wouldn't sleep with any male boss. I didn't give any of them the chance. Perhaps if I had, I would still have my job.

I'm much more aware of myself now. I didn't have friends for a long time. There were a lot of decisions I have had to make. Every decision I made, I would think, *Is this okay? Does this look suspicious?* I don't want to think like that any more – and it's getting better now. I'm closer with LGBT people. I went to my first LGBT meeting a year ago. It was a bad period of my life. I had just lost my job. I had no friends. I had to fall back on family. I had to go back home. I went online – which I had to be very strict and cautious about. This was after my ex-girlfriend's boyfriend had threatened me, so I had to be extra careful. I was trying to make friends online. I went on Facebook and looked at the pictures. If I felt the person looked like me, I felt comfortable and tried to talk to them. There was one site I went on where I met a girl. We never visited physically but it didn't go well. I think she was a bit dubious. I found a total stranger had pictures of me that I had shared with her. Coincidentally, I got talking with the guy who had threatened me, as I thought this was necessary. It was also to help myself clarify things. We got talking and he told me he had seen my pictures somewhere. I had only shared them with her and they had got to people I had never even met – I don't quite know what happened. That was scary and I went back into my shell again.

Then I found the group. I told this guy that I lived in ___ and he linked me up. He also linked me up with a girl who was lesbian and an activist. I got talking to her. They had a meeting in ___ and I was invited. Both were significant points when I had a turnaround. It was fantastic. I was like, *Wow, there are people like me.* That was liberating. Since then, I've met more people like me. I've been able to think about things outside concentrating on my sexuality. Now I can feel normal. It's not like being LGBT is abnormal, but when you find people who are like you and you can relate to them, you think less about this burden of secrecy. You are able to get over that and face the struggle. It's a great thing.

In the society we find ourselves in, we need to start doing something, no matter how small. Even we, the LGBT persons, need to start having courage. A lot of courageous efforts are being made to change people's minds. Even though our efforts may seem small now, it has started and I believe it's going to expand. It has to. A few voices have come up in support. They are like tears in the sea compared with the inhumanity and injustice we are seeing. They're small – but they're important.

– *VA, age 35, Lagos*

Everybody In J-Town Is Now A Lola

'No other country has as many lolas as Nigeria – we have the most on the African continent – but you don't know because everyone is low-key.'

Content Note: Intercommunal Violence, Drug and Alcohol Addiction, Bereavement

I'm from a family of eight. I'm in the middle. My family has a division of love. My younger sister was my dad's favourite, my first sister was my mum's and I was just an introvert. I kept everything to myself. I was very close to my grandmum before she died. I felt she was the only one who understood me. My friends were always telling me I was weird but my grandmum understood me.

I'd say I grew up on my own and with the help of my elder siblings, peer groups, friends and all that. Our parents were always busy. They'd leave early in the morning and come back late. They'd spend the whole day at work, so spend very few minutes with us. It was obvious that it was a partial love. Your parents don't have your time. Okay, they have school fees that they have to pay but it was just money, money, money. When you needed money, you could talk to my father and he'd be there, but money is not all that is important. You should be able to know your child, understand them.

There should be a relationship but there was no room for that. There was a time I had a fight with somebody in school. I injured myself but it took them a week to notice the mark on my face.

I didn't understand my mum until three years ago. We started spending more time together then. There was no mother–daughter relationship before. I was a good child. I would do all my house chores. I went out of my way to please my dad. It was just me and the younger ones at home. He felt beating was the right thing to do to correct a child. All the responsibility was on me so I was beaten a lot. He was really brutal. Up till today, I can't even stay together with my dad. If he wants to communicate with me, he goes through my mum. That father–daughter relationship is not there. So I grew up with this mentality that I was always wrong. Everything I do, I'm on my own. I felt nobody could understand me because how do you tell them? What do you want to tell? Who wants to listen? Nobody. Growing up was really terrible.

My earliest memories of being attracted to the same sex are of the first girl I kissed. We were very close neighbours, with just the fence demarcating us. She was two years older than I was. I was in primary four and she had just got into secondary school. I didn't really understand the feelings. I just felt that this was the only person who liked me. Whenever I was with her, I was open. I could talk. I could share my emotions. I didn't know what I was doing. I didn't know it was bad. I didn't know that what I was doing was called attractions or emotions. She would come to my house and help me do chores. I felt she liked me because she was always coming around to help. She was my friend. I saw her as my big sis.

One time, we were home alone, watching a movie. They were kissing on screen. She was like, 'How does it feel to kiss?' I said, 'I don't know. I don't even like watching this scene.' You know, that mentality. A few days later, she told me that kissing was cool and that she was going to teach me. She was already in JSS1 and I was still in primary school. I made her promise that it wouldn't get me pregnant.

That was the first time she kissed me. It felt awesome. I thought it would last for a minute or thirty seconds, but it went on for like five minutes because there was something else too. She was older. She was more mature. She asked me to touch her in some places. Initially, I felt it was bad, but after that, I felt really cool. It was nice. I asked her, 'Who taught you? Because you are really good.' She said she had a school mother who did it to her and she liked it and that's why she was teaching me.

I was shy. Very, very shy. I stopped going to her house. I always said I was busy. She came when I was home alone and asked me why I was avoiding her. I told her I didn't want to kiss her again. I didn't feel it was right. She felt really bad. She promised me she wouldn't tell anybody and she knew I wouldn't tell. Then it happened again and again and again. It kept happening and, with time, I liked it. It got to the point that we couldn't do without each other.

It lasted for two years till I got into JSS1. Then her dad sold the house and they packed somewhere very far. I hated the fact that I fell for her. She was the first person I loved. It was terrible. I was always crying. I couldn't eat. Nobody even understood why. Nobody knew about it. We kept it secret. I didn't tell. She didn't tell. The love I had for her, I have never even felt for my own mother. I felt so bad. Though she kept visiting for some time, she stopped after a while.

JSS1, JSS2, JSS3, I had best friends, but I didn't feel what I felt for her till I got to SS1 and went to boarding school. There,

I met N___. She was friendly. She would come to my hostel and help me do my laundry. We started seeing each other after classes. There's something we call AP – appointment. The hostel was always busy. We couldn't see each other there so we met after classes.

One day, we met for the AP and she was like, 'What do you feel about me?' I said, 'I like you.' But she loved me. I told her, 'It doesn't matter if I've kissed a girl or not, I just like you as my friend.' Okay, fine. She asked me to hug her goodbye. I hugged her. She asked to kiss me. I said, 'No, you can't just kiss me.' She got angry and left. She stopped talking to me – and she was the only friend I had then in secondary school. I felt bad – why was it always me? I had to go to her hostel. I wrote her a letter, apologising. She said that before she would accept the apology, I had to kiss her. I kissed her and the whole thing started. I was 15.

She was a professional. She was really perfect. Compared to the one I had all those childish kisses with, she was more mature, more professional. When I met her, it was as if something in me awakened. We would meet and kiss after classes. There was this small, quiet room where you could go and rest if you wanted. That was where we would go. But we broke up after second term, after six months. She was always complaining about not seeing me, that I wasn't there when she needed me. This was a hostel for crying out loud. People who were mature could tell what we were doing so I had to be extremely careful. I broke up with N___ and started going around with my senior. I dated her until she graduated.

Only once have I ever felt anything for a man. We were very close friends. He was in love before we got together, but I was with N___ and then with my senior. After my senior graduated, I wasn't with anybody. He started to tell me what he felt for me. I found myself thinking about him sometimes. We dated for a few months. I loved him. That's the first and only guy I ever had sex with. I was 15 and in SS2. He was older – 23. He was cool. He was gentle. He was caring. He said he was Muslim, thinking I would get scared and end the relationship. I'm Christian and Christians don't love Muslims. He was testing me to see how strong my love for him was. But even if he had been pagan, I would still have been in love with him. I would have married him.

Then the Jos crisis happened. He was driving past the Bauchi Road. They slaughtered him in his car. His sister called me and I went to the mortuary. I needed to see him. What I saw, I can't erase.

I didn't love any guy again. Everything about love died the day he died. It was as if I died with him. Initially, after he died, I became very wild. I would date ten girls at the same time. I felt love was bad, that since I had kept one and it ended up bad, let me have a lot of them. I dated my juniors, my seniors, my mates – and it was chaos. I did it to make myself feel better. I didn't care if they loved me. It was terrible because I didn't have a heart.

I enjoyed kissing more but most of the girls liked sex. I'm quite adventurous and love experimenting – in life and in sex. I don't like tomboys. I don't like the way they fuck, the way they have sex, like the way guys have sex with you. Come on, we are doing girl things. Why do me like a guy? I don't like it.

I was doing everybody. I think I dated half the lesbians in Jos. I also started taking drugs, hard drugs, like codeine, white ashes – I think that might be cocaine. I didn't sniff it. I injected it. I took a lot of other hard drugs. They helped because there was no love. This lasted from age 15 until just now.

During that time, someone tried to blackmail me. Someone told my mother that my friends and I were lesbians. She came to my room and searched. I don't know what she was looking for. That alone can provoke the madness in my head. It is an offence. You don't invade my privacy. When that happened, I was so bad – the only thing I did not do was to kill someone.

It was my brother who was blackmailing me. He picked contacts from my phone and added them. He chatted with them. He was using logic and figured out what was happening. I got a chat from an unknown number saying I should stop what I was doing. When he felt the thing was getting too hot for him, when he noticed the thing was getting out of hand, because my friends and I all came together to try to find out what was happening and handle the situation, he told my mum.

I found out it was him because he wouldn't sleep at night and he would be in the parlour doing some tiny calls. My girlfriend told me that the guy who was calling them was always speaking quietly, late at night. So, one morning, I logged into his WhatsApp. I saw the chats. I deleted them and formatted his phone. When he came back, he didn't know who had touched it. My friends wanted to do something to him. They even paid some guys to beat him up. I said, 'No, this is my brother. He didn't hurt anybody. Even if he did, it was me he hurt.' So I prevented them from beating him up.

I was very wild at that time. It all changed because I met C___. I hadn't been faithful since my boyfriend's death. I had always been a player. But when I met C___, it was different. She was straight. She was always coming to the library with her friend. I like highly intelligent girls. Even when I didn't want to read, I would check if she was around. I had this particular spot I was always sitting in. She had her spot. I couldn't stop staring. She was so beautiful. I was harbouring feelings for her. I used to think, *If I ever date this girl, I wouldn't date any girl again.* But I was scared to talk to her. One day, she caught my eye. She wrote a note to me: 'You are beginning to get me nervous with the way you stare at me. Any problem?' I wrote back: 'There's no problem. Sorry, I'm not staring. I'm just glancing.'

She didn't talk to me again. I crushed on her for more than a month. I couldn't say anything to her. One day I decided to speak with her. I thought, if we can't date, at least we could be friends. I was trying to start a conversation so I told her, 'You're like someone I know. That's why I've been staring so much at you, because you look like someone I know.' She asked what that person's name was. I said C___. Surprisingly, it turned out that was her name too.

A week later, I was reading when she came up behind me and tickled me. Goodness, my heart raced. I'd never felt anything like it. I've been a player. I've dated different girls, all lesbians. At 15, I dated a 27 year old teacher – that shows you how bad I was back then. So, she tickled me from behind and I was like, 'Can I have your number, can we talk?' I had always wanted to call her but I didn't have her number. She was like, 'How much will you pay?' I said, 'Give me, then we can negotiate.'

She gave me her number and that was it. I started calling her. We started talking. We started meeting outside the library. We met outside the university. She invited me to her house. On the phone, I told her I was in love with her. She said that she knew but didn't know how you could have feelings for a girl. I told her that I would come over and tell her that I loved her. If she bounced me out of her premises, I would never disturb her again.

I was tongue-tied that day. I told her how much I loved her and how much I wanted to be friends. I had never asked a girl out but with her it was different. I loved her sincerely. I would have respected whatever she told me. She said she'd never dated a girl before. I told her that there's always a first time. She replied that she was straight. I said, 'I know but I love you, and I'm gay. If you don't want me to have sex with you, fine. I just love you, I'm not after your body.' Then she kissed me and told me that was a yes.

I felt goodness. I felt so happy. I have never been in love this way. She is too good. She has a very nice heart. Even when I get her angry, she forgives me easily. We started seeing each other and she started wanting the sex. At a point I even said, 'Enough of this, it's too much for me!' I'm not really a sex freak. I just enjoy kissing a lot. We've been together for four months now and the relationship is perfect. I told her everything about me. I've never told a girl my weaknesses – and she still likes me. I told her that I'm really bad and she's good. She's from a very nice family. I told her I feel I shouldn't have her because I'm not worth her. I told her that I had lied to her a lot – that I smoke and do drugs. I had not told her because I believe first impressions matter a lot. Now, I'm born-again. I still drink alcohol but when I told C___ the truth, she made me promise not to take drugs any more.

That was three months ago. The first week was terrible. There have been times where I would smoke a packet of cigarettes a day, there was no kind of strong liquor I wouldn't take, and I couldn't go a day without drugs.

When I tried to stop, I was already so addicted that it was like I was losing my mind. It got easier with time. I used to drink extreme amounts. Now, just a glass is fine by me. I only smoke partially. I look healthy. Initially, I looked as if I was going to die. Now, the only time I get tempted is when I see my friends taking it. I don't stay around them now though. She made me cut myself off from some friends, people who supplied the drugs. The guys who sell drugs are everywhere in Jos. All you need to do is to signal them. If you have your money, it works for you. I would get just enough for the week. He'd know that I would buy next Monday so he'd come around. But I told him that I'm not doing it any more.

I am focusing on school now. When school is on, I spend the day there and try to read for at least three, four hours every day. I like my subject so much. I have a passion for it. I'm inquisitive. I want to know everything. I like it a lot. As well as studying, I run a personal business. I graduated from secondary school with N300,000. I spent N150,000 doing drugs, partying, living a wild life. Then I had to sit down and bite myself. I spoke some little sense into my head and used the rest of the money to get a keke. I gave it out on hire purchase and that yielded more money for me to start up my business.

I was supposed to start it with my friend. We thought, *We have the money. Instead of clubbing, partying, drinking, smoking, doing drugs, let's do something good for ourselves rather than spending and not having any income.* I ended up starting it alone because the plans with my friend fell through. With the money from my personal business so far, I have my own car, my own house – and my parents don't know. The only person who knows is my sister.

When I bought the house, I needed privacy for my girlfriends and to do drugs. Now, I'm hoping I can use the money I make for further studies. I don't want to depend on my parents, especially my dad. I don't like depending on people. When you are independent, you can make your own decisions. If it goes well, fine. If not, it's your own money. By the time I'm done with uni, I should have come up with something reasonable to even fly out of the country and attend school abroad.

I may not want to depend on my parents but my friends are my family. They know everything about me and they don't care. Both the straights and the gays, they're fine. No problem whatsoever. My sister once saw me strafing a girl. It was our stupidity. We were the only ones at home. The house was locked and we didn't hear her banging. She went through the other door and the window was open, so she saw us. She never told me and her attitude didn't change. She only spoke to my friend, saying, 'I'm so sorry for meeting you in that act.'

I think everybody in J-Town is now a lola. We host parties from time to time. The parties happen as often as people have money to throw them. Sometimes lolas host it. Sometimes tibis host it. They are usually separate parties, although lolas can go to the tibi parties if they're invited. I can throw a party and invite only lolas. You will get to meet people only like you – for once in a lifetime. You meet people who accept you and don't judge you. You can be completely yourself. You can kiss a lola outside and everyone thinks it's cool.

But some of them go into this for absurd reasons. These days, it pays – the sugar mummies, you know. Even the street girls – if you're coming with money, they'll do it. And they're cool with it. But most of them do it because they are lolas, not because of the money. I recently spoke to a street girl who was in love with a lola. She told me that lolas know how to take care of their babes.

Do I think we're sinning? Hmm … I love my God. Whatever I do, God first. I go down on my knees and ask God for mercy. Even if I was strafing a guy, I would say, God have mercy. So long as you're not my husband and I'm not married to you, I think it's a sin. I mean, I don't say I'm sinning. The way people see this whole thing, they think it is clear. But you are dating a guy who's not your husband and I'm dating a girl who's not my wife; it's the same thing. From my own mentality and sense of reasoning, it's the same thing. The judgement that goes with that one is the same that should come with me.

Not everybody will like you and not everybody will hate you. There are guys to whom you could say you're gay and they will make you feel like the worst thing on earth. But, I've got to the point where you can't make me feel convicted by the colour of your heart. No matter how pure your heart is, there's a fault you'll have. I'm not judgemental. I might be a terrible sinner because I smoke. I might be a terrible sinner because I lie. It takes us all to hell. There's no special role there. We all go to the same hell. I'm not going to hell. I can't. I'm always at peace with God. I pray. I do everything I need to do. I'm not religious, I'm just a Christian. I think what God is after is the state of your mind. I can't act all good, act all religious and then see someone who smokes and say, God forgive him. That is being religious. You are already judging him. You didn't judge him openly but your actions did.

No other country has as many lolas as Nigeria – we have the most on the African continent – but you don't know because everyone is low-key. When they brought that law here, Goodluck bounced it and our senate president minuted it and half of the people in that House wanted it. It's made the situation worse. There are young people there, young kids who are practising these things, and they won't be able to come out and tell you because they are scared. Ten years ago, it wasn't really open. People didn't even know people like us existed. We could go out with a girl, hang out with her, hold her, but now it's crazy. People are very, very afraid.

But, at the time they were passing the law, they started talking about it on air. They had these radio shows, talk shows. A lot of people wanted it to be legalised. There was a man who called in who was married with kids. He said, People have the right to fall in love with anybody, it is their feelings, give them that right, that freedom. Other cities are even more open than Jos – like Port Harcourt. I went to see a friend of mine in PH and she took me out to a place where there were lots of her friends, lolas like us. And they all asked me if I had a girlfriend. They were so open. A friend of mine was in Abuja and a girl walked up to her and asked, 'Are you good to go?' She was shocked. We thought J-town girls had mind but we're not seeing anything. In Jos, I'm not sure people are as free as in PH and Abuja.

I think that if you are a lola, if you are a tibi, if you are bisexual, you should be able to be comfortable with who you are. You can't change it. Some people tell you it's a spirit. What spirit? It's your emotions. People should not see others as being abnormal. They are just humans like you. It's their feelings. Not every guy will fall in love with a girl. Not every girl will fall in love with a guy. You might be straight and get married to a guy. But your kids – how sure are you? So don't judge them.

– *AG, age 21, Plateau*

I Want To Be Myself Around People I Care About

'Most people I know don't really want to settle down because of the society. We already know that the society doesn't allow it, so why fool yourself?'

Content Note: Domestic Violence and Abuse

I grew up in Lagos and have always lived here. I am a Lagos girl to the core. I was schooled in Ogun but it was part-time so I got to come and go. I was working while in school so I had to be in Lagos most of the time. I would consider living somewhere else if my partner would.

I come from a large polygamous family with six brothers and two sisters, so I am a bit of a tomboy because I grew up around boys. I have five boys and one sister ahead of me. Growing up carefree but trying to fit into school and be girly was hard. Both my sisters are very girly and it was a little tough because I didn't really know what I was at the time. All those stories of people saying, 'When I was in secondary school' did not apply to me. Yes, I felt an attraction in secondary school. I would see a girl and I knew that I liked girls but I never did anything about it. I was a slow bloomer. I never had the liver to push for more. There was this cute girl. I never talked to her. I was quiet so that was out of the question for me. I would always just stare at her in class, but nothing was done until a year after secondary school. Way after secondary school, all I could do was online dating.

What we used in those days – about twenty years ago – was Yahoo chat and Messenger. My profile was very bold. I had a sign that said 'Likes girls' on my profile and that was very risky because my picture was there and my name. It wasn't so frowned upon then, so I was bold enough to do that. We could chat via webcam, as that was the video at that time. It was kind of like our own Skype. It was frustrating cos in between the thing would cut off, so you would have to redial and try to get that person back. I had other girls who were kind of exploring. We would talk, sometimes talk dirty. Most of them were not in Lagos so nothing could be done. Until I met Q___. She was in Lagos so I think I sent her a message. We met and hit it off. We actually dated for quite a while. She was my first girlfriend. My first experience was beautiful. I think I am always the person who makes the first move. I am not bold enough when it comes to face-to-face but over the computer, I say a lot of crazy things. I think we chatted for like three months before we met and we dated for three to four years. My job was flexible so I had a phone. This was way back when and I had a massive Blackberry. I must have been one of the first people to have a Blackberry and I could do all my chats on my phone. When I got home, I could use my brother's computer. It was sneaky but nice. Nobody ever suspected, so nobody ever had any inclination to check my chats. It wasn't rampant enough for people to frown upon at that time. But now it is everywhere. Girls are a bit more obvious. I was a tomboy but I wasn't obvious.

I have dated guys, but it is not it for me. I have not felt

any attraction to men but sometimes you do it to tell yourself that you are really not into men: Let me try this and convince myself that I am not missing out on something. I once had a thing for a boy in school who stayed on my street. It wasn't really a crush but we would talk and walk to and from from school together, like puppy love. It was nothing more than that. He once asked me to be his girlfriend and he tried to kiss me. This was a time when your mother told you that if a boy touched you, you were going to get pregnant. So he tried kissing me and I slapped him. But I kind of warmed up to him at the end of secondary school. There was this other guy I met after school when I had started working. We talked and kind of dated. I don't know if I would call that dating though. We hung out a lot, he came to the house, my family knew him and everybody thought I was going to marry him. We were together for almost two years, between 18 and 20, but it was pretty serious. That was when I thought, *Okay, you know what, I will get married and get it over with. This is what everybody wants me to do.* I kind of thank God I didn't.

At that point I was already dating girls. Apart from my first girlfriend, I was still playing around. I didn't call it dating but I tried to play the field, trying to make sure I wasn't the only queer one out there. There were a lot of people out there and it was easy to meet them if you were on the right website. I don't know how I found them. Sometimes you just search for websites you can use to meet girls. You join the website, create a profile etc.

I didn't know queer people growing up. I grew up in a kind of controlled environment and my family was close-knit. I didn't have the opportunity to meet people and even when I did I was too shy and quiet to even ask questions, so I never knew a queer person. I was a bit clueless. You might have been gay and sitting right there and I couldn't even tell. Now I have gaydar. You can tell even with the girly girls from their reaction to you, the way they stare at you, the way they talk, that they have an interest in you. But back then everybody was trying to act straight, so it was harder. The first queer person I met was when I was about twenty-five, through a friend of a friend. I didn't even know people were out there; I thought everyone was living codedly and stuff. But I met her, I went to a couple of parties and I was blown away. I thought, *Wow, so we are out there.*

I am Igbo so my family is a bit too by-the-book. It was hard to even acknowledge that I liked girls let alone do anything. And maybe because I couldn't really express myself then, I was always into myself. I could stay in the room and not come out for the whole day, sometimes longer. I had terrible mood swings. I found it hard to express myself and let people know what I was thinking. I read a lot of books, anything that would keep my interest. I hung out with boys. My brothers had a lot of friends. You would see my sister with her female friends, playing with dolls and stuff, but I would be on the balcony with the boys, carrying weights. All they did was lift weights and talk about girls. And that was where you would typically see me. So I grew up being the only girl among the boys, even to date.

None of my siblings knew I was dating girls. And I still haven't discussed it or come out to any of them. I have a feeling a few of them know, but we don't talk about it. Nobody brings it up. Don't talk about it, don't rub it in their faces, and they don't ask. I know some of my family members know. My half-sister, who is older than me, she definitely knows.

But it is not something I can say. I can't say, 'Here, meet my girlfriend.' Or hold hands with her. But I want to. Everybody wants to. I want to be myself around people I care about but I can't. I know the family I am from. The minute you do that, it is going to cause a rift and I am not ready for that. I have come pretty close to saying fuck it and telling everybody, but then I think about how I am not so close to them right now anyway, so what's the point? If I tell them now it is going to cause a bigger rift. And I am okay with the way things are for now. Probably in the near future.

Everybody lived together. At one point, my mum got separated from my dad and took us, her kids, away for some years. And then they made up and we came back. Everybody lived in the same house, grew up in the same house. It was a bit tough because there were two wives and ten children. There were bound to be clashes and stuff, but we were close growing up. We couldn't even tell who was half or full, but eventually a rift grew between us. Although it was fun when we were young. My house was like a barracks. We had a massive compound so everybody's friends liked to come to hang out to play outside. We always had kids in the streets coming in to play. We played ten-ten, suwe, or that my-mother-told-me game, skipping rope, those kinds of things. This compound in Surulere was huge. We eventually moved out as the other kids started moving out and getting married.

I worked with a relative who had a clothing store. You know how clothing stores are: you sit down and wait for your customer. Half the time you are there for like thirty minutes to an hour without anything happening. I worked with her for seventeen years. Leaving was tough but I am trying to set up my own business. I have an online store coming up soon. I also work for a registered cab service on the side. I have too much time on my hands. All I do is monitor my drivers online. The rest of the time is spent setting up my online store.

The first girl I fell in love with was about three years ago. It wasn't that long really. I really don't know how but I felt for her deeply. She was a tomboy, is still a tomboy, maybe more so now. In that relationship, I had to be less tomboyish and more of the girly one. So there were a lot of clashes. People still have this thing about who is on top and who is not and who is the guy and who is the girl. These roles were transformed in the bedroom. You know when you have someone who is in charge but allows you take charge in bed? I kind of liked that. We had unspoken roles. In Nigeria, everybody just knows the tomboy is in charge. And she was a tomboy, she was older, so she was in charge. But I had issues with a lot of things even though I cared deeply for her. We were together for less than a year but it was beautiful and the break-up was tough. She broke up with me. I never did anything wrong, or at least she never told me that I did. We were just in different spaces. It was getting too serious and she was not ready. That's what she said. I was looking for something grounded and she wasn't, although she was older than me. I guess people have different priorities. I have always wanted something stable: date someone and be with that person.

I have met people who were ready to settle down, but with guys. I have also met people who do not want to settle down even though they are way, way older than me. They tend to have excuses as to why they do not want to settle down or why they are not ready to settle down with you. It is not something they feel they can be open about. You can't say you are settling down with someone, you can't even hold that person in public or kiss that person, so what is the point? But most people I know don't really want to settle down because of the society. We already know that the society doesn't allow it, so why fool yourself? Some people decide to have live-in lovers.

I currently live with my partner. We share bills, run the household together. We have been doing this for two years now. There have been ups and downs but nothing major. It is tough living with someone, and I was so used to living alone. I moved out of home fifteen years ago. I have been living alone for all that time, although I lived with a girlfriend for like two years within that time. I prefer living alone but nobody is an island, I guess. I love living with her. I am still enjoying living together. Sometimes we want to kill each other but it has been fine, good so far.

There was a girlfriend I dated for about three years. She was my second serious girlfriend. (I have had five serious girlfriends, including my present partner.) As usual, she had a boyfriend and got pregnant for the boyfriend. That was it for me so I got a place of my own and moved out. I knew she had a boyfriend but he was not in the country for years so I didn't think it was anything serious. She married him. They have two children together. We still talk once in a while. I think she identifies as bisexual. It took me by surprise that she was pregnant because she hid it from me until she started showing. I noticed she was gaining weight and her tummy was getting bigger. I kept asking and she never told me. Until her sister and my family came to the house. They didn't know; they thought we were close friends. I can't even remember what we were talking about but her sister let it slip: 'Oh this your baby, when are you due?' And I was shocked. I said, 'When is who due?' That was the beginning of the issue we had. Because the boyfriend used to come and go. He wasn't around, so what happened? How did it happen? She eventually told me that it happened the last time he was in town and that killed it for me.

I am godmother to the child. When she had the baby, the boyfriend wasn't even in the country. I was in the theatre with her. I was practically her husband, even after the child was born, because the boyfriend came back once or twice and then left. I was the one doing everything for her and the baby … just like a husband would.

Then the boyfriend came back and the next thing I hear is that they are engaged. The baby was between eight months and a year because by the celebration of the first year the boyfriend wasn't there. But we threw a big party. It was huge. I did everything. I was in touch with her. Everything. She made me understand that she was never going back to him so I was there fully. I wanted the child. We were still in a relationship. We were raising the baby. The kid's school was right around the corner so I would take the child to school and when school closed, I was responsible for picking the child up. The baby stayed with me at work and she'd come to pick the baby up later. Then I'd go home to meet them because I close from work late.

It was our own little routine and then, all of a sudden, the guy came back into the picture. He had his house and that was where he stayed, but he knew she was into girls. He knew everything, but when he came back fully, he started getting jealous and moved out of his house and in with us. Things got very awkward. She got so confused. At night, she didn't know where to sleep – my room or his. There were three bedrooms: one was unoccupied, one was mine, and the third one his. It caused a rift.

I started looking for an apartment. I didn't tell her when I got the apartment. I didn't even tell her where. The day I moved was the day I told her I was leaving. I just moved out. I didn't even break up with her, so to speak. I just moved out. And she took it like I broke it off. But I was trying to ease her into it, because I couldn't be in the picture while she was doing this with this guy. That was it.

With another girlfriend, well, it was short. I don't know if nine months is short but it was serious with this girl I loved. Friends, everybody knew how I felt. We both felt the same but I was very, very far away, on the outskirts of Lagos. I didn't even mind. I close work at 8pm every day. I drove all the way to her house every night. I went from her house to work every morning. My house even got neglected. I was paying rent just to have my stuff there. In a week, I would stay at my house for two, maybe three days and the rest at her place. I guess I was a bit too serious for her so she broke it off.

My current, we had a mutual friend. In Surulere, most of the gay people know each other. Mostly the girls, because the guys are just drama queens so we don't hang out too much. Anyway, there was this friend of ours who was way older than all of us. She had a store that sold clothes and everybody would close from work and often end up there. We would bring drinks and gist and talk. When she passed away two years ago, we went back to her store for the last time after the burial. That's where I met my partner. I had been going to that store for years and I had never met her. The death was very hard for her and she was out of the country when it happened so she had to quickly fly back for the burial. Everybody was at the store. People were just talking. Some cried. She came to me. I was in a relationship then. She'd asked around who I was and they told her I was in a relationship but she didn't care. She got my number. We started talking. I cheated on my other girlfriend with her. I had never done that. I don't do that. Part of the reason why the other one broke up with me was that she came to my house and met her. That was brutal. You know how you do something bad and you know it but you get caught red-handed and try to wiggle out of it: 'No, she is just my friend, we are just friends.' My then girlfriend came to my house early on a Sunday morning. She was on her way to church but she stopped by and met my now girlfriend in shorts in the kitchen, cooking. I couldn't even lie and say she just came or anything. I tried but it didn't work. She cried and stuff. I begged. I was confused. I didn't know who I wanted. But after I realised that they knew about each other, well, I thought whoever wants to stay can stay.

She had her own key but I had my key on the inside of the door so she couldn't open it. Then she called me. Thank God, I didn't lie. She asked where I was and I said I was at home. My car was outside, obviously, and she was already at the door so she knew I was home. I was in the room so she said, 'Come and open the door.' I froze. Then I got up and opened the door. I told my partner my girlfriend was at the door. She was actually butt naked and shorts were the fastest things she could find so she wore them. She went into the kitchen. I think she did that on purpose. She made matters worse by starting to cook. It pissed my then girlfriend off and she started yelling: 'Who is that in my kitchen doing all that and feeling so familiar with everywhere?'

I had to take her to the living room. She sat down. We started talking and she cried. I had to beg. She didn't do anything bad to me so I felt bad. And, at that time, I didn't want to let her go because she was my girlfriend. But my partner was like, 'Well I don't care. If she wants to stay, whoever wants to stay should stay.' She liked me and wanted to be with me. If my girlfriend wanted to be there then she should stay but if my girlfriend wanted to go then she could take a walk for all she cared. And I liked that. At the end of the day, my then girlfriend left crying. After she left, things escalated with the one in my house. We kind of broke up with my girlfriend. And that is how I found myself. I think I made the right decision.

We were not so religious but we did the whole go-to-church-on-Sundays thing. I am Catholic so we went to Mass on Sundays. I grew up in a religious household. I don't go to church any more. The whole idea with church right now is not something I want to be associated with. I would love to be a bit more prayerful than I am right now. I think I can pray to God on my bed in my house without having to go listen to someone else interpret the Bible for me. I can read my bible and understand it. If I don't understand then I can seek help. But I am not really a religious person. I am trying to change. People are trying to change me and I will welcome the change when it happens but for now, nah.

I only experienced homophobia in subtle ways. When I heard people make snide remarks. But on the street, you hang out with friends ... I look like a tomboy, right, and someone walks in who looks ten times more of a tomboy and people say stuff like, 'That one that looks so gay.' You find out that most of these tomboys are not necessarily gay; some of them are straight and they are just tomboys. You just hear it in snide remarks. I won't say that I have experienced homophobia, in fact, because I do not put myself out there. It is not deliberate, it is just me. Maybe it is just something I grew up with, not putting myself out there. Not letting myself be known. I would never do this on a normal day. I do not put myself out there for me to even get that kind of remark. I know people tend to talk behind your back but I don't experience it.

You hear it all the time, on the news, and because I am on Twitter, I hear a lot, I read a lot of comments and maybe that is where I see my own homophobia. You read people's comments and you hear some people say that it is nobody's cup of tea if someone decides to sleep with a girl. If a girl decides to sleep with a girl, how is that your problem? But you also see people say things like, 'Yes, if they catch them, burn them on a fire. Let them be naked and if they are women, have guys rape them. Rape them till their sanity is back.' You hear and read things like that. But apart from that, no.

People in my circle right now, even my straight friends at that time when the bill was passed, were like, 'How is this such a big deal that the government had to sit down and pass such a bill to restrict people from doing what they do inside their houses?' If you say something like gay people shouldn't walk on the street or hold hands on the streets or kiss, that is different. But you are saying that they should outright abolish it. I have straight friends who are saying, 'No, that is not their business,' but I also know people who are indifferent and I know people who are like, 'Yes, that is the right thing.'

I don't have friends who are totally against it. I have friends who really couldn't care less and I have straight friends who will tell you that if a gay guy should come close to them, it is disgusting. But a lesbian will be invited to bed. You have friends like that who want to see girl-on-girl: 'Kiss her now, kiss her, hold her, I want to see.' When they see gay guys they go, *Urgh*. And I think, *Why?* Either you like gay people or you don't. Don't tell me you have issues with hanging out with gay guys but we the tomboys hang out with the straight guys and they know. We don't come out to tell you, but you know, especially because you see us with girls. They see one or two girls around us, pretty girls, so they don't have problems with that. But the minute you say this guy is gay, everybody is just, 'Make e no sit down here oh, don't let him sit down here. If he near me I fit slap am.' Why do you automatically assume that a gay guy is interested in you? You are straight; he knows that.

My family just did not talk about it. I mean, I have had discussions with an aunty. I can't remember how that conversation started. She was a big aunty. She was driving us in her car and I think that was when it was legalised in some states in America or something and they were talking about it on the radio, so she brought it up. We started talking and I said, 'I am for it. I love the fact that they were able to legalise it.' She is one of those liberal people; she really doesn't care. She had tried her best to raise her children to have an open mind about people and their beliefs and orientation and whatever, but she didn't see why it had to be legalised. So she said, 'So you are for it?' And she asked it in a funny way. She said, 'Are you for it because you are one or because you know people who are?'

I froze. That was my opportunity to come out, at least to one person. But because of the age difference ... If it was my sister, I would probably have said, Yeah I am, but because she was older I just froze and I said, 'No, I am not, but I know friends who are and they are very good friends.'

She said, 'Really, and they live in Nigeria?'

'Yes.'

'And they don't have issues? People don't attack them?'

I said, 'Yeah, because people don't necessarily know.'

I was a bit scared but that is what made me think maybe she had an idea. As I said, my family doesn't talk about it. But that is the closest I have come to coming out.

I don't think I have come out to anyone who isn't a gay friend. I try to not put myself in a position where I have to come out first and then find out that this person is straight and has to look at me in a funny way. So I try not to. Especially if I am not sure. If we are in a neutral place and I notice a few things that she says, and I am not sure if she does or not ... I am a blunt person, so I can come out straight and ask, 'So do you do girls?' And you usually have to answer me yes or no. A couple of people answer honestly. I feel that a few of them do cos they already know that I am, so they have nothing to fear. So they come out. But I feel that if I were girly and they were not sure, and I asked that question, they would not come out and say yes. A few of them have said yes and thrown the question back at me. I say yes, I am. And then we probably, maybe become friends from there, exchange numbers and talk. And then most times I find myself on, like, gay BBM groups and stuff.

Most people don't know they are homophobic until they meet someone who pings their gaydar. That is when you can judge how they will react to meeting a gay person. And it is not just for me. I hang out with friends and my partner doesn't want anyone to know for now. She is trying to finalise her divorce so she doesn't want anything to tarnish her divorce. And I don't want people to assume that everyone they see me with is gay.

I have never been in a relationship with violence. If there was going to be any violence, I probably would have been the violent one. I am not a violent person, but I have only been the dominating one in relationships, apart from that tomboy I dated for a few months. Every girl I dated has been a bit more submissive. I am always the dominating one.

I have heard a lot of them talk. Especially about the substance abuse and relationships where they get treated badly. I have actually had to separate a tomboy from the girlfriend she was beating on the streets. I had to throw her girlfriend into my car and drive off. This was years ago. The girl told me her story, how the tomboy beat her up and didn't want to see her talk to any other girl, let alone a guy. Even just to say hello to someone was a problem, and she got into hard drugs. She smoked weed and codeine with weed to get high. They do a lot of different things that I never even knew were possible to escape their problems. She got high and slept because she couldn't make friends, couldn't even get away from that relationship. This was five to seven years ago. I tried to be her friend but I guess she was a bit into that relationship and wasn't ready to leave so she was taking that abuse. She was with that girl for years. It went on for so long. I tried to bring her out so they could come see me but some people seem to misread that. She thought I was hitting on her and the tomboy even told a few friends who came to me and told me to stay away. I was just trying to help but eventually I had to delete her number. If that was what she wanted for her life, fine; I was only trying to help. I know stories like that but I don't know first-hand. I have pretty much been a boring lesbian.

The law hasn't affected me in any way. It has even helped

because, before the passing of the law, I stayed in my house and my partner stayed in her house and we visited each other. I have been able to live with my partner since the passing of the law. It doesn't really affect me so far, as I don't put myself out there. I don't let people know who I am. You have to be more careful, and sometimes try not to be so tomboyish. I have heard stories of tomboys being harassed on the road by policemen. If you look too much like a dude, they tend to harass you and collect your phone to see what groups you are in, your pictures and stuff. If you have anything incriminating, they tend to take advantage so I don't want anything like that happening.

I have never feared for my safety. I am too careful. Maybe because I hang around straight people as much as I hang with queer people. In fact, I hang around more straight people, so people are not so sure. I tend to not put myself in such situations. You have to monitor where you go. Even when I go to a gay party, I want to know beforehand where it is, whose house, how safe I'm going to be, if there will be people filming things with their phones. I don't want anybody taking a picture of me holding or kissing my girlfriend. You never can tell – pictures go viral. All those things have to be put in place. I have to know before I can even say, Okay, yes, I am going to go to that party.

A lot of parties take place in Lagos. In houses mostly. Maybe a gay friend who lives alone throws a party. On 26 December, we went to a friend's house. It was just gay people smoking, dancing, you know, but I got so conscious cos one or two people had their phones out and they were taking pictures so I didn't really have fun. Gay parties are not usually fun for me. I would like to go to a party where everybody left their phones outside, no cameras, nothing, so everybody can relax. But most people will not want to drop their phones so …

I want to be married. Obviously married somewhere else, then come back and coexist somehow. Nobody has to know we are married. I know it is going to be very, very bad. In fact I am preparing my mind to be disowned because I know that might happen. I am positioning my mind to get to that point where I really will not care if my family disown me. But right now, I would care, because there are a few things I still do. I run a business with my brother so it would be detrimental to my business and financial security. But if I were financially secure enough to stand alone, I would be willing to make that decision.

We would probably have her surname in between and have mine as the major surname cos I am the dude. I don't like having a label to it but when it comes to the household chores and stuff, I do most of the things a guy would do, like the generator, make sure that power is on. My partner keeps the house tidy, does cooking and stuff. So it has already been labelled even without us knowing. Unconsciously, it is already there. I think I am comfortable with it right now. I don't want it to be specified like that, or rigid. When she is cooking, I can come in and help cook, clean and stuff. But I still want her to know that it's me having to go out and work and do whatever it is I need to do to provide for the family. I am willing to do that. I am a hustler. I can hustle. I come back, the generator is faulty, I am a handy person, I can fix my generator, I can make sure the power is on. Stuff a typical man should do, I do already. I am fine with the way it is right now.

I want children, possibly two. I don't know if I will carry them; that is still something we are talking about. Probably my partner will carry them. She wants a boy and I want a girl, at least for the first child. I have talked to her about her carrying a child for us. We have talked about having our eggs harvested, then have a sperm donor, and she carries it to term. I don't think I can carry it. It is too painful. I have witnessed it too many times, so it is no. Yes, I admit I can be selfish in that aspect. It is not something that I look forward to. It is something that I would do if I absolutely had to, if there were no other option. If, for example, my partner can't carry a baby, I will do it, but I don't know. Maybe when that time comes I will know if I absolutely can, but right now, nah. I would rather adopt and be a parent. We would probably use an anonymous donor, but at this point, I'll take what I can get. This topic is something my partner and I are still figuring out so we'll see how it goes.

I imagine I will be rich, because of my business plan, because of what I have planned. That is one of the reasons why I don't want to live outside Nigeria – I know my business will thrive more here and I am going to do well. So living outside Nigeria would be a problem.

I hang out with younger people but I am not necessarily friends with them. Most of my friends are older, or maybe a year or two younger. Young people are too dramatic. They tend to not understand that you don't want to be put out there. Young people are the ones who you will have a fight with at a bar. They will take it and blow it out of proportion and everybody will be like, Why is she fighting with you? Are you guys together? I don't want questions like that asked. I want someone who can have a fight with me in the midst of straight people and nobody even knows. And then we can sort it out at home. I want to be in a more mature relationship.

I know young people, I know of them, I have been in BBM groups with them, we have met at parties, they know me, I know them. But friends? I am not approachable in that way. I want to think that I am someone you can talk to, and people have always been able to talk to me, but I also know that I am not that approachable. Only when I am drinking; then you can tell me stuff and I will give you the best advice ever. I am approachable to an extent.

At one point, I had friends who would tell me the problems in their relationships. My ex-girlfriend who I cheated on is now dating a very good friend of mine. We had a falling out, because they were being sneaky and I felt like my ex was holding me to guilt because she caught me. I didn't catch her but I felt like they were dating long before we broke up. My friend and I fell out for a couple of months and now she is suddenly trying to rekindle the friendship because we were quite close. So now she talks to me. She is a tomboy and she talks to me about my ex. It is a bit awkward because she has always been able to tell me stuff, but now it's about my ex. So it is a triangle like that.

I would like to participate in more LGBTI activities, but in Nigeria it is very risky. I would like to be involved if there was a way to be silent and anonymous about it. That is why I was willing to talk to you and have this interview.

If I came back as a young person, I don't think I would be different. But I probably would be a bit more gay sometimes. I won't even let it get too late before I get into being myself. I would have been myself from a lot younger age. For young people, be yourself. If you know you are queer and you have the opportunity to be queer, be yourself, do it. Do not let anyone restrict you. I felt a bit more restricted and maybe that is why I don't have many friends who are queer and why I don't know how to relate to people who are gay.

I would advise everyone to be open, to be bold enough to come out to your family. What is the worst that can happen? They could disown you. I know friends who have been disowned and years later, the family still comes back. It might not be easy, but with time, they learn to accept you. That is what I am working myself towards. If I had come out to my family years ago, they would have gone through the process of disowning me. By now they would have been accepting. That's what scares me at this age. Do I want to come out and be disowned at this age? I mean, it won't make any difference, but am I willing to not be with my family for a while at this age? I don't know.

So be yourself, come out. The worst that can possibly happen is that you will get disowned and be on your own for a while. It will be tough but you will get through.

– *RL, age 38, Lagos*

What Is Happiness?

'Everybody was like, "Boys are bad". But nobody ever said anything about girls. If boys were bad, then girls had to be good.'

I am a woman looking for money. Jesus! Money brings the most happiness in life. Let me expatiate. Money comes with options. Money gives you the independence to do exactly what you want to do. I love to help people and money allows me do that. When it comes down to it, a lot of the issues people have are due to lack of money. I would love to be able to make money, to be able to have the kind of life that I think I deserve. That life involves helping people.

I have been travelling all my life and my earliest memories are of setting up house in other countries. There was no single childhood home but I remember what every one of them felt like. They all had interesting stories. The houses we stayed in were huge. Some had massive backyards. In Guinea, there were so many mango trees. You could not avoid being under a tree. You could not go out at night because massive mangoes would fall on you. If the mango fell on your head, it was yours because you had suffered the pain of it. My fondest memory is a combination of all the holidays my family ever took when I was growing up. It is an unending silent movie with road trips, eating in the car and drinking milk in unripe coconuts. I hold on to that memory. Every time I am sad or miss my family, I go back to those holidays.

My mum is the strongest person I know. She has been through a lot and she is one of those annoyingly positive people. When I was depressed once, I told her I was tired of everything. She said, 'I understand, but you cannot let it get you down. You cannot say you are depressed.' She applies that to her life when she has issues. My parents are, oddly, very progressive. My dad even more so than my mum, even though he can be quiet. I would say my parents are good parents. They would give everything they had to us, but as individuals I have issues with them.

I was an imaginative child. I spent most of the time playing alone. My siblings were the busy ones. I spent my entire childhood half between reality and imagination. Like every child, I played and I had toys, but I would also lie down under the big dining table for ages and dream up alternate realities. Thinking back, it was weird but it was what brought me the most fun. It was also what started my life as a storyteller. I enjoyed all the stories I used to tell myself or see in my head.

When I was younger, acknowledging that you were in love with a guy was taboo. Everybody was like, 'Boys are bad'. But nobody ever said anything about girls. If boys were bad, then girls had to be good.

Pretty much all the voluntary exploration I did when I was younger was with girls. There was no first time when I felt an attraction to the same sex. The basis of my attraction was curiosity. I was surrounded by older girls. I had some age mates around me but many of them were older. So I had seen what their bodies looked like and it was interesting. I wondered, *Am I going to get like this?*

I wanted to know what others felt like. It was more curiosity than attraction. People tell me that one of the annoying things about me is my constant need to know things. I am always asking people why. Even now, if I am attracted to someone, it is because I am interested in finding out what they look like. I want to know what they feel like.

I was young and I was curious about girls. I think everybody is curious at that age. Like, I know what *my* body feels like. Can I touch your body? I had friends who I used to do that with. I think that is just innocent exploration. My first kiss was when I was younger, maybe 9 years old. I thought it was disgusting.

I took the curiosity further with this one cousin. Ever since we were kids, we had been exploring each other's bodies. We would pretty much finger each other. There were no boobs so that was the only thing we could do. We took showers together. Everybody in the family thought we were inseparable but no one had any idea. I was 13, 14 or 15 years old when I realised she had started growing pubic hair. It was awkward.

My first love was quite recent – my ex-boyfriend. I learned about patience and compromise from him. I also learned the importance of knowing your worth. My ex is wonderful, but the person I was when I was with him is not who I am now. I like me now but I did not like me then. As much as I adore him, I do not think I can go back to him. I know this growth is because of my acceptance of everything about me. I am finding every part of me beautiful.

Right now, I am going through what I call my 'ho phase', which is just lots of exploration. There are a lot of people you have this unseen connection with. You meet some people and you think, *God, I want to make out with you.* I think it is unfair that, because you are in a relationship, it is only you and this one person. I probably liked that at some point but I do not think that is who I am now. Regardless, I do like relationships. They allow people to be a lot more honest than they would be.

I am not in an exclusive relationship or sexually monogamous with anybody. I am opening myself to new experiences. There are so many types of relationships. What covers the breadth of my curiosity is a good situationship. I am currently in situationships with a few people. I want to date both men and women. Interestingly, while my earlier life was generally around women, my adult life has just been men.

It is not because I am running away from women. I just feel like men recognise that I am some form of queer but women do not see that in me. Or maybe it is because I have not been around queer women and I want to. I would love to be around queer women. I am actually looking forward to it.

Situationships are not easy. Somebody is going to be the main bae even if you do not want that to happen. The hardest thing is when everybody I am involved with somehow becomes friends. Then I have to be cute with them all without anybody suspecting. I am open about the fact that I am not exclusive to these people but I also do not want to hurt their feelings by letting them know who the other people are. I feel it's rude. Sometimes I struggle with balancing when I am around more than one of them. Still, I have been good, so far.

I have begun to enjoy sex as I just started having penetrative sex. I love to have sex with someone I am attracted to. But then, there are some people who I may seem attracted to but nothing is going to happen. I channel that attraction to something else. I believe in trying almost everything at least once. I do not have that many hang ups about sex. It is just sex.

If I am fucking you, then it is you. It is not the you that existed, like, ten years ago, it is the you now. I think that is how I am able to justify things. One can get jealous when someone is like, 'I've been with fifteen other people.' But if you ignore everybody else and just think, *I am with you now*, all is good.

I am the people I am attracted to. I choose to have sex with people for myriad reasons. All the people I am involved with have a certain something about them. Having sex with them is a combination of knowing who they are. They become part of my identity in a weird way. I get a certain something from them that is a bit out of the ordinary. You are you, I am me and because of who you are, I am a bit more of something else. Imagine if you met Picasso and had sex with him. You might have had a good connection and everything, but at the end of the day you had sex with Picasso. It has made you a bit more of something else, do you know what I mean?

I was reading something in *Nat Geo* about a guy who was marrying his car. He had been in a longterm relationship with his car, a very ugly thing. I judged him. It was not even vintage. If I met that person, I would laugh and be like, 'What is wrong with you? How are you attracted to a car that is not pretty?' and, 'Why are you not attracted to a Lamborghini?' I would say, 'You know what? I get it. I think you are a bit weird but it is just an ugly car.'

His choices do not harm me. I think people focus too much on the sex that others have and forget the fact that those people are human beings.

I encounter homophobia with everybody I know. For all intents and purposes, I am a Christian. Sometimes I pray and read the Bible. Sometimes I go to church on my own. I have a relationship with God but my religion has no bearing on my identity. I talk to people when they make homophobic statements. I warn them not to say that around me because it is incredibly offensive. Why insult people you do not even know? I try to educate and yell. This is not because I am queer. I believe so much in living like this: if someone is not hurting you, you do not have the right to hurt them. You might not agree with what they are doing and you can judge, but you keep that judgement to yourself. Sexuality and lifestyle are such tiny parts of who LGBT people are. You judging is you being petty. It says a lot about you.

In terms of sexuality, I am fluid. I do not tell everybody I am attracted to women but when people ask me, I may tell them, depending on who they are. If I think you are the kind of person who should know, I will tell you immediately. I do not hide who I am attracted to. I do not have that many queer people around me. I feel that when you choose to be around a group of people because of who they are, you are fetishising them to some extent. I would not want to set my friends based on my sexuality. I am surrounded by a lot of expressions. If I make a new friend and they happen to be queer, amazing. If they are not, fine with me. I do have friends who I can gush to, saying, 'Oh my God, I saw this woman and she was stunning.' But I would not want those to be the only kinds of people in my friendship circle.

With my friends and family, I am a private person. My mum has only ever known about one person I was dating. If I ever got into a serious relationship with a woman, I do not think I would tell my parents. They are homophobic even if they do not know why they are. At work, I am a designer and I adore it. I do not believe my colleagues should know who I am. I am just not an open person. I am not worried about colleagues finding out because I do not share my personal life in the office.

At the moment, I am trying to build a career. I want to be a household name in my industry. I want to have money. I want to be independent. I am unhappy that I am not. I want to be successful. That is what drives me. Success comes in so many ways. I have this boss. She is eccentric, absolutely mad. She is the head of my department in my huge company. Her name is not one of the first that comes to mind when you think about women in the industry, yet you cannot mention her name without somebody knowing who she is. I want to be like that.

Right now, my professional life does not factor in marriage, but in my future, I see myself being with a partner. I think we would be in a committed relationship, but are we going to be married? Because of who I am seeing, the answer is likely yes. I am scared of marriage. There is one among the people I am seeing who, if he told me to marry him, I would say yes. My idea of marriage is: let us be together, just us, away from everybody we know. That is idealised. When you think about it, marriage is families coming together to be one. People become invested in your marriage and you have to let them be. It is so scary to me. I know my mother would have a stroke if I told her I did not want to get married. I think the reason I am scared so much is due to societal expectations and also that horrible day – the wedding day.

I do not like divorces. I think they are sad. I am not a

cold-hearted person. I am romantic, so the end of anything is just heartbreaking. Divorce is one of those things. It is final: I made a big mistake in my life. You are not who I should have got with. I feel so heartbroken every time I hear about a divorce, regardless of what happened. I mean, I would be happy if someone were to tell me, 'Oh my person was abusive' or, 'We were not compatible.' I would cheer them on ... and I would still be sad. I do not want that to be my story; I really, truly want that happily-ever-after thing. Yet I factor in my need to know other people. Can I commit 100 per cent to one person, forever? Does that mean I would never know people as much as I want to? It is all selfish.

I think I want kids but they are such a big responsibility. I adore kids. Right now, I am not mature enough to have one. Same thing with marriage. At 25, you are a child. Your parents might say you are not a child but you are. Even if my mother thinks 25 is old enough, to me it's a big age for an idiot. If I was going to get a kid or something, I would be 30. Thirty is a nice, good, adult age. When I get to 30, you cannot say 'I am a child.'

The most important thing to me is identity. I think I am beginning to create one for myself. I am beginning to come into who I thought I would be as a child. It feels affirming. Getting a job was pretty sweet. Graduation from university too. But I have to ask, 'What is happiness? How is happiness supposed to feel? Does it mean that everything at that point in your life is good and as it should be? Is that what happiness is?' I struggle with being alone. I mentioned earlier that I adore my mother. A lot of the choices I make are because of her. I would say the most unconditional love that I have ever felt came from my family. But we are never around each other so such moments are rare. I struggled with depression for a long period of time. Every significant moment when I should have been over-the-moon happy, there has been something holding me back. I think I am happy but any time I look back it feels like I was pretending. I want to be happy but maybe I have never been happy. I do not know.

– *ZH, age 25*

When I Die, I Just Want To Be Remembered

'It feels good knowing people who are queer. With my straight friends, I have to act proper, talk of the perfect guy, weddings and the Bible, but with my queer friends I can be myself and talk about everything.'

Growing up was growing up. I did normal stuff like going to school, coming back, eating and playing. I had friends in school and I had friends at home. I used to play with my neighbours a lot. When they were not available, I had a lot of toys to play with. I loved dolls. I had a lot of dolls. With my friends, we played hide and seek, ice and water, police and thief – silly games like that.

I liked school and I did well, but then I guess I lost focus. I was a loner, a little quiet. Initially I was very noisy and I used to destroy stuff. I loved the screwdriver, so anything that had a screw was my hobby. I became quiet when I entered my early teens. Till now, I am quiet. I don't like formal education; I prefer informal education. After graduation, I plan to go into business, I don't know which one yet. It will definitely be rendering a service not selling products, but I am not sure what it would be.

My mum was a career woman. It was normal for her not to be around. My relationship with her was always very good and she is the most important person to me. She is a great person. She is strong. She is a very good Christian, religious. She is just like any other person's mum. She is funny, confident, determined. I love her.

When I was younger, I wanted to be a cardiologist because the name sounded fancy. I thought by 23, I would be in medical school. I also imagined I was going to be married to a man, have a fancy house, maybe two kids. But I like the decisions I have made and I am enjoying my journey so far. My happiness doesn't come from anybody.

My first kiss was with a girl. I think I was in primary 3. We went to their house and we were playing when she said, 'Okay, let me show you something.' She said I should close my eyes, so I closed my eyes, and then she kissed me. I pushed her away and started spitting. I said I would never kiss anybody again.

The first time I fell in love was secondary school. I attended a same-sex missionary boarding school. She was older and she was my senior. I have always liked older people. I get bored with my mates. I don't know why but they bore me. I don't flow with most of their gist but with people older than me, I learn from them so I think that is why I prefer them.

I was in JSS2 and she was in SS1. She had a girlfriend in her class and she had other junior girls too. I don't think she was being a player. It was just the norm with almost all seniors. I wrote her letters, then I got gifts for her: sweets, chocolate, stuff like that. At that point, I guess she knew. Then I think she told her friends because they would tease me. Sometimes they would force me to spend the night at her place. It was intense. My feelings were satisfied but not necessarily reciprocated because this was secondary school. But she cared about me. Yes, she did.

In SS2, I got into my first official queer relationship. It was with my friend's neighbour, who also happened to be my friend's elder sister's friend. I was really shy but I never miss my heart when it jumps about a person. Being too shy to speak to her, I stargazed at her, awestruck. Finally, she noticed me, but she felt I was too young for her so she chatted me up like you would a kid: 'What school are you in? What do you want to be when you grow up?' It was annoying but she was talking to me! Anyways, when I returned to school, we would write each other and then she started visiting me at school. Barely a year later, we were dating. Dreams do come true, lol.

That was not the first time I slept with a girl but it was the first time I was attracted to one. The first person I had a sexual encounter with, the first girl who gave me oral sex, I don't even know how it happened. I just know one day we started making out. The funny thing is I think I was in Primary 4 or 5 and she was a year behind me. She wasn't in the same school as me but she was my neighbour and my friend so we used to hang out together. This was mostly at my place, since Mumsie wasn't at home most of the time.

There was this day she was at my place and we were together when suddenly my mum came home. There was no light. The power was out but I heard my mum's voice through the gate and I just jumped off. I lowered the lantern and told her to get dressed while I ran to the gate. By the time Mumsie came she was like, 'Ah, why is there no light? Why didn't you switch on the lamp?' I went into the house and she was already dressed so I picked up the lamp, turned it higher, and then we came out together and she went home. I didn't even know what it was called then but it was a regular thing until we packed out of that place.

I knew a couple of people liked me in secondary school because we had toms. We knew they were toms mostly because of the way they walked and stuff like that. In my secondary school, they punished people like that. People who were termed 'lesbians'. Sometimes, the principal would do the punishing. Sometimes they could give it to the Reverend Sister. Sometimes they could be suspended. I knew I was really attracted to girls but I didn't define it and besides I hadn't had contact with boys yet so there was really no comparison.

I had a particular friend but we are no longer friends. She was the first straight friend I came out to and she left me because of that. I think that was when I made a decision that no straight friend should know about me. We were gisting one day and I said, 'There's this girl I really like. I just met her. You know I'm into girls too, right?' She was shocked at first then she started asking me weird questions like, 'So you suck pussy? How does it taste? When did you know? How did you know?'

She seemed cool with it, then like two months later, she started withdrawing. She wouldn't visit. She would never be around if I wanted to visit. When I confronted her eventually, she said, 'So all the while I was dressing in front of you and spending the night with you, you were fantasising about having sex with me?' I told her it didn't work that way but she wasn't convinced. She said stuff like, 'It's not normal. I'm not like that. God didn't create anybody like that, blah blah blah.'

She was preaching to me one day and I remember telling her,

'Look, you have sex with your boyfriend. That is fornication. I am sleeping with a girl. Fine, that is lesbianism. We are going to the same hell, just different compartments. Your own section would be different but we are still in the same place.' There is a place in the Bible that says 'Your righteousness is as filthy rags before Me.' It means it is not by power or might, contrary to what people think. It is not their effort or because they are good. It is about grace. I try to remember that.

I think I am mostly attracted to androgynous girls first, then toms. By toms, I mean girls who act like guys. I tend to be slightly feminine in my relationships. I think the thing with dating women is that there is a kind of emotional fulfilment that you don't get dating a man. I think that is basically it, then I think I like the sex part. I dated a man four years back and it was cool. It lasted six months. I found sleeping with a lady more interesting than a guy.

I am currently in a complicated relationship. In an ideal world, we'd be made for each other. We talk on and on for hours. We don't even know what we are talking about but we just keep talking. Our line of ideologies is not that distant and there is just something about her. But unfortunately, we can't be together because she is getting married. It is difficult being with someone who is about to get married. I have not met the man and I do not want to meet him, but I want to continue seeing her.

We met on an online lesbian forum. We started chatting. I liked her but I knew she wasn't available so I didn't sweat it. About a month later, she asked me out and it was magic since then. Some of our friends felt we were rushing but I've never been a believer in the 'love grows with time' paradigm. For me, love happens at any time and however it wishes. Many times, she had to post me for her fiancé, understandably, and that hurt like hell, but I love her and that was all that counted to me. The first time we met in person, it was kind of awkward, like, you've chatted with this person through so much social media – Skype, BBM, WhatsApp, emails, calls, then you're standing before each other and you're tongue-tied. We were blushing and all that stuff but we adjusted to each other quickly enough.

Sometimes, I think I will leave this country. Lately I have been thinking, if I get married to a lady, we might live apart at a distance. If my girlfriend happens to be younger than me, then maybe I will have her be my personal assistant so she will have to be everywhere with me and the world will not ask questions. And other times, I think that only our families will know or maybe we will have a secret door so that it will look like everybody is entering their own room but we can share a room.

Dating is cool. It is not difficult. The best thing about being in a relationship is the emotional satisfaction. Knowing there is someone who already cares about you, someone who has your back and who you can call when you are down. I think those are important things concerning a relationship. The worst part, I don't know. It depends on the personality you are dealing with. Like when you are in a relationship with someone who plays around, then the jealousy stuff comes up. Or when you are with someone who is very authoritative and annoying. I think it all depends on the personality sha.

To me, a relationship is when you say I love you. I don't know. I like formality. Like, when you either ask the person or the person asks you, 'Will you be my girlfriend?' Or something like that. That is it for me. I think relationships are great. My longest relationship was three years. I can't remember how many relationships I have been in. I get over it early. I hate to count. I think it's childish to count.

Obviously, sex is very important in a relationship. It's like the baptism at the beginning of being a believer. At the beginning, you have given your life to Christ. First the altar call, then the baptism. The altar call is when the pastor asks if you want to give your life to Christ. That for me symbolises the 'asking out' phase, when you ask a girl to be your girlfriend or you agree to be her girlfriend. After that, in the Christian religion, you have water baptism to show your commitment, that you give your life to Christ. That's sex, at least for people who aren't players. Then again, people have walked out of church after their water baptism, right back into the world, so some relationships don't necessarily survive even after this phase.

To me, sex is sex. Whatever you like, it is what it is. It is just in your mind you know. There is making love. There is fucking. You should be able to know the difference in what you are doing. For me, making love means emotions. Fucking is just like a ritual, like you are not thinking. You are not being all romantic. Your emotions are not really there. You can actually fuck.

Women who sleep with women and think they are still virgins – to me that is naïve. They believe that until the hymen breaks, the lady is still a virgin. There are a lot of ladies who don't finger. They don't use toys. It is just oral and scissoring so the hymen is still intact. Then there are ladies who don't let anyone touch them. They just do the touching. Making out is maybe kissing and foreplay.

It is never a subject I have had to think on but to me,

sleeping with women counts as sex. If I am giving her head or there is complete nudity, then that is sex. Oral sex, fingers, scissors, toys, they are all sex. There are also no roles in sex because you can be anything. I can interchange roles depending on what I want at the time. There are times I want to be dominated. There are times I don't want to be. I want to do the one dominating. It depends; whatever I want, or whatever we want.

I wouldn't consider myself sexually adventurous. I don't know, maybe I am too uptight. But it is by choice that I do not want to be sexually adventurous. I was not sexually monogamous at the time. But now, I only have sex with the person I am dating or people I am dating. I don't use sex toys, not because we do not have access but because I don't like dicks. I dated a guy, so for me toys are an artificial dick. I know a vibrator is not a dildo but even stuff like that, I am not a fan. I think I know two websites where you can access sex toys and they are in Lagos. I have seen a few on a popular shopping website but they are not nice. I think straight people use strap-ons in their relationships though. I have seen porn videos where girls have sex with guys using strap-ons on the guys.

My identity should be who I date, not who I choose to have sex with. Who I have sex with is a completely different thing from who I date. I have straight friends but they do not know I am queer. There is a separation. But there are rumours that I am not straight. I am not out to other people but my close friends know who I am dating and their reaction is welcoming and open. I have a lot of friends who are queer. Some were girlfriends who I broke up with but am still in touch with.

There are rumours about my queerness. For those who

come to my face to ask me, I deny it. I act angry, but for others I act indifferent. I no longer wear my rings and chains. I stopped wearing my rings partly because of what they were saying and partly because, at the time, I was dating this tomboy. She said there was a lot of gossip about her already and it wouldn't help if I came out looking like a queer model. So I stopped. My current girlfriend doesn't like them either. I stopped using a lot of those things, to reduce the suspicion.

I wouldn't want people knowing in school because it is not healthy in Nigeria. We have die-hard homophobes like crazy. They don't mind raping a girl or stuff like that. I don't want that. I am not so worried about queerness being in the way of my getting a job because I am not thinking about getting a job. I am thinking about creating jobs.

I have had more in-person relationships than long distance so far. Typically, when I am in a relationship, I wake up in the morning and, if I have lectures, I go to class and come back. The person I am dating comes around, we spend time, we gist, cook, eat, maybe watch a movie, maybe make love or go out, just stroll, then say goodnight. Things are different, depending on who I am dating. When it is a long-distance relationship, it is calls, calls, calls, chat, chat, chat, Skype, stuff like that. I prefer meeting people online, because when you meet people online, they are more open to you.

In reality, there is a fear of being wrong. For example, you have leg chains to recognise each other, but now some people use it for fashion. They don't know what it means. They just saw someone use it and they liked it. Of course, it is a gay symbol. Or when you wear a ring on your right toe, a ring on the thumb and forefinger or the forefinger and the pinkie. Queer people usually wear a silver ring on the forefinger, pinkie or thumb. Some people wear it but it's always confusing because people in straight relationships wear rings on these fingers. If you wore a chain on your left leg, I would think you were just wearing it for fashion, but if you wore it on your right, that is saying you are queer.

I think marriage is good. I want to get married. I want three kids. My plan is, if I end up with a guy, then we are probably going to get married along the line and will still be in Nigeria. When I am done having my kids, I will file for divorce and full custody. If I get married to a lady, then we will definitely be abroad and I could see it lasting a lifetime.

I like kids. I think they are cute, especially toddlers. I want a liberal home, like everybody is just open: open communication, do whatever you want to do, stuff like that. That is what I want. Liberal to me means no strict rules. I don't want my children raised under any religious setting. I don't want the brainwashing that comes with that. I want them to be individuals and be non-judgemental, open. If I had kids with a man, I don't think I'd have to bring up the topic of homosexuality. If I can make them non-judgemental, that issue is solved. They will not judge people for being different from them. They will understand that life is about peculiarities. That is why, even with flowers, God gave us different types of flowers, different colours with the birds, the feathers and stuff like that. I think if I can raise open-minded individuals, I do not have to bring up homosexuality with them because in every aspect they will be open-minded like that.

If my mum knows I am queer, I think she is in denial because she has never said anything about it. I have had ex-girlfriends come over. Some even stay over. I sleep out once in a while but sleeping out, I think, has to do with trust levels. I have always been a good kid and my mum is always happy to see friends come over because then she will know who they are. So when I go to sleep over, she doesn't mind because she knows it is a girl and she knows who the person is. I do not plan to come out to my mum in so many words but maybe in action. Like, this is it. I am living with a girl.

If I get married to a girl, I will just leave. I will not say anything to my mum. She will feel really bad about it because she will think she was the one who went wrong and that is not true. I read a lot into philosophy and I have a lot of philosophy in my life so I know that people are individuals; you don't really shape anybody, even as a parent. But I don't like her thinking she did something wrong, that she didn't bring me up right.

I think I am part of the LGBTI community, especially online. I have a friend I met from NaijaLez who is talking of starting an NGO. The money will go into a women's and LGBT centre. It feels good knowing people who are queer. With my straight friends, I have to act proper, talk of the perfect guy, weddings and the Bible, but with my queer friends I can just be myself and talk about everything: what bothers me, sex positions, whatever we want to talk about. The offline community knows me too, but when the rumours started, I had to make myself scarce. I deleted myself from BBM groups and stuff like that.

My role models change as time goes but I think my mum is my biggest role model. I like Ibukun Awosika and Genevieve Nnaji. I look up to them. I think Genevieve is strong. Having a kid when she did and being able to withstand pressure and make something so amazing of herself despite all the rumours.

She has not been fazed by any of it. She doesn't even stoop to respond to those rumours and that takes a strong personality. Ibukun, on the other hand, has been very successful and has been able to give back to society. She has a lot of people on scholarships, entrepreneurship programmes and is making a difference practically. I think that is a good thing.

Life is short and a lot of people are dead. When I die, I want to be remembered as someone who lived (in every sense of the word). Someone loving. Someone open. I want to tell other queer people to be open to life and the experiences of life. To not let themselves be boxed up by religion. Explore. Always have an open mind. Don't judge anybody. If people decide to judge you, it is their problem but you do not judge. Live life. That is what I tell people. Whatever you do, live!

There is a quote I have always liked: 'The heights by great men reached and kept were not attained by sudden flight, but they, while their companions slept, were toiling upward in the night.'[1]

– PD, age 29, Abuja

---

1   Henry Wadsworth Longfellow

To Anyone Being Hated, Be Strong

'When they started hating me, I hated myself even more.'

Content Note: Physical Violence, Deliverance Sessions, Verbal Abuse, Depression, Sexual Violence, Attempted Suicide, Corrective Rape, Self-Harm

Being an African lesbian, an out lesbian, especially with my folks, here in ___ State, is a blessing. I came out to my parents years ago and they finally accepted it last year. They said okay, fine, but I shouldn't rub it in their faces. My family give me space. I have sisters and there is always pressure – marriage this, my grandkids that – but for me, it's fine. When they see me with some girls, my mum always goes, 'Is she your friend?' I know what she means by that. But then, it's very scary because we live in a community, especially in my area, where there are church activities. There's this zonal fellowship. Christianity and Islam really, really affect our community.

My family is very religious. My father is a politician and my mother was in government. They're not high profile but they're known. One thing my father said to me was, 'Be careful. You know, they can use you to target me. They can use me to target you.' So, that is one of the reasons why I have to be careful. We're from a Christian background and we have Muslims in my family. And of course, religion frowns on the LGBTI. I've not had it easy. In fact, I doubted myself. In the early stages, I thought I was possessed.

My father is from a large family with over twenty surviving brothers and sisters. We're not close because of their mentality. We are all girls and they look at us like we don't exist. I'm closer to my mum's side because they're more accepting. They embrace us. In fact, some know my sexuality and they're cool with it. I have a relation who is married to someone in the National Assembly and they're cool. From time to time, their daughter asks me about my girlfriend. She has started asking me questions. I'm like, 'No. Stop. You have to grow up before we talk about these things.' But, of course, there are some people who detest it. They are homophobic.

I'm the quiet, friendly cousin. I don't rub it in their faces but my mum always goes, 'Be careful. Be careful.' She says that because, growing up, people have heard, people have suspected, people have said, and now I'm older, they go, 'When will she settle down?' Some people look at me and can tell: 'This one is different.' I play football, volleyball. The mentality is, because she's a tomboy, she's a lesbian. In fact, someone has suggested I marry a homosexual so society can accept us. We can be married and do our things behind closed doors. Yes, it's tempting, but I don't think I want to live a lie.

Growing up, I was confused. Everyone around me was religious. My uncles are priests. We have family devotions every day at 8am. I was wild though. I had the opportunity to travel and meet different people who were open and willing to try stuff. It was exciting but it got to the point where I asked myself, *Is this who I want to be?*

But let me start from the beginning.

I remember being the outgoing kid. The sporty one. I was adorable but stubborn. My father had this 'London mentality'. My cousins used to tease us. We were the kids who wore socks and shoes. We were proper. We would sit at the table to eat lunch. We would have dinner together and pray together. We went to really good schools. My home was a loving home. We never hit each other. It was never abusive. Growing up was really nice. I know many people are not privileged to have that, especially in this part of the country.

My primary school was mixed. I'd always want to be the dad or the son when we were playing. I didn't want to be a girl. I felt like a boy. I still do. My father and I were close. He would sit down to fix something and call me up to show me. The first thing I fixed was this fan. He gave me the screwdriver and watched me fix the motor. He was so proud of me. He went, 'You're just like a boy.' I remember feeling, *Of course I'm a boy.* I was 5 or 6. Up until today, I'm the one who takes the cars with the drivers to go and get fuel. I go to the mechanic. I pay the bills. I go change the gen. I don't go to the market. I don't cook. My family has accepted that that's my role.

Around the same time as the fan motor, there was a girl I would play with. She would rub up on me when playing Mummy and Daddy. Then one day, her mum caught us. We were just cuddling but I think she saw the tendencies – or maybe there was something about her we didn't know. She really beat us and told my mum. I stopped going to their house. I knew I was attracted to girls but I didn't understand it. I couldn't tell anybody – my sisters were busy being older sisters. We were not allowed to play with the area children but I would sneak out, play football, and come back. When

I was 8 or so, there was my older sister's friend. She was 18 and really pretty. I fell in love. I knew I liked girls before but this was the first time I felt emotional attraction. She was an angel. I didn't want any harm to come to her. I didn't want her to want anything. I worshipped her.

That was my first crush. I started experimenting sexually at a very young age. I was in JSS1 when things started. My older sister's friend was 12. We were in school and she would come to me and kiss me goodnight – on my cheek or my lip. One day, this kiss was different. It was very … tonguey. I had read novels so I knew what that meant. My sister was always reading M&Bs, Silhouette Sensations, the *Real* magazines. I would pick them up. I liked the sexuality of them. They made me feel things. I would put a pillow in between my legs, cross them and read. The part that really got me off was when they talked about their penises. I just felt, yeah, that's me. Especially when women gave them head. So I was very angry when she kissed me. I wanted to be dominant. I was supposed to kiss her because I was the man. I followed her one night into her corner in her room. She was in bed. I sat beside her and kissed her. It made me feel good.

This went on for two years. I learned on her. I listened to her and I knew that, if she made a sound, it meant she liked it. She was the first person I went all the way with. I was 10 when I gave her head. I read novels to prepare. I underlined the sexual parts. Anything he did, I knew I was supposed to do. I was nervous. Before that, all we had done was kiss. I was remembering all the lines I had underlined: *Okay, he did this. Okay, is this what they are talking about, the flower bud? Doesn't look like a flower. It tastes like pee. Ewww!* I knew she really liked it because I was listening to her sounds. She held my head there and I thought, *Well, fine, let me please her cos I like it too.* Oh, I was hooked. From then, I just knew.

I didn't like her touching me though. She came to visit my older sister when I was in university. I told her that I had so many new tricks to show her and to come back later when the house would be empty. She tried to reciprocate. I still didn't let her touch me. I didn't let anybody touch me until I was 20. During all this time, it felt good between my legs, it was warm in my chest but I was scared of being caught. My sister never found out. None of my sisters know I've been with their friends.

After her, I started trying with others. Apart from my sister's friend and one other girl in SS3, I would just kiss the others. With these girls, it was casual. I was their guy. Some wanted to learn. They would come and ask, 'Teach me how to kiss.' I would kiss them. They would keep coming back. We would kiss and kiss and kiss. It became like a chore. So I stopped.

I was 11 when I went to a bigger school. I will never forget my first impression. I was being driven in and they were all checking me out. I knew what it was for a girl to look at me in a certain way. So I could tell, *Okay, this girl knows what's up. Okay, that one. Oooh! That one too!* Some would look at you with disgust. There was someone who actually said, 'Another one!' And I was like, *Another what? Oh, so there are other people like me in this school? Yes!* I knew this was going to be fun.

It was hidden, but that school was very sexual. I picked up from where I stopped but made it a challenge. I would go for the prettiest girls, make them like me, then leave it. It got sexual with one particular girl. That was when I evolved from one stage to another. I was 14. Before then, I had enjoyed it, but now I knew this was me.

I liked the way I was even though it was hell. Seniors would punish me and staff would come after me. There were other lesbians there but I was their sacrificial lamb. I was set apart. I was abused. I was beaten. I was punished for no reason. But then I excelled in sports so some staff asked me and I denied it so they put me under their wing. Seniors would come and demand I have sex with them. They would punish me for saying no. I couldn't tell because nobody would believe me. There was this particular senior who got caught and was asked to write a list of girls she had been with. She wrote three lists. In all three lists, my name was number one. I had never been with her. In fact, I hated her with a passion. So some friends and I beat her up. It made me feel good. It made me feel the strength and the masculinity: I'm a guy here so don't mess with me.

It was at that school that I fell in love. Everybody was running away from me but she would hang out. She would listen. She accepted me so I loved her for that. I told her I really liked her. She shot me down. Heartbroken. I was devastated.

One day, she was putting cubes of sugar in her mouth and saw me looking. She asked if I wanted some. I was like, yeesss ... so we kissed. I was so unsure of myself because I didn't want to mess it up. In our final year, last term, we had sex. All the way – everything I had read, everything I had done, everything I had practised, and everything I knew ... That was the first time I came just by knowing she had an orgasm. I felt this was the love of my life. I was going to marry her. That was the first time I considered being with a chick forever. And then we graduated.

Many of the girls at my school are now married with children but they still see other girls. Some are scared to even try it again but want to. There's one who is a doctor now. She recently asked me, 'Do you still do girls?' and said we should hook up. I keep telling people there's no girl or lady who is 100 per cent straight. None. Even our parents. You just choose a path – the most dominant one for you.

I felt there was something wrong with me. At school, everybody was constantly talking about boyfriends. So I had a boyfriend, but to me he was my friend. He tried to kiss me once. That was the worst feeling ever. It felt out of place and uncalled for. I told him never to do it again. Later on, after secondary school, I still felt there was something wrong. I called a friend: 'Let's try and have sex.' I just couldn't. I saw his penis and I took off. It was ugly. It was not mine. I'd pictured myself going into someone, not someone going into me. It was just wrong.

I was so confused. I was trying to be good. I was trying to be Christian – altar calls and all that. Nobody even suspected. Then I got into drugs. I wasn't really keen about drinking but I liked the smell of cigarettes. I liked the effect of weed. Then I started going higher and higher. I tried crack, I tried cocaine, to get my mind off things. It felt better when I got high – or so I told myself. I went crazy. I shut down. I was depressed. But here in Africa, you don't know what depression is. They say, 'She's not well. This one, ah, you know …' I knew I was depressed because I read a lot.

I had a friend who I could talk to. At that point, she hadn't told me she was also a lesbian. I was scared. I didn't want her to feel I was weird. And she, too, was going through the same thing.

I opened up to my mum about it. I told her I was a bad person. I told her I'd been with girls. For like four, five minutes, she was silent and looking at me. She said, 'It will pass but I don't want you to smoke. I don't want you to drink. It will pass.'

Now, looking back on it, I wonder what she meant. My mum was very sporty. She was outgoing. She was like me, but feminine. There were always women she would talk about. She was this Hausa girl, sporty, travelling, so they looked up to her. There's this woman who, up till today, calls her 'my husband'. So I wonder, did it pass for her? I tried to ask her about it and she just went, 'Don't', very quietly – so I left it. We started praying. My mother was there for me.

And then my sister found a pack of cigarettes and a cigar in my jacket. All hell broke loose. She called my dad, called everybody. My sisters were evil. They started searching my room. They checked my phones. I had kept letters from old girlfriends. That was how they found out. I was 18. I have never seen hate like that. My dad beat me. My sisters treated me like shit. All of them kept telling me I was of the devil. I was going to die young. I was dirty. I shouldn't come close to them. I was a filthy lesbian. I didn't even look human. The one that really, really hurt was that I didn't deserve to be alive – and in days of old, they would stone us to death.

There was a time when I was in a coma for a month. They had given up. They'd dug my grave in the village. Then this Indian man came in and said they should give me my father's blood and some medication. I woke up as if from sleep. It was a miraculous recovery. They looked but nobody had seen any Indian man. Of course, they ascribed it to God. So, when all of this came out about my sexuality, they kept saying that if God had not saved me then I would have died and this shameful thing for the family wouldn't have come.

That was the worst three years of my life. When they started hating me, I hated myself even more. School was messed up because I couldn't concentrate. I quit school for a year. I went deeper into drugs. I was rebellious. I was wild with girls. In a week, I would be with four different girls. I attempted suicide. I slit my wrists. I still have the scar. They started blaming my mum. I felt I had brought so much sadness to her I shouldn't exist.

I was taken for deliverance. They would wash me. They would anoint me with oil. They would pray and pray and pray and bind and cast out every demon. 'Bind and cast out the spirit of homosexuality, the spirit of lies, the spirit of the demons holding her, the chains tied around her!' I would wonder, *Is there a demon that's about to come out? I'm hot; does that mean the demon is coming out of my chest?* I believed I was possessed. I felt less than human. I felt I was better off dead. But they would make me understand that God had given me this life so I should dedicate it to him. They brought this preacher I was supposed to marry. You should have seen this guy ... but even he didn't want to be associated with the lesbian convert.

The sessions sometimes lasted days. I was just allowed to eat, take a bath and go back. Afterwards, I would be reformed because I would lock up. I wouldn't leave the house. I would go offline. I'd come back and watch myself. I wouldn't even think some thoughts. I'd make sure not to say some things in front of them. There was a period of time – this is why I even thought I was possessed – when I'd just zone out and be somewhere else in my head. There are days I can't remember. There are years of my life I can't remember.

Around this time, my dad shot at me. He picked up a gun and pulled the trigger – because I'm a lesbian. I had no money, so I came home and took N20,000. I told him I had taken it when he asked. He got annoyed.

That's when I heard the gun shot – *tkh tkh tkh tkh tkh*. But I had bent down so the bullet hole was in the wall. My sisters ran to the room. My mum pushed my dad down. She started hitting him, calling him a killer, that he wouldn't kill her child. He disowned me, said he never believed I was his child, that I was different. My sisters were silent. The gun had fallen. That was when I knew, *Okay, you have to leave now.*

I still don't like my dad for that. He apologised to me later. We went for counselling. I've forgiven him but I can't forget. Even though he has now accepted me, I can't. What if I didn't bend? What if my mum hadn't jumped on him? Would he have shot again?

I moved out into students' quarters. My parents didn't know where I was. I changed my lines. I went off grid. I would put on my number and call my mum once a week. I would tell her where we could meet and make her promise not to tell anybody. My mum was always saying they didn't understand, that I needed love, even if I was going to change.

I spent over a year away. In the end, my mum convinced me to come home. The priests, the bishop and some others got involved. One of them had gone through something similar – he wasn't homosexual but he was a womaniser and into drugs – and he was now in the Church. So, he understood. He was just happy I wasn't doing heroin.

The bishop took me to church, St ___. He said, 'Yes, the religion has taught us it is wrong,' but told me to look at the cross and asked me, 'Do you believe in the cross?'

I said, 'Yeah, I'm a Christian.'

He asked, 'Do you believe Christ died?'

I said, 'Yes I do.' I actually do.

'Do you believe that it is God who will judge?'

'Yes.'

'That's all.' He told me he didn't have a right to judge. He couldn't say this is wrong or right. It's the Bible. It's what I believe. At the end of the day, it's between God and me.

Of course, he doesn't speak publicly like this. He has spoken out against same-sex marriage in church. He told me that that is what the religion has said, he's a man of God and he preaches the word – but it is between you and God. He said this to me one-on-one but wouldn't say that openly.

My mother also spoke with me. She told me God does not make mistakes. The same God that we always say, He's this, He's that, knows He's the only one that will judge. It's true. Even if I sin – because we all sin – it's between me and God. My mother made me learn to love myself. I believe that, in my religiousness, God understands and knows me so there's no need for me to pretend.

Church is very homophobic though. Today, we were treating Revelations and the return of God. We treated Joel. It's a poem of destruction and the wrath of God on those who don't believe. Of course, homosexuality was there and the woman drummed on it. She went on about how they've legalised same-sex marriage now but not in Nigeria, and these fourteen years are not enough. You could see everyone nodding. It made me feel like crap. My sisters were looking down because they didn't want to look at me. They thought, *Okay, is she getting this?* I see my younger sister getting confused. She knows about me but the church is saying this, so why am I doing it?

It has made me doubt and not want to go to church or Bible study. It helps that my cousin knows about my sexuality and we always sit together. She will hold my hand and we'll sit through it. Or, I'll pick up my phone and start playing Candy Crush. After all, I live better lives than many of them. You see what these same people do. There was this day where we all went for a picnic. We were seated and gisting. Then I saw this usher in a short skirt grinding on this guy. Before you know it, they're making out. Some Sundays later, I realise she's married – to somebody else. This is an usher in my church. They stand up there and go, 'Homosexuals will die. We will stone them. Fourteen years is not enough!'

Come on, who are we kidding? Why do we pick on only some sins?

Around the time of my conversation with the bishop, I got a job. I started providing for myself and believing in myself. Then I got robbed and everything went to shit again. They blamed it on me: It's because you're not living a good life. You're still doing your nonsense. I decided to start a business. Then I got my first staff member and was like, *Wow, I'm actually paying someone.* I felt good. It was like a stigma before, that I had not schooled well, but now I can be proud of myself. I can bring something to the table. No one can tell me, 'Do this.' I have the option of not living at home.

I'm still not having it easy with most of my sisters, who are outright homophobic. I don't even talk about my sexuality with the sister I am closest to. We pretend it's not part of my life. With another, we say hi and that's it. I have one sister who is really cool with me. She told me all those horrible things but she has changed. She says the only thing she hates about my life is that I did drugs and still smoke and drink: 'If only you didn't do that. Do you know where you would have been today? You had a scholarship. You blew it.' But if I have a problem with my girlfriend, she will give me advice. She was the one who spoke to my folks and went, 'See, she's the way she is. It's been dragging for years and years and years. The best thing is to accept her and love her. If she will change, it's love that will change her. If she won't, she's still family.'

All of this has not been a good experience but it has built me into who I am. It has helped me to know who I want to be. I want to be my own person. I don't see myself living under a man. I've not had sex with a man until today. In fact, I don't see myself as a lesbian. I say to people I'm straight but in one direction. Honestly, I'm lesbian because I'm female and I'm here in this time and place. If it were different, I wouldn't be. I'm not happy. I'm not complete. I feel it's wrong when I'm on my period. I discovered I had some issues there and wanted to take out the uterus. My mum tried to convince me it's correctable, that there's a fifty-fifty chance of having kids. But that's not my place.

I'm very conscious of my body. That's why I learned to cover big. Before all my health problems, I loved my body being fit and trim and muscular. I'm stronger than the average female. My stamina is greater. I feel safe where I can defend myself. But being this way, I can't even defend myself because, *Ah, she's a woman.* I have to act a certain way because I'm female. I have to be gentle. I feel I'm lying to myself. I would find myself getting into fights with men, and they'd be, 'But you're a woman.' And I would say, 'To hell with that.' I feel it's an insult to hold back, but if he hits me, it's cool.

I'm not thinking of being transgender yet. Maybe I've not yet accepted it. But if there were an opportunity for me to take out my uterus, cut off my boobs, then of course I would do that. I'd feel safe. I'd feel real. We've seen the movies, *The L Word* and all that and how you go through the medication and the surgery. My folks and everybody will not accept me as transgender. I'm not ready for them to outright reject me. I love my mum and that would just kill her. But, if my mum is no more and maybe my dad passes away and if I have the means, I know I will go for surgery, perhaps in another country. I don't want people looking at me and condemning me here. I've had enough of that in my life.

That's why the community is so important to me. It feels good, knowing there are other women with you. It's like a family, especially for some of us. I always have this picture on my BBM: Family is not all about blood, it's about those who love you through thick and thin and can hold your hand even through fires. These are the people who are family, not just blood. After all, my own sister told me some weeks back that the only thing connecting us is that we came out of the same womb.

When I look at the community in other countries, yes, they have their difficulties. But here, I can't even express how painful it is. I know at least ten people who are lesbian and bisexual but because they are married, they're not safe. They can't even be part of this project because they're going to jeopardise their marriage. In this country we're in, you're either hated by your family or shamed by your community. You lose your job or you're exploited or you're raped.

I know of a girl, here in ___. She was raped because she's a lesbian. She went to buy stuff. This guy had been asking her out and she was feeling cool about it. So, she said, 'Sorry I don't do guys. I only do girls.' She was staying on her own in students' quarters. The guy comes to her door. He knocks. His friend comes in. And then they rape her. They rape her and rape her and rape her. In her own place. They rape her until she passes out. The next day, I see her crying in the car and she tells me. I don't believe it because I know this guy. Come on, I know him ...

I lost it. I didn't have him arrested because they'd blame her. They'd probably lock her up, fourteen years. Nigeria. I paid some soldiers to beat him up. I told them he robbed her. He went and reported he beat up a lesbian and she got her lesbian friends to mess him up. Well, he reported to police and I reported to soldiers, so ... This is Nigeria ... Of course, everything died down.

I heard there are cultists who raped another girl in ___. I've heard of three cases plus that one. The first girl who came to me, I took to the hospital. But the others, I don't know. For you to be raped is something to cover up. It happens a lot but they keep quiet about it.

We need a safe place but there is no safe place. Even when you think you find one, you find people trying to gain off you. It's painful when your true self is being exploited at the one place you think you're home. Or you lose your friends because this person is bad-mouthing that person. Why can't we have a secure place where lesbians can just come and be? A place where you can come with your girlfriend, you can come with your wife, you can come single, you can come to mingle – why can't that happen? Why can't I do that? Just create a place for this group of women who just want to be safe?

All of this has made relationships rocky. I was going through shit at home and needed them to understand. For some of them it's fun. They're just trying this out. My last relationship, I knew she was bisexual but I expected that meant one at a time. But she had me and she was going with this guy. When I found out and I spoke to her, she said it was financial. It put me off. It made me think, *Do people actually take me seriously?* These girls, they believe this is who they are but they compromise themselves. I've been deprived of food because I am lesbian. I expect to fight and struggle. Not compromise myself.

My current girlfriend is married and her husband knows about us. I'm her first girlfriend. They've been married for five years. She was very depressed because they didn't have kids. We were friends, then stuff started happening. He noticed she had changed and she was better. So he encouraged it – this relationship, this friendship. For me, it's not easy. The thought of them being together, because they have to try to have kids ... I can't sleep. She'll call me at, like, 2am and we'll talk. He knows she talks to me after they've just finished trying for a child. It's messed up but I love her. I used to be so promiscuous but since I started dating her, I've not even looked at anybody else. She makes me feel whole.

It works for all three of us. He respects my opinion. He respects our relationship and I respect their relationship. He wants to have a kid, I want to have a kid and she wants to have my kid. They're trying but we've planned that, next year, we're going to try with my egg and get sperm from a donor. I want my kid to be very fine so I want to try to have a mixed-race child. I think her husband is likely to be polygamous. His people are saying, 'Your wife is barren! Five years!' He's running for political office and has to go to his state, ___. She will leave him if he takes a second wife. He will move to his state. And we will be together. That's my hope.

But the situation has got worse lately. When we were young, it was not known as LGBTI. It was just known that they were the different people. Those people who liked their sex. It was not labelled in the same way. My mum told me there was a house like a brothel but for guys, dan daudu, and another one for hajiyas where you could go and be with other women. A brothel of women for women. Here. In ___. People would pass it. It was known. Up till today, it's practised in Northern Nigeria – Sokoto, Kano ...

People are now outspoken as they feel the law is on their side. There's a big label. But being LGBTI and even identifying with them is putting a target on your back. Back then, you could support them and nobody would ask why. If you said, Because they're human beings, people would be like, Okay that's fine, that's your opinion. But now the law has come, it's legalising the criminality and stupidity. They feel the last government gave fourteen years and this government should improve on it. We have a new president. Some Christians go, 'He's not even doing anything because he's Muslim.' Then the Muslims go, 'Ah, why isn't he doing it when he's Muslim?' If you do anything as a female, they can accost you, kill you and claim you were a lesbian.

You would see people at the clubs, outside the clubs, kissing. People were like, 'Ooh, what's that?' But now they go, 'Ah, we're going to report you to the police!' We are more susceptible to harm. Not only can we be beaten, but they feel they're justified. If it was like this when I was growing up, my life would have taken a different turn. The law and all that nonsense gives room for young boys and young men to abuse young girls, to threaten, to frame them. It doesn't make sense. I know people in government who are homosexuals.

I even helped one get a friend to talk to and he just started dating this young man. Hypocrites passed these laws.

But I think it's going to get better. In this generation, we are learning to speak out. We will be heard in the nearest future. I believe that in my heart. There's nothing you can tell a homophobic person that is sure to make them change their mind. But you can try. For the religious person, I tell them that God is love and God will judge so leave the judging to God and just love your neighbour as yourself. The traditional ones don't even have a point. Most traditions in Nigeria accept that a woman can be with a woman, or a man can be with a man, if they lose a spouse or whatever. They're just adding the ideology of culture and tradition to their hate and trying to impress it upon people. They should really research.

To anyone who is battling and being hated, I tell them to be strong. You feel it's the end but there's always a better day. I'm living testimony of that. I've cut myself. I've bled in a bathtub. But right now, I can't see myself not living my life. We must not all be the same. Fingers are not the same. We don't have the same fingerprints. We're free to be different. That's why I'm letting them hate me. I'm not killing them for hating me. But my life matters. Let us just live.

– BM, age 30, Plateau

Your Sexuality Doesn't Define Who You Are

'I find men don't have a problem with lesbians, only with gay men. They say, "The more the merrier." They want to watch. I have never met a homophobic guy who says it is disgusting to see two girls.'

I have one younger sibling, a sister who is quite stubborn. I am three years older than her. My sister and I were like cat and dog when we were growing up but we are okay now. We were always fighting, like we could never agree on anything. She was stubborn. She had such a big mouth and was always spitting out nonsense. She is moody. I try to understand it but I can't. Now she is better. I think she understands that you have to try to improve your persona for the people around you. Even when she gets into her mood now, she finds a way to get out of it.

I was a normal kid, a very good kid. I watched TV, played ten-ten, suwe, gossiped with friends, that's it. I had normal friends, nothing spectacular. We were all just kids. I used to watch the boys play football. I didn't play a lot. I was always indoors, trying to help out in one way or another. I also loved to sing and dance. I still dance these days and I like karaoke.

I can count the number of times I was beaten. But there was this one time a girl told me she wanted to be my school mother. I was in primary school and the whole idea of having a school mother was exciting. She said I should steal money and give it to her. Well, she didn't specifically say I should steal but she said I should carry money, and then she would buy me a pack of cabin biscuits. And because I knew where they kept the money, I did it until I was caught and flogged. There was also a day I hid under my friend's bed cos I was having so much fun I didn't want to go home. They looked for me in the house. Even my friends were looking for me. They eventually found me that night and bundled me home. I was crying, 'I don't want to go home,' but they were like, 'You have to go.' I was about 6. Looking back, I wonder what exactly was I thinking.

It is hard telling someone about myself. I was really shy in my early teens. Mood wise, I could be an introvert and I could be an extrovert – more of an extrovert. I used to be more of an introvert, then I met people who wanted to make sure I wasn't quiet. I heard I talked a lot as a kid. I could say what was not and what was.

At the beginning, I hated boarding school and I wanted to leave. It was horrible. I didn't like being away from home, the punishments, everything! But in JSS2 it got easier. When I started having friends, some good, some bad, it got better. There were the friends for food, the ones who wanted to spoil me, the ones who wanted to take me to church, and the normal ones who just wanted to hang with me. I can't even remember all of them now.

They say, 'Come I want to show you something.' You go with them and they kiss you, and they touch you, and you are left wondering what just happened. There was this very cute girl. She is married to a man now, but apparently, she had done more things than I did. I just found myself being used. I was around 11.

I was in class during night prep and this girl said, 'Come with me, let's go and do something somewhere.' We were just chilling and gisting on the bed in her room and before I knew what was going on, she kissed me without warning. I can't really remember everything but it was my first kiss. I don't remember if I responded or not, but I didn't pull away so she started touching me. I thought, *Okay, what is going on here?* We weren't undressed but her hands were under my clothes and she was touching me. I think she was touching herself too, kissing me and getting off and when she was done, she left me.

I wouldn't say I enjoyed it. I was still wondering what just happened. I think she was a year older than me and she was really advanced. I was looking around me and trying to understand. I don't know, I was just there. I was so young ... and I haven't gone into these memories in a while. They aren't fun to remember. When we were done, we acted like nothing happened. There was someone else in class who kissed me too and it was not nice and I ran away. I never said no; I never really said anything. I never even did anything.

Then, finally, I met someone I really liked in SS1. She was in my class: pretty, cool and dark, but I was too much a chicken to do anything. I told her I liked her and we started having something but it was nothing physical. Just an exchange of notes and she officially became my lifey. That is the term for a special person in your life.

The first time I felt attracted to her was the first time I saw her. I thought to myself, *How can somebody be this fine? It is not possible.* I passed it off as being in an environment where you were allowed or it was the norm to be attracted to a girl. It was okay as long as it wasn't physical. We became friends and started talking. I wrote her a note. She was attracted to me too. I sent her Valentine's gifts, exchanged notes in class. My friends knew I liked her and they used to tease me and say, 'Oh she is coming, she is coming.' I was very shy around her. I couldn't shower around her. It was ... I don't know, just something that was never gonna happen.

Eventually we got over that cos I started staying in her room. We started to shower, share a big bucket of water, whatever. And it wasn't a big deal when I became okay with it; it was just normal. Everybody knew she was my lifey. I stayed in her room a lot, slept on the same bed, but then she couldn't deal with the senior students always on my case. She sent me a note that said she couldn't deal with the fact that any time she wanted to see me, there was someone calling me and asking for me, so she was going to take a bow. I tried to get her back but I guess her mind was made up. I still call her the one that got away. I even saw her at university and I was like, *Damn, she is still hot!*

So yes, the senior students being on my case was bad. I didn't like it and it landed me in trouble a lot. I was always punished for nothing. Once they even fought over me and I landed in the admin block for a fight I knew nothing about. I think it was after the fight that she told me she couldn't deal with it.

At that time, there was this girl who was a year my senior. She liked me and gave me a card, and that was why they fought. Funny enough, I liked the one who gave me the card. She was cute. She asked me openly to be her lifey and I said okay. But she got de-boarded from the hostel cos they beat some junior students.

Then her friend, whom I thought was trying to look out for her friend's lifey, made a move on me. I didn't know she wanted me for herself but it was fine because my relationship with card girl ended and I started with this girl, who turned out to be the greatest lifey I had in school. With her, it was physical. I kissed her. We had great chemistry. I remember the first time we spent the night on the same bed. We couldn't sleep because it felt so electric and we were trying not to touch each other. We kept tossing and turning and then at some point our faces met and voilà, we kissed. But that was it. We just kissed and touched our bodies, but nothing serious. That was the highest I did then.

I really liked her. She was cool, very stubborn and too much of a tomboy. She beat me one time, and I thought, *What?* It was because people knew we were together, so when I did something wrong, they would report me to her knowing she had to punish me somehow, as she was a prefect. People were watching that day so she had to, but that night, she called me over and apologised. I loved her any ways and it hurt when she graduated and left school. I cried at nights. It was so bad and everybody expected me to cry, to be down. I would wail, but I put up an act during the day. When I got back to my pillow, I would cry a lot. She wrote me a book, sixty long pages of stories, songs and poetry. I still have it in my room.

When she left, I became a player and had many lifeys. Anybody who liked me, I was like yeah, I am available. Then I met someone else but we weren't officially lifeys. We started as friends but we had an attraction for each other. She understood that people liked me and I knew people liked her too. She eventually moved into my room so we just became very good friends and beneficial friends sometimes. We are still friends. I called her my lover from the beginning. I used to call her baby. Even in front of my friends and her friends.

I didn't have anyone I was pinned to like the one lifey who

had graduated, so I floated around with people who admired me. There was this junior student who was very aggressive. I was friends with her. She was not a school daughter but she used to come around to my room. I never let her spend the night. She wanted to but I would say, 'It's time to go.'

Hell no, nothing was going to happen, but I liked her because she was bold. I didn't want to have anything with my juniors cos it was too much of a hassle. She told me she liked me, bought gifts and made a dozen notebooks with my face on it. When she brought the books on my birthday I was puzzled. I thought, *Is it that I don't have notebooks?* There was no light so I asked for a torch, and then I screamed. She wondered what was wrong and I said it was because my face was on the books. A dozen of them with my face.

I am really attracted to dark girls and someone I can hold a good conversation with. Also, people who are deep, less materialistic and less judgemental. I do not like extreme tomboys but I do not like very girly girls. If you can switch, the better for me. I switch roles too, so I don't mind. I can be a tomboy if you want. I can be girly if you want. I don't mind. I am all for that but I like girls. I want a girl. I don't need you to try to be a boy. If I want a boy I will find one. You don't need to be a boy. You do not need to pack and sag for me.

With men, I think penetration counts as sex. With women, I am not really a fan of finger penetration so I consider head to be sex. Before that, I would just think we were making out. Sex is very important to a relationship. There is a connection that comes with sex. I also find that if you have sex a lot, you fight less. The insecurity and unnecessary quarrels don't come up because you are basking in the euphoria. Sex, love, you are happy. I fight a lot in my relationships when I have not had sex in a while.

When it comes to sex, I think I am a giver cos that is satisfying. I consider myself very sexually adventurous. I am even open to toys but I find that I do not want a dildo with a girl. I am with you because I do not want a dick. There are other ways we can have fun but I am open to trying out a dildo and whatever it is when I am with you – the whips, the ass, everything.

I am still friends with my first boyfriend, J___. Good friends. I met him through his cousin, who was the first boy I ever kissed. The cousin was so cute and I liked him. He was the first guy I really liked so I chased him. He had a girlfriend. I didn't mind, because I knew the girlfriend liked someone else. I was about 17 and had graduated from secondary school. The girlfriend was someone I knew from school and she lived across from me. She always came to my house to see him but I couldn't tell him, 'You can't be killing yourself for a girl who is not killing herself for you.' I was there trying to get what I could.

One day he kissed me and I responded. Well, what happened was I went to his place, early in the morning. My mum used to go to work early and then I would stroll out to see him. He had this job at a cybercafe. So I went to his place and we just kissed. It became the norm. Every morning, I would go to his house to kiss him before he went to work. It was just kisses before we started making out but we never shagged.

Then I met his cousin J___ at the cybercafe. When he left for school, I found out that J___ had a crush on me. I stumbled on J___'s journal, where he wrote about me every day. So I wrote a line in it for him: 'Make hay while the sun shines.' He saw it and called me. He asked me if I wrote it and I said I hadn't written anything. But after that we started gisting and hanging out more often. Soon we were dating and we were together for a while. He loved me to a fault and he was my first but we broke up when we went to school. Also, he became a born-again, or at least that was the excuse he gave me. Although I suspected he also had a girlfriend cos I called him once and the girl picked up. Glo used to give free sms's and he sms'd me on her phone. I called the girl around nine and she said, 'He is here; let me give him the phone.'

My first girlfriend in university is who I consider to be my first official relationship. She was a bit of a tomboy. Pretty girl, but she had four brothers so it was understandable. The first day I saw her I was like, *God, who is this human being?* She was weird! She had blue hair. She would sit and put her legs over the third floor balcony and I always wondered, *Who does that?* I was attracted to the weirdness and I would come out when I saw her outside. I would bring a chair and sit outside just to watch her. Then we started talking.

One day she said to me, 'You know, your eyes talk. You don't need to say anything to me.' I spent a night in her room. She spent a night in my room. We really didn't do anything. We would just cuddle. We were too chicken to do anything else. Then one day, I was supposed to travel, so we got a room at a hotel and we still cuddled. Naked. The next day, when I went home, I was sad. Waste of a room, now that I think about it.

One time we decided to leave school for a change of environment. We lodged somewhere in Imo State. Finally, we had sex and I had my first orgasm.

We were together everywhere at school, holding hands. They even started talking about us. That did not stop us. The only thing we did was reduce our PDA. We used to hold hands all the time, but that was so scandalous at the school.

We didn't live in the same room. We would have killed each other with drama. We fought a lot! She was meticulous. I am meticulous. If it wasn't her way or my way, we'd have a fight. So we needed our space.

She was a flirt and I didn't mind. I was too in love. It used to break my heart whenever I went to her room and saw a lot of girls. A lot of people were attracted to her. She was so diplomatic, jovial and nice. To me, it felt like she couldn't say no. I thought, *If someone likes you, you should just say no, it is not by force.* But she flirted with them. She eventually cheated and I forgave her countless times. We dated for about three years and I forgave her every single time. It was a lot of times.

I think the anti-LGBTI law is stupid because we have more issues, pressing issues in Nigeria. We're wasting our time discussing same-sex marriage or same-sex relationships and fourteen-years rubbish when I know most of them are into it. How hypocritical can we be in this country? The problem we have right now is hypocrisy. We are too engrossed with removing the lock from people instead of trying to make better versions of ourselves. We would rather find someone to correct. It makes us feel better about ourselves.

I don't know if this is the way it is in all African countries but in Nigeria it is terrible. I have had instances where I was walking with a short dress in the market and someone came to ask, did my mother see me before I left the house?

I never really gave a thought to the law when it was passed, but right now, I wish I could be with my girlfriend and marry her. Even though I am Igbo, I cannot take a wife for myself, despite popular belief. You can only take a wife for your husband. She is called your wife, but she is for your husband, so that she can give birth when you can't. She might be your wife, but it doesn't mean you are allowed to touch her.

I want to get married. I am not particular about the gender of the person. It just has to be the right person. I want to have kids, one or two, but one is fine. I want to carry the baby even if I end up with a woman. I want the experience. I hope my partner, whoever it is, is willing to go through the experience with me. If I end up with a girl, I would rather have one kid. I am not against adoption. I want a kid and it doesn't matter if it is mine biologically or someone else's, as long as, at the end of the day, it is my child. I want someone to spoil and beat – yes – and dream with. I do not imagine bringing up my kid in this country. Especially if I am going to end up with a girl. I want her to be in a community where she understands that there is nothing wrong with having two mummies. And that she is loved like whoever has a mum and a dad. That is it.

It isn't easy meeting other people. You don't know who is queer. You don't want people going, 'Oh my God is she looking at me and saying all these things to me?' One has to be careful. I met my first girlfriend because we had a lot of chemistry. All others, I knew about their queerness from someone else. And I have not dated a lot of girls. I have been with girls but I haven't really dated them. I have dated two girls, been with more than that and dated four boys. Most of the girls you meet at friends' places or at school.

You know how people like to be holy. I try my best to be spiritual so I do not have to be identified with a church or a religion to have a spiritual connection to my creator. I used to be a lot more spiritual when I was much younger, especially in my early days in secondary school. My girlfriend has asked me how I reconcile my faith with my sexual identity and I said that I feel like God wants us to be happy. He is not sad, and wants every creation of His to be happy. And I feel like He has to be aware. If not, He would not have created an earth where we came up with the idea of same-sex relationships or having orgasms together or explosive sex. Come on, it has to have come from somewhere. I am not religious but I am spiritual. Are you trying to say that, despite being good to my neighbours and everything, I will go to hell because of my sexuality? It doesn't make sense.

I spend my time at work and then I see my girlfriend. The first time we had sex was at her childhood friend's house. My girlfriend is actually out to a lot of her friends and I envy her. She comes to my house and has met my family so everybody knows her as my friend. I am not out to my sister but I think she has an idea. She can see, I guess. I am not out to anyone in my family, except some of my cousins. I casually mentioned to them that I liked this girl and we were having something. They took it like it was nothing. I knew their minds and they weren't myopic, so I told them. I know I will eventually come out to my mum and my sister. Those are the only important people in my life. But I do not intend to tell my extended family.

If I come out, I imagine I will sit them in the house and say, 'There is something I want to tell you and I know you are not gonna like it. I have a housemate who is not exactly my housemate. She is my wife ... yeah.'

(I don't want it to be in this country. Maybe when I am living somewhere else, they come to visit, and then I say it.)

I would want my sister to be at my wedding but if it would to be too much for my mum, I would spare her that. But I don't want a big wedding. I want to wear pants, not like a suit but fitted pants and a tube top. Still look sexy, cos I like to look sexy. But my girlfriend and I talked about it and she wants a dress so I am gonna wear a dress. She loves to wear a jacket and pants so I imagine she will look gorgeous. I think it will be on the beach, without shoes, in the Maldives, not more than fifteen people, just people really close to us. I am not particular about flowers, but maybe rose petals. No bridesmaids, just my friends. If people come in bikinis, that is also good. We are just gonna get hitched and party.

Some of my friends already know but not many. The first person who knew about my sexuality, we never even had to have the conversation. She just figured it out and I was like, yeah. There was a guy who really liked me and I said to him, 'You know I have a girlfriend, right?' He said, 'Yeah, the more the merrier,' and I was like, 'No, I am serious. I have a girlfriend.' Then the day he met her I said, 'Oh yeah, I told you about my girlfriend so here she is,' and he was like 'Wow, I have heard about you.' I had a friend. We used to have a crush on each other. When I put up my girlfriend's picture on my DP, he asked, 'Is she the one?' I asked, 'Who is "she"?' And he replied, 'Is she the bae?' Eventually I said yes and when we met during a wedding we all attended, I introduced the two of them.

The terms/slang I have heard are 'gay' and 'dyke'. Things like 'lele', '3737' and 'lifey' were in high school and nobody uses them any more. They actually call you 'lesbian' now. I think Nigeria will change but it is going to take a long time. I won't say never, but it is far-fetched. I do not think it will be in our generation because we are still hypocritical. Maybe in twenty years it will be better, because in this city, a lot of people in the LGBT community are able to go out on dates. People might know. They won't openly say something but they have an idea so I guess some cities are becoming ignorantly accepting of it. I say ignorantly because they know but they chose to ignore it. But that is for cities where people are enlightened. What will happen to the other cities, the other states, where they do not have a lot of enlightened people? They are never gonna get there.

I do not imagine my future in this country. I think maybe Canada, because it is cold. I like the cold, my girlfriend even more so, and I want to make her comfortable. And the LGBT community there is widely accepted. They also have better jobs and employment opportunities, so we can feed ourselves.

I think traditionally we have a problem with homosexuality. I always hear people say, 'In the Bible is there any case where you hear animals do this?' But that is the thing with Nigeria: they don't seem able to distinguish between religion and tradition. They hide under the cover of religion and join a lot of things to it. Traditionally, they will tell you that they only know the forefathers and they married the opposite sex ... and nobody was aware of same-sex attraction.

I have experienced homophobia. In the community, if you ask them why they do not like people who are gay, many don't even know why they are homophobic. The stereotype is that if you are gay you cannot be a good person. I found myself often saying that your sexuality doesn't define who you are. You could be an awesome person. It doesn't change the fact that you like the same sex.

As for the guys, they don't want you to come near them. They say, 'Don't touch me, don't touch me. Why will a guy come and tell me that he likes me? I will punch him.'

You find out that the homophobia doesn't have a substantial explanation. I find men don't have a problem with lesbians, only with gay men. Because they say, 'The more, the merrier.' They want to watch. I have never met a homophobic guy who says it is disgusting to see two girls. They are like, 'No, you know they can touch each other ...'.

One of my happiest memories was when I gave my girlfriend a Christmas gift. She didn't expect it. I had told her I was going to give her a Christmas gift a month before, then some days to Christmas I said to her, 'Baby, I don't have money, I hope you understand. I wish I could but I can't any more.' And she was like, 'It is fine, you don't have to do anything, I just want to spend Christmas with you.' In the early hours of the twenty-fifth, I told her I was just gonna get something downstairs, and then I came back with the gift she wanted and picked out without knowing it was for her. It was a wristwatch and she kept saying, 'Oh my god.' And I thought, *Oh baby, this is so cool.* It made me so happy. I like that I surprised her.

If a straight homophobic person was reading this, I would like to tell them to look past the homosexuality to the person. Our sexuality doesn't define who we are. We have terrible people who are straight, and we have terrible people who are homosexuals. Same thing with being good. Sexuality has a minute part to play in being a good person.

– BW, age 29, Abuja

Same-Sex Relationships Are A Choice

'To say I am born gay is to accept the empathy of naïve homophobes. So, no. I am not born gay. I choose to be gay.'

When I think about how hard it is for my friends to come out of the closet, especially to their family, I am convinced I was dealt a better hand in life. What felt like a sad story became the core of my strength. At 17, my mother became the shame of the family because she had the audacity to lose her virginity before marriage and get pregnant. She told me many times how she couldn't take the shortcut and hide her shame by aborting the pregnancy. At 17 she was a child herself and didn't have the means to care for me. I was eventually raised by my uncle and aunties and lived in the company of cousins who might or might not have liked the fact that I lived freely in their house. This taught me a great lesson: independence is key.

I had my first sexual experience when I was about 7 and it was with a girl. She was a neighbour where I lived with my uncle and she was about 9 years old. I knew I had a special affection for her even though it didn't have a name, nor did I have anyone to talk to about my feelings. I only found out she felt something for me when we played this game called 'Mummy and Daddy'. The game is quite popular with kids who are left at home to care for themselves while their parents go to work. In my case, my uncle left me at home for work. The game requires acting out the role of a mother, father and kids in an attempt to mirror what we are taught is an ideal family. So, this girl declared she was the mummy and I had to play the daddy. We staged a night scene and told the other kids to go sleep. We had a little corner that we claimed as daddy and mummy's room. That was when it happened. We were wrapped up in a duvet and I was dying to kiss her or touch her, so she could know I had something for her. Still unsure how to profess my feelings, I heard her whisper, 'Kiss me.' I didn't know what that meant. I was so scared I would mess it up, not knowing what she wanted. But at the end of the day we kissed and she told me how to touch her. That is the most I remember about my first experience.

I think I had my first relationship when I was 16. A neighbour again. She was the most beautiful person I had ever seen. Her skin glowed and in my head, I was like, *Oh my God, how can someone be this pretty?* I think she noticed how drawn I was to her. One day, I was home alone and we watched a movie called *Body of Evidence*. It had a lot of sex scenes.

Around that time, she was struggling with her sister having boyfriends and didn't understand why she should have boyfriends. While we were watching this movie, she said, 'So what attracts a girl to a guy, or what attracts a girl to someone else? Why is my sister always liking boys?' I said 'Maybe because the kiss felt good.' She said, 'Really? I have never kissed anybody before.' I said, 'Do you want to try it?'

She just shrugged. She was probably nervous too. I wasn't sure if I could kiss her well, so I started with her ear. I nibbled on it. It became so tensed that she brought her lips. Then there was no question as to whether I knew how to kiss. It was more about what we were feeling at the time.

My first relationship with a girl lasted about five years. It became an on-and-off thing after the third year or so. She had to leave the country in pursuit of a better life. Distance meant nothing to me because I was genuinely in love for the first time. It wasn't the same for her. She brought up religion as an excuse, but she had a relationship with someone else in the UK.

For a while, I believed her 'religion' and 'wanting to be a better person' excuses. I assumed that if I put all my energy into dating a guy then maybe it would work out. Maybe I was not trying hard enough. Maybe I had a soulmate who happened to be a guy and I just had to find and commit to him. I cried and I prayed. Then I felt that, since I'd cried and prayed and God must have answered my prayers to take my desires for women away, it was time to do the work.

I dated a guy named P___ for a few months. I went against everything I wanted. I only dated him because I wanted to get rid of the gay part of me and see if I could correct it. I had sex with him without feeling anything. I just lay there like a log. He was grunting and saying, 'This is so nice. You are so beautiful' and I was like, 'Okay.' During the relationship, I used to calculate or schedule the sex. I told myself I would have sex with him twice a week so that at least I would know that every week I tried to remove the gay in me. Until one particular day. We had already had sex twice that week the way I had arranged it in my head, but then he wanted more. I couldn't take it any more. It felt funny and I said, 'No, I can't do it.' He said, 'If you can't have sex with me, then I am going to have another girl.'

I ended it. That was the last time I ever saw him. I became celibate, but after a while I couldn't stay away from sex with women.

I think love is a choice. I think everything about us is a choice. I can find a combination of things that take my breath away in a woman but I am also aware that the little things I find interesting in her are the result of choices I made. I do not believe in love at first sight. I have had three relationships with guys and only consummated one. I had my first boyfriend right after secondary school and shortly before I met my first girlfriend. This was a tale of two teenagers experimenting with each other's bodies, but we never got to the finish line. I think I was able to cope then because he was a little bit girly. So I thought, *Oh he looks like a girl ...* but I could never bring myself to sleep with him. My second relationship with a guy was with P___, the one I slept with twice a week. He was the one I really wanted to work it out with, but I just couldn't. The last one was when I was still in university and I wanted to try again. I sincerely think that boy loved me but I couldn't bring myself to sleep with him because I knew it would be a lie and I couldn't take myself back to how I tried in the past with P___. So I cut ties with him.

Same-sex relationships are a choice for me. I feel I must have chosen to enjoy emotional entanglement with a woman. What other reason can ever be sufficient as to why I am gay? I was not born gay. To say I was born gay is to accept the empathy of naïve homophobes. So, no. I was not born gay. I choose to be gay. I would rather stand as a woman with all of my intrinsic rights and affirm my choice.

I have never really struggled with my identity. I have always known I loved women, but at some point I wanted that to change. I wanted a chance at being 'normal'. I have, however, come to realise that I am normal and it's okay to be gay. I do not think my sexuality is a phase. I know I am gay because I choose to be. I am not going to bow to society or what they think. I didn't know at 7 that I was a lesbian but I knew I wanted girls. I see everyone from the spiritual part of life. I think everyone is a spiritual being and who you fuck doesn't really matter. I believe marriage or relationships do not exist in heaven so why not have enough of being gay, straight or asexual while you are on earth? I am a spiritual person and I practice spirituality. I used to have problems reconciling that with my sexuality but I have made my peace with being gay.

I am out to a few people. I used to think coming out was unnecessary, like, why do you have to explain to anyone that you are gay? Why does anyone need to explain why they love to eat pizza not pounded yam, then march on the streets with plaques saying, 'Hey I love pizza'? However, my perspective on coming out has changed. I went from, 'Ooh I can live a quiet life and mind my business and all will be well,' to, 'OMG! People need to know it's okay to be different. It's okay to be gay.'

The part of me that believed gay pride was an unnecessary parade of gender-confused people has been permanently dissolved. I owe this generous, mind-opening occurrence to a colleague who tried to out me after I had to terminate her employment. She had obviously heard a rumour that I was gay and decided to give me one final kick as a parting gift. She screamed, 'You bloody lesbian! I will deal with you!'

The entire office heard her and I felt like my world came

crashing down. I wanted to hide my face. I wanted to scream and cry. In all of this, I also asked myself why I felt so bad, so guilty. Had I done anything wrong? No! No! NO! I had not.

I felt a sense of betrayal to myself. I thought I had my life together. I was wrong. I had not dealt with my coming out. I'd told a few people about my sexuality but it wasn't enough. It certainly wasn't enough to disclose my sexuality to a few 'safe' folks. I was still afraid. Afraid of my choices. This opened a big, invincible hole in my head. I questioned myself and my perspectives, the ideologies that had been so buried in my everyday decisions.

I have handled folks who ask me if am gay pretty well, in my opinion. With some folks, I affirmed their suspicions. With others, I bluntly asked what business it was of theirs to know if I am gay. I have had to deny my sexuality on a few occasions. You see, I am an androgynous-presenting woman. Sometimes I am all butched up and folks are like, 'What's up with you?' And then they see my friends and they say, 'Uhm, what's up with them?' One time at home, a neighbour asked me if I was gay because only gay guys and girls came looking for me. He is an older person and I think he knows I am gay, so I said, 'Well how does that affect the neighbourhood?' I think he got the message. He replied, 'Well I am just asking,' and said that he actually likes gay people. I think if I confirmed it to him or to other neighbours, they would be very judgemental. Nigerians are a judgemental people.

What I still don't understand, though, is why was I so afraid of anyone knowing that I am a same-sex-loving woman? I am on a journey to find the answers to that question.

I assume colleagues know I am gay. I am friendly with them. I liked one person at work, but because I am her boss I disregarded it. I had to teach myself to let it go. I try not to do romance or date somebody at work. At law school, I hooked up with one person. She kept asking me weird questions like, 'What secondary school did you attend? Have you ever been into women?' I knew she was gay but I pretended I didn't know what she was talking about. I didn't want any kind of work or school complication so I have never dated anyone at work or at school. I told her I was straight. She kept on trying to woo me and bend me until one day I just looked at her and told her I was very gay, not straight. She said, 'No you are lying. It can't be true.' I said, 'Okay, let's kiss and then you will know.' So we kissed and she asked me why I had been lying to her. Anyway, she booked a hotel and we did it.

I am out to a few people. I told my cousin I like girls and she said okay. I think she likes girls too but she hasn't come to terms with it yet. Since I told her, she says, 'How is your girlfriend?' once in a while. Then I told a few friends, the ones I think are cool. I do not like straight people, so the ones I think are cool are the ones I told. I try to judge our friendship on whether you will accept me or not. And if you won't accept me then that is the end of the friendship. Because I think the only reason we were friends is because I thought you might be able to tolerate me. And if you can't, then there is really no point. I have very few straight friends, maybe three. I have more lesbian friends, so we admire girls, but I have gay friends too.

I think my parents know. There was one time I had a girlfriend over. My younger sister was about 5 or 6 then, and I thought she was sleeping but she saw me kiss my girlfriend. She asked my mum if it was okay to kiss a girl. My mum asked her, 'Where did you see that?' When my sister told her, my mum didn't even talk to me about it. She went straight to the family and they called a family meeting. Then they asked me. My straight best friend at the time called me before the meeting so I knew. We were really close and they had already asked her questions. She said, 'I think you should deny it. Don't tell anybody ...'

So, when I got to the family meeting, I denied it, but I think my aunt knows. There was one time I was at my aunt's place in Ibadan and I was supposed to go and do some stuff in Lagos. I knew it was just going to take a few hours but I was into one chick so I said it was going to take me three days. I stayed at her house and even the day I was supposed to go back, I tried to push it until finally I couldn't push it any more and I had to go home. When I got home, my aunt took my phone and called the last dialled number. Behold, my lover answered. I think she was very smart cos my aunt started asking, 'Who are you? You have been calling her. Who are you?' Because they had been suspecting me, my lover started saying, 'I can't hear you ma' and eventually dropped the phone.

I was really scared cos my aunt said she was going to take me to the police station and I should stop this way ... So I started crying. She preached the gospel to me, then I cried and we never spoke about it again. I think they know but we don't talk about it. Like my uncle met T___. Every time he comes, he asks me how my new in-law is. I say, 'She is fine,' but we don't talk about it. I will come out to my family later in life. I think it is important that I do that.

My mum tries to talk about marriage but I am not close to her. One time she was like, 'Just have kids. Let our family line continue.' I told her, 'Look. You have two other kids. Expect marriage from them.' She said, 'God forbid! You will marry, you will have kids ...' I have to remind her that I am going to have kids, just not get married. Yes, I will have kids, two biological kids and adopted kids. Maybe three girls and three boys. I want to have twins then adopt four at the same time.

I want kids but not a marriage. I don't believe in marriage. I don't see why some paper or a court should tell me, 'Now you are together with this person.' And getting out of that means I have to go back to the same court? I don't believe in that. I believe two people in love with each other should keep their word and their promises and say they want to be with each other because they want to be with each other, not because of any other thing. And that alone should be stronger than a certificate. I am not even a pro-marriage person. Relationships and the like can be tricky, sha. I usually watch the person I am dating. I try to take my time.

Right now, my days are simple. I wake up, I try to say my prayers then I go to work. I work, work, work and come back home. In between work, I talk to the girlfriend, talk to people I am flirting with, come back home, watch a movie if I can, chat on social media, Twitter, Instagram and go to bed. On weekends, I wake up late, watch movies, go out or hang out. I am currently watching *Empire*, *Blackish*, *The Originals*, *How to Get Away with Murder*, *Game of Thrones*, *Suits* and many other dramas and comedies. I also can't stop listening to *Zero* by Chris Brown.

I like girly girls. I like intelligent girls. I like girls with big clits. I like turquoise blue. I am a morning person. I like tea with lemon. I like Angelina Jolie and if there was a guy I had to shag, it would be Adam Levine. If there was one person, dead or alive, I had the opportunity of meeting, it would be Angelina. I prefer flat shoes to heels. I don't get why I should make myself uncomfortable because I want someone to think I am sexy. I like boobs more than ass. Boobs because I couldn't get over one girl's boobs. She had these really huge breasts and they hung low. I don't think I have ever looked at ass and hungered, but those boobs left some imaginations in my head.

I live with my partner now. We see each other every day, except when she is in Lagos. For the first time ever, I have someone taking care of me. I wake up in the morning and she is there with a cup of tea. It feels good to have someone there. I feel really loved by her. She is the first person I've lived with. I have always liked having my space so it took a while to get used to it. I am not even sure I am used to it yet. I find peace important. I don't want anything to disturb me. I just want to be at peace with myself. I want to be able to glow by myself. Recently something hit me, that love is different. You experience different kinds of love in different relationships and you learn some things. I have been gay, like, forever, but in my twenty years of being gay I realised that humility is one of the strongest aids you have. If you have a partner who is humble, it makes life easy. It makes everything different. I had to learn that recently.

When I was a kid, I always wanted to get a proper home. I imagined that when I was older, before getting married, I would have fucked all the beautiful girls. But now I have a comfortable house and I don't fuck all the beautiful girls I see because I like the way I have my house to myself. So, it is definitely different from what I imagined. I thought I would be randy and fucking around but now that I can, I don't.

When I think about the future, I want to have an empire. I am trying to build one now that would basically end hunger. I want to achieve that. I want to help people. I want to save lives.

I want to do something, be known for something. I want to be successful. I want to have an organisation that focuses on ending hunger. I already have it registered. I am going to have units in different parts of Nigeria. There are three different parts. The first part is the NGO part and is responsible for influencing policies around agriculture and making food available. Because it is important that people don't worry about what is going into their stomach, what they have to eat. Then they can focus on other things and dig into their potential. I want to be part of that, removing hunger from the equation and seeing what everybody can bring to the table if they are well fed. The second part is having a website where food is sold at a discount, meaning farmers are registered to sell all they have, because sometimes they have products but they can't sell because of transportation or networks or something. I want to have this platform where local farmers can sell their stuff and we will have restaurants register on the same platform to get fresh food without a middleman. That would make their food cheaper too. The third part is creating jobs, because having food and money is not really fulfilling. People need a sense of duty and accomplishment. So providing food, work, everything. I imagine employing thousands across different parts of Nigeria from this publicly traded company. I think there will be a time when Africa realises its potential and lives up to its true strength. I think we have a lot of instability because we haven't realised that, in the unity of all the states of Africa, we can compete with the rest of the world.

I like life. I want to enjoy life. I don't care how long that takes and I am not scared to work for it. I am the kind of person who plans, and if I want to get, say, a phone by next year December, I will.

I think in ten years, queer people will be so strong that straight people won't be able to do without us. Queer people will be having all the fun and getting all the fine jobs and all that. I think if a lot of Nigerian artists deem it fit to come out and live their lives, people will just be okay with it.

When I look at the future, I imagine I'll be living in Abuja with my partner, the kids, a cat and a dog. I will get the dog before the cat and maybe even a monkey. I will be in politics and I will be part of an LGBT activist group. I don't think we have strong LGBT activism yet, not the way I think there should be. I would want my kids to go to a Christian school. I don't care if my neighbours know about us. I think they will suspect us because I am not sure I will be able to hide that part of my life. I think the law would have changed by then. I think even now people are beginning to change their views. I imagine Fashola might be the president, the Super Falcons will still be on top of football on the continent, but the Super Eagles will be dead.

When I think of mentors, I think of strong Nigerian women like Lola Shoneyin. I think she is awesome. I like what she is doing and how she gets things done. I want to follow in some of her footsteps. I haven't been to Ake Festival yet, but I hope to go there and meet her one day. I also look up to my aunt. She shaped me into this disciplined person and I owe all of that to her. The fact that I like to work and get my money is because of her.

– *HK, age 30, Abuja.*

There Is No One Way To Be A Woman

'To be a woman is more limiting than to be a man.'

I currently live in Madrid, Spain, where I teach English.

My mum died three months ago. Right now, my family is me, my dad, my stepmum, my brother and my two step-siblings. My dad was born in Ivory Coast to Yoruba parents but raised in Ghana. I just found out that my mum is from a group of Brazilian people living in Nigeria. After she passed away, a whole bunch of family started reaching out, trying to get in contact with me. None of them had Nigerian or Yoruba last names. Rather, they have Spanish-sounding last names like Da Costa. I asked my dad what was up with that. He told me my grandfather and grandmother were descendants of escaped slaves from Brazil and sent me a few articles about them. So, my mum's side is Brazilian and my dad's side is Ghanaian. To be honest, I do not even know what community I belong to. I do not understand the concept of community because different people raised me. I guess I am Yoruba–American.

The earliest thing I remember is having picnics with my family. We always used a blue and white blanket whenever we went to this park. The park was near a building that had, like, a giant pink glass of milk on top of it. My mum and dad were not living together although they were not separated. My dad worked in Washington and my mum was in New York, so I only got to see my dad once a month. When he was around, he would take me to jazz concerts. Then, after 9/11, I started living with my dad and it was the opposite. I would not see my mum often.

Growing up, I was a lot quieter than I am now. I was afraid of everything. I used to have a lot of fears. Now I do not have that many. I spent my time reading. I read a lot when I was young. I read a lot of big books, long books, fantasy and history. I read Shakespeare and *The Tale of Genji*, which inspired me to learn Japanese. I loved Greek and Egyptian mythology for the longest time. Anything related to ancient history fascinated me.

I think men and women are gendered differently. To be a woman is more limiting than to be a man. I am not saying that men are unlimited. I feel being a woman is an exclusive cult that you are either part of or not. It is very, very small. It is not something that you can join but that you are forced into. If a man is viewed as feminine, he will still be regarded as a man. No one is going to view him as less than a woman, even if they call him a woman. Transgendered women, even though they portray all the traits that people consider feminine, are still viewed as men disguised as women.

I do not think that people take the concept of trans-ness seriously, no matter what gender it is. I feel like trans men do not have much to do. While they have a lot more to deal with, people generally will accept them more than trans women. For example, comparing trans men to lesbians, I feel like people despise lesbians because it is like, 'Why don't you just become a man?' Whereas trans men are considered to be what lesbians want to be. The way gender is conceptualised, only a few people get to be called 'woman' or fit into the idea of what a woman is supposed to be.

For a long time, my gender confused me because I never fit any of the things that people said women were. My mum always tried to make me more feminine. She told me that I needed to accept help from men and know how to let a man be a man. But that was not what I saw from her. She made more money than my dad did. My dad is the emotional one, not my mum. My mum was the independent woman. What she was telling me was contradictory to what she was doing. I preferred to be the independent person that she was instead of the docile person she was trying to make me be. Because she was telling me that the way I acted was not feminine, I felt that I was not a woman. Up until recently, my gender was a confusing topic for me. I have since realised that there is no one way to be a woman. I can be a woman whatever way I want to. Now I am perfectly fine with being a woman.

The first time I felt attracted to someone of the same sex was awkward for me. I was not afraid of being gay or anything like that. I did not necessarily believe that it was evil. I did not have any gay friends and just did not know what to do with the feeling. I was in the fifth grade, maybe 11 or 12. I had just found out a week before what sex was while watching a cartoon on TV, and it grossed me out. This disgust stayed with me until I was 17 or 18 years old. I had a relationship with someone when I was 16 but his penis was gross to me. Sex was just nasty.

The week after I discovered what sex was, I went to Florida to see cousins I had never met before. They thought I was sleeping and started watching lesbian porn. I was awake and watching it on the screen with them. I grew aroused. *What the hell is going on? Why am I so attracted to this?* Heterosexual sex disgusted me but then I got aroused by lesbian sex. It was all so weird. I did not know what to do with it and ended up having a wet dream that night. I did not understand what a wet dream was, so that, too, was awkward for me. Since I did not know how to deal with all that, I decided to bury it in the back of my head and never talk about it again.

I have no idea how I would describe my identity but who I have sex with is not part of it. Sex is more about my personality than my identity. The way I have sex is lot more different than most people. My roommate was explaining it to me. She said that I love sex as much as men do, but my motives for it are dramatically different. When I have sex, it is to get to know people. Most of the people I have slept with, I only slept with once and never again. Instead, I kept them as friends. Once I have had sex with them, I know them. Sex especially does not have an impact on my identity because I have not had sex with women yet. I have only had three relationships, one with a girl and two with guys.

About three years ago, when I was in college, I had a girlfriend but I was afraid of her. The relationship was me trying to find out who I was but I was so afraid of being gay that I was kind of cold to her. I was not reciprocal towards her touching or kissing me or even showing me affection. I cared about her and found her attractive, but I did not want people to know this about me.

Sex to me is mutual orgasm, and especially enjoyment of the act. Pleasure has to be in mind and both parties have to enjoy the act. We never had sex. I went down on my girlfriend but she did not go down on me. That could still be seen as sex but I was just trying it out. It was something I had never done before and it was not something I was doing for her pleasure. It was not enjoyable. That was not the focus. I did not know what I was doing. I was not comfortable in the relationship until towards the end. Then, I warmed up to the idea of telling people I had a girlfriend and found that everyone was okay with it.

I am liberal so I do not feel like I have to be in a relationship to have sex. If I were to get into a relationship with someone, I would have to see a future with them. I like relationships because they are an opportunity to learn about yourself. They are an opportunity to know who you are and what you can tolerate from others. I do not believe there should be roles in relationships, but I do play one whenever I am in one. I like being the more submissive and feminine of the two. I also like being the opposite of my partner. If someone offers one perspective, I will offer the other.

I will be more dominant if we are two feminine people because I believe one of us has to be the backbone. Backbone here does not mean control. There is always one person who displays themselves more than the other. You know how different people have different ways of expressing themselves? Some people are passive-aggressive. Some people do not like competition. I do not mind being competitive. If I am the person who has to raise issues or sit down and talk or be the one who is approachable, I can be that person. If my partner is stronger in those aspects than me, I will let them be that person.

I used to think about marriage when I was 16 or 17 years old, due to family pressure, but now I do not care. I am 22 and I have a good fifteen years before I need to worry about marriage. I do not have any animosity towards children. I love kids and think they are adorable. It would be awesome to have my own kids. If I did not have them, I would not care. It bothers me that this confuses people. One minute you want kids, the next minute you say they are disgusting. I am just like, yeah, I can want someone who looks like me and has similar traits to me. I can also want to pass on information to the next generation. At the same time, I understand it is hard work. I am in control of someone's life and the way that they perceive things for the rest of their lives, even after I die.

I want to treat children like I treat adults. My children may not have the capacity to tell me how they feel but I have to trust that they know what they experience. I have to value their perspective while letting them understand mine. I do not believe that children want to damage themselves. For example, eating vegetables. My parents and I never had a problem with that. I understood that vegetables are good for you. I knew that I was eating vegetables, not because I wanted to do it but because it kept me healthy. I learned to take pride in my body and my health. I do not see the point in hiding one's sexuality from one's children. It is not like I want to have sex with my partner in front of my kids. I think it is okay to let them know my sexual proclivities. I would need to let children understand that sex is a natural part of life. I do not see myself finding it difficult to talk to my kids about sex at the age of 4 or 5. It is just normal.

I am afraid of my job. I never realised how much power teachers have over the perceptions of kids until I became one. There is a transgender girl in my class. There is a lot of pressure. I have to make sure that my kids learn everything, that they become good people in the future. It is stressful but I like it. I just wish my school was smaller and that I spoke more Spanish. I want effortless communication with my students and fellow teachers. Right now, I do not talk to the teachers much except for those who speak English. Most of them are twenty years older than me and we do not have much to relate to. None of them know about my orientation or have any idea, but they are going to know when gay pride comes around. I doubt they will say anything about it.

I do not know many queer people in Spain but I have met enough black and Nigerian people here. I do not need to know gay people or be part of a gay community here. All my friends in America are gay. I do not know if I have straight friends. It was something that happened at random. Maybe because of my politics, I do not have time for people who I do not agree with. With my friends, I can talk to them about anything and they will understand. Here in Spain, I find myself having to explain things that should be normal. It is a different culture and many of them do not have the same background.

I told my mum about my sexuality but not my dad. When I came out to her, she advised me not to tell anybody else. My mum has always been the most supportive person in my life. She is the one who taught me to be independent and always question things – even though she did not like it when I questioned her.

I feel like my relationship with her has strengthened since she died. I now see a lot of what she had been trying to tell me when she was alive. It kind of sucks because I wish I could show her how much I have changed. I can only hope that, one day, we will reunite and she will be proud of me. I remember talking to my dad when I was younger and asking him what a gay person was. He was like, 'You are not allowed to be that.' I asked him the same question a few years ago. His perception had completely changed. He told me that they are just people. In the course of five years, things had changed.

My relationship with my family is good. It is a lot better than when I was younger. I was angry for a while. My parents pressured me into doing things I did not want to do. Especially with education, religion, all the usual Nigerian bullshit. With religion, I believe in a higher power but I do not complicate it by adding things to it. I do not have time for practising any doctrine, but my family is Christian.

After or during college, I realised that they are going to die one day and I will only have myself. I could not continue trying to convince them that I can make the right decisions for myself. I realised that I do not have to be angry with my past. I am allowed to disagree with my parents. Even without a reason; I can just choose to disagree. I am the only one who can conceptualise my feelings and I must do what I feel is correct.

As a child, I thought I would be a lot happier but it is okay. I will achieve my happiness in the future. The happiest moment of my life was coming to Spain and realising that I can be happy here. I thought that I was going to hate everything but I have felt so happy and free. I guess I just needed freedom to be honest. I needed to be free from the pressure to be perfect, to never fail and to be one type of person. Here, I can be whatever I want. It is not easy to move to a country where you do not speak their language and you do not know anyone. It has only been a couple of months and I have made enough friends to host a twenty-person Thanksgiving dinner. Still, there have been hard times. My power was cut off for four days and I had no idea what to do. Also, my heart has been broken by various guys who were ashamed to take me home to their families.

I thought I knew what I wanted for my future when I came here but I do not know. Now, I try to take things one month at a time and one year at a time. My goal for this year is to become fluent in Spanish and save a good amount of money. Next year, my goal will be looking for graduate schools and programmes I can apply to. I do not do relationships any more, although I am seeing someone at the moment. We cook for each other every weekend, either at my place or at his. I do not feel the need to call him my boyfriend or to not see other people because I appreciate what we have.

Sexual monogamy does not matter to me. It depends on the other person. I will talk to them and ask them what they want but I do not care. With me and the current dude, he does not care who I have sex with. But I have chosen to have one partner because it makes things easier for me. I find that a lot of men are comfortable with telling me what they want and that they prefer that I be more dominant in bed. A huge number of men have wanted me to eat their ass or do choking and slapping. Some people are into that. I am fine with being submissive because I am lazy.

Rather than focusing on relationships, I have body goals. I want to be able to run 12 kilometres in under an hour without stopping, and to lift my own bodyweight in a pull-up.

What brings me happiness is travelling. I love meeting new people and exploring different areas. When I went to Dublin, I was hanging with a random group of people I had never met before. Someone started playing the guitar, then more people joined in playing instruments. Even more people came into the circle, then more and more people joined. All of a sudden, we had people from Dublin and Brazil and Iraq and Jordan and Nigeria. We were all different people sitting down, drinking cider and playing music together. That is my most precious moment. It was everything I wanted: a multicultural group of people who do not really know each other but are somehow connected enough to care for each other like a family.

– CG, age 22, New York, USA / Madrid, Spain

This Is Not Our World

'This is a heterosexual world. And until they come to realise that we are not going anywhere, that we are as normal as they are, stop exhibiting yourselves.'

Content Note: Sexual Violence, Domestic Violence and Abuse

I grew up in Lagos in a family of three. I am the last. My brother is ten years my senior and my sister is twenty years my senior, so each of us was practically raised as an only child. I was naughty. I liked watching films; I still do. I was a tomboy. It was very obvious, so girls would come to me. I liked having my girlfriends visit me. They still do it. I like sleeping with girls. I still enjoy female company.

I had fun growing up. I wasn't close to anybody at home, not my mum or anybody else, so I was close to the people in school. I had toys. Any toy I wanted, they would buy and keep in the house for me. I had a little motorised car that I drove around the compound. I built with my Lego set. I went to school, came back and did my house chores. It was a gated house so everybody was inside. You just stood inside and saw people outside pass you by.

I didn't even play with sand, just expensive toys. Till tomorrow I will not play with sand, except on the beach. My friends still insult me for that. I just played with toys, rode my bicycle, read books and, later on, discovered Mills and Boon. In most of my childhood pictures, apart from those taken when I was in the mosque, I was wearing shorts, then trousers. During my primary school send-off, I was in a complete three-piece suit. I have been wearing jeans, trousers and proper shoes since I was little. It was what my mum used to buy for me. So I grew up with those kinds of things.

I never grew up with homophobia. I grew up like this, not wearing feminine clothes. I don't know how my mum coped. Maybe she was even the one who turned me into a tomboy. I didn't have feminine clothes. Even my shoes were canvas, gladiators, male shoes. My school shoes were Cortina. My sister and brother were already used to my dressing. The community and my neighbours knew that that was how I always dressed. If I wore something different they would be surprised.

I dress in what I am comfortable with. Nobody had issues with me growing up. We did not discuss it, just like a regular Nigerian house. Nobody asks, nobody wants to know. I am in my forties and nobody has said, 'Why are you not married? What is going on with you?' You know that fight, that pressure to settle down; I do not get it. And I am like, 'Is it because my parents are late that nobody is asking me?' Sometimes I feel funny, like, 'Why is nobody asking me?' The only people who ask me are my friends and colleagues. And I get pissed with them and go, 'What is your problem? Why are you asking me? Are you the one feeding me? How can you ask me those stupid questions when people who are supposed to ask me are not asking me?'

I was a very naughty child. I told someone one day that I do not want to have a child who is like me. I look back and see the way I treated my mum and I am like, 'God, what kind of child is this?' I started having girlfriends at about 15, a very young age, and they would visit me at home. The only way I would do anything at home or any chore was if I was about to have a visitor. If my mum asked me do this thing, I would say, 'Abeg, abeg I no dey do.' I would just go and find somewhere and sleep. She would scream, scream, scream and then I would realise, *Shit, that girl from my school is coming,* so I would get up and fix it so that she would not embarrass me in front of my friend. My mother would just be looking at me like, *Is this not the same person who refused to move an hour ago?* But if nobody was coming to see me, I would not lift my hand. We had house helps growing up. I do not cook till today because we had house helps to do that. The first time I lit a match was in secondary school.

My dad died when I was in Class 6 and even when he was alive, I always told him I was not going to get married. He didn't understand what I was saying and I didn't understand why I was saying it, but I always said it. I would never say, 'Oh I want to get married to a hunk,' and then say, maybe while watching TV, 'That is the kind of person I want to marry.' I realised early on that I was attracted to girls. When I started primary school, towards Primary 4, I was attracted to my best friend and her cousin who were in my class. I cannot remember most of my primary school but these incidents I remember vividly. I still picture what they look like and how our desks were right next to each other. Until secondary school, we were in the same school, the same class, everything.

I initially went to a girls' day school but I got distracted. I had three girlfriends in SS1. Two of them were best friends and I thought they knew that I was dating both of them. I thought that, because they were best friends, they would talk to each other and tell each other everything. I only found out when one of them asked me accusingly if I was dating the other, and I was like, *Oh shit.* I said, 'No I am not.' That thing spoiled their friendship anyway. There was a guy who was toasting me and I said no to him. He continued to disturb me and since he was the cousin of one of my best friends, he invited me to his house. So we went to the house and when he went to buy drinks for us, his younger sister went into the bedroom, came back with something she'd written on a paper and put it in my hand. She had written something sexual: she liked me. Before the guy came back, I had already gone into the room, spoken to her and she had even kissed me. She and I were steady for a couple of years but I never slept with him.

I am still in touch with everybody, from the first girl I dated, who is now married with kids. There was a time we were very, very close. I only stopped being close to her because she was trying to hook me up with her husband's friends. I told her, 'It was a phase for you but this is not a phase for me. This is me.' And then she wanted to start preaching. I was just like, 'Fuck it, I do not need this. I know what you are and now you want to come and start pretending with me. I do not do that. Even if you feel you are now born-again and you don't want to go that way, I am not asking you out, I am not trying to sleep with you again. Let's respect ourselves.'

I decided to cut it. She is on my BBM. We still talk once in a while. She has been begging me since. Her kids know me. They have been begging me to visit but I don't want to go. I talk to them on the phone but I won't go. I don't even want that conversation to come up. I do not want to get angry.

After her, I made up my mind not to visit secondary school friends who are married. Because they feel my life should be like their life. I sit down sometimes and think of some of them and wonder, *So if this girl didn't get married, would she have these things that she has right now? This is what you want, this is everything you have achieved …* I look at myself and I have all those things but I am not married. I didn't get them from any man, while everything they get is from a man.

I have never wanted to get married, never. Even marry a woman; sef that one too comes with its own problems. Funny enough, I believe in the union of marriage. I don't do one-night stands. I have never had a one-night stand. I have one-month stands, two months, three months, but never a one-night stand. If I get a casual, I usually keep her for a month or three. Because I would want to be friends with her, we would talk. I need to get to know you. I am not the kind of person who just meets you and wants to sleep with you. I have to have a connection. We will talk, because after you have done what you are doing, are you just going to say, 'Okay come and go home?' She will probably spend the night in my house, spend the weekend, but we have to talk. We have to be able to communicate. If not, I will just look at you. I will say, 'Let's watch TV.' I have never had a casual one-night stand, although nobody believes me. But there is this notion everybody has about me because of the way I talk. I talk a lot so they think I have been with every woman who has been around me. I just look at them and think, *You people don't understand.*

If I found the right woman, I would tell her, 'Let's be life partners.' I have found that people are very comfortable in relationships but once you put a title of marriage on it, it changes them. My ex-girlfriend H___, whom I dated for two years and five months, told me she didn't want to be the wife, didn't want to be the person who got told, 'Okay stay at home,' while her spouse had girlfriends outside. She wanted to be the 'whore'. And everything I did, we did together, but then all of a sudden she started saying, 'My husband, I am the wife ...'

I just looked at her and thought, *Okay the narrative is changing now.* And then she said, 'I will stay at home, we will get married and I will raise your children.' I thought, *Okay, this is not a problem.* And because she was doing 'wife', I would say, 'Me and the guys are going to go and hang out.' If she wanted to come I would say, 'Come to where? I said me and the guys; do you see any girl there? Do you see any chick there? We want to talk. You know if you are there we won't be able to talk.'

I wasn't trying to provoke her but I am a human being. I should be able to say, 'Babe, I want to go hang out with my friends. You are my girlfriend, but you have your own friends – go and hang out with them. If you tell me now that you want to hang out with your friends, I will not come along with you. You are going to be gossiping and discussing things that have nothing to do with me so I will tell you to go and I will hang out with my friends too.'

She started saying we were all girls and since we were all toms she could contribute. I was like, 'No, maybe one of us has one issue or another and we want to discuss it.'

She said, 'No, you people just sit down, you are drinking and when girls are passing ...'

And I said, 'Is there something wrong with that? We want to gist and talk and say oya, this is what is happening to us ...'

I did not understand why she would not let me hang out with my friends without her coming along. I was like, *You are turning yourself into the wife you are not supposed to be.* A girlfriend doesn't follow you everywhere. If I am at work and somebody suggests grabbing drinks after work, she will say, 'Let me meet you there.' Why do you want to meet me there? Why? I didn't invite you. But then she'd start to talk and I'd say, 'Come, let's go.'

And then my friends stopped inviting me out. I didn't know what was happening with my friends any more. I'd hear that they were hanging out. I would see pictures and when I said, 'You guys didn't call me,' they would say, 'You know you were very busy.' I didn't like it. They felt that anything they told me, I would discuss with her.

After a while I felt alone, and I told her, 'You and I can't exist alone; we have to have people. The day you and I have a big issue, who will I talk to, who do I call? Maybe we break up; do I start building up friendships all over again?' So we started having issues when I went out. I eventually said, 'Bullshit, fuck it.' I felt she was blackmailing me emotionally. I told her she was nagging me and we had to break up after a while. She broke up with me nearly every day and then I told her that there would come a time when she broke up with me and I would actually just tell her, 'Fine, it's okay.' And one day I just told her, 'Don't bother.'

If I don't like you enough, I will cheat. See, even when I like the person, I still cheat. I practised monogamy, but I started with the last person I dated in Abuja. That person also had issues with me. Every time I went to work or went on a shoot, I would get home and she would take my phone and start scrolling and checking for stuff. She even checked for new numbers on my phone. I asked, 'Is it that you went through my contacts so you know every new number? How do people have the stamina to do this? You actually picked my phone and studied all the numbers, so you can pick out every new name.' That is how bad it was. We were live-in lovers but I got tired so I said I couldn't live like that.

I also told her, 'I will cheat on you. Because this thing you are putting me through, I just can't. I need to let out steam.' It was really bad. I would get to the office, sit down in a corner and cry. I was like, 'Is this life? Can't I have friends? Am I not a human being? You go about and come back talking about a new friend or talking to them on the phone and I do not question you. But the minute I tell you, I went for an audition today and some people wanted me to see if they were going to get a callback so I took their number, you will collect my phone and start looking for people, saying I am going to toast them. Why don't I think you are going to toast new people?'

Anyway, I got tired. I cheated and we broke up. When I started dating H___, I told her the story of what happened in Abuja. I said I cheated because of what she was doing to me and that I didn't like it, and I kept warning her and begging her. And then H___ started this same thing. And I was committed to her until she started stressing me. I was okay with her for two years and five months. I only cheated on her after she moved out of the house. At least a month later.

We did have roles. She used to tell me, 'The kitchen is my office. I will take care of the kitchen and you bring the money and do other things.' She would say, 'You are the man, you are the butch, you take care of the house' and I was okay with it. I didn't have issues with it. I always have the masculine role in a relationship, always. It comes naturally to me. Why, I do not know. I did not learn it from anybody.

I didn't learn any of this from anybody. The first time I

kissed a girl, she just brought her lips to mine and pulled me and started kissing me. I kissed her back, which was my first experience with a woman. I didn't have a lesbian friend or a lesbian adult. They locked us inside the house. It was a gated house, always locked, and we stayed in when we got back from school. We did not go out. The only friends I had were in school and I only saw them during school. We watched TV. There were no gay scenes then, just heterosexual couples. I didn't have anything then that I would say influenced me. I did not know any gay person. I did not know any gay movies.

My first experience was that day in secondary school in SS1. Even though I was a year older than her, I was a novice. She had been coming to visit me. We would play, play, play, she would bring stuff for me, and then one day she brought pictures for me to look at. When I gave them back to her, she said, 'No, take one, I brought them for you.' I think she had been waiting for me to do something and when I didn't do anything, she just came on her own through the window, pulled my head out by my uniform and kissed me, so I kissed her back. It was a wooden window, it was open, and I was sitting down on my chair, so when she came from outside it was easy to drag me and kiss me. After that she left and waited for me to go and meet her, but I didn't. Later, she came back and said, 'How far?' I said, 'I am coming to your classroom.' So I went and sat down with her. And then she used to follow me home. I didn't know that in her mind we were already dating. We never talked about it. We just went on from there. And this was why I thought her best friend knew what was happening. Because the day I kissed her best friend, she was there, although she didn't see me kiss her best friend. She was feeling sick so she was sitting down beside me and her friend was on the other side of her. It was in the classroom at the end of the school day and she had an upset stomach, her period, I think. Her best friend reached over her head and we kissed. I thought she knew. And we just kissed innocently. That is how that relationship started.

I am sure that if I had had somebody older who had taught me, I would be worse than I am right now. I did not have any role model or anyone who taught me anything or molested me or gave me sexual orientation. I was touching them but none of them touched me. I was the one touching them. I was always fully clothed. I would touch, lick, suck, but they did nothing to me. It all came to me naturally; how, I do not know. I enjoyed it all the way.

I had boyfriends though, even from secondary school. I had three boyfriends. All my friends were dating and when boys came after me too, I just said yes. And we kissed, just normal kissing. When they wanted to get down there, I would say no. I was sexually active with the girls but not the boys. I dated the boys for a very long time. There was even one who came back after me recently and I said, 'It is because I did not sleep with you in secondary school that you want to come back again. The reason why you people are coming back is cos I did not have sex with you and now you all want to do that thing you did not do.' I only tried it once, after university, because there was pressure on me. At that time, I was like, *Maybe there is something wrong with me because I have not tried it, so let me try it.* At least I am a woman – I can be bisexual. At least I have dated men, kissed them. There was even a guy who I taught a few things to. I sucked his breast and that was his first time experiencing it. He was shocked. He screamed. He said he had never experienced such a thing before. I even wanked him till he came. But when it came to more, I said I wasn't ready.

My one experience having sex with a guy was after university, around 2001. My best friend at the time said it was the devil; she kept saying, 'Something you have never tried; how will you know if you would enjoy it?' There was too much pressure on me from all my friends. Too many people were beginning to talk. There was this army guy who was in lust with me. I went to his place and slept with him. While he was on top of me, I started screaming. I became stiff, my eyes were closed, and I wanted him to get off. I was thinking, *What are people enjoying? This thing is so painful.* When he came, he got off me. I don't know if he enjoyed himself but I just got up. I was disgusted. I didn't even talk to him. I got up and left. To this day, I have not gone to his house. I have not talked about it. He wanted to talk about it with me. He wanted to ask me if it was something that I had never done but I didn't even want him to talk to me. I was too disgusted. I went back to my friend and I told her, 'Never in your life pressure me again. If I am not, I am not. If I like something, I am adventurous, so I will go into it myself. For me not to have gone into it, means my mind, my soul, my body was not into it, so please respect yourself and stay in your lane. Don't ever try it again. Because if I tell you now that I experiment with girls, you will say I am demonic. So don't tell me to experiment with this bullshit thing, don't even bring it up again.'

She felt so bad. I had been hurt. I felt as if I had been raped, I told her. I was traumatised. I still think about it and wonder why I even attempted it. Was I trying to prove to the world and myself that I was not into this thing? And then I went and hurt myself. I am not doing it again. That is why

I tell people growing up, 'If you are not into it, you are not. Don't force yourself.'

I no longer stop people from touching me. Now I will touch and be touched. I don't know what it was. I enjoy touching but I don't always enjoy being touched. I could have sex with a girl for one month now without her touching me. My pleasure is in her coming. I enjoy seeing her come. Sometimes I even feel asexual. I just like to touch them, see them ... I do not have to come. Me making you come, that is the koko for me. I am not really a sexual person. You don't really have to touch me. Me touching you ... that is it for me.

If I can get a partner who can help me get a kid, I will get a kid. But it is too expensive and most times it doesn't work. Or maybe we will adopt, but this country is a mess. I tried to adopt twice and the process was ... in fact there is no process. You can't adopt as a single mum. But my friend just adopted in Kaduna and she spent about N600,000. It is very difficult to adopt a child around Lagos unless you want to be shady. I wanted to do it the legal way and they told me that, if you are not married, no hope for you. I went to the orphanage. I spoke to the chaplain. They asked if I was married and when I said no they said, 'So why are you even here? Why are we having this conversation?' I just hissed and walked away. I don't think I will try again, unless I get a fake marriage certificate. But they investigate those things so you have to get married. They will come to the house to make sure you are living together and the house is conducive. They will ask people who live around you questions ... I am not ready for that. If I had a partner who could carry a baby I would consider it. But then, what if you break up? I know someone who adopted her girlfriend's son. When they broke up, she took the child away.

I was born a Muslim. My family members are still Muslim and then I joined the church. One of my girlfriends took me to church and I liked it so I started attending. Then one of the pastors started toasting my girlfriend so I left. There was a time in my life when I was very much into the church scene but I was not spiritual. I later realised that every time I became committed in church I got tempted. All those girls ... When I was in Abuja, I was quite committed, and a girl who was in the choir came after me. Then when I was in Lagos after my youth service, another girl in the choir came after me. We were together for a very long time.

If I am supposed to go to church to have a renewed mind, then there is no need. Let me just stay in my house and pray since this is what happens every time I go to church. That was how I totally stopped going. There was a time I nearly followed my brother-in-law to do Eckankar. They are called Eckists. I was reading his books about all this spiritual travel and soul travel and I got scared. I nearly started doing things like sitting down and soul travelling to different places so I just stopped. I thought it was too much for me, too spiritual for me. It was getting like a cult.

I attended Christ Embassy and nobody talked about being gay. In that church, there are a lot of gay people. I knew a lot of them and they were in the choir. Not that it was a more accepting church, but they were not interested in your sexual orientation so long as you did not rub it in their faces. As long as you don't come acting feminine as a guy in the church, nobody cares. I always tell my male gay friends, 'Act macho, you are a guy, walk like a guy.' If you are within the community, then you can do what you want, but when you are outside, try to be more macho before they lynch you. Your boss could be homophobic and could sack you for that reason alone. You won't have a livelihood any more. Your family will throw you out, your friends will deny you. And even the ones who are gay, if you do not have a source of income, how long will they want to remain friends with such? I said, 'Please conform. I will not put you up in my house; I wouldn't want my landlady to throw me out.'

Our community is not a trusting community. I am not trusting of it. I can't. Initially I trusted before I started making too many friends. When I was younger, I didn't have too many friends in the community. I just had the ones in my school who I was sleeping with. There is a lot of backbiting, treachery and all in the community. Now, I have many friends in the community and I don't trust any of them. I fully participate in community events and nearly everybody knows me. By name or by reputation. A lot of places I go to, they know me by my nickname. My name has gone beyond where I have got to. I know a lot of younger people also. Some of them even call me daddy. A lot of them say I am a figure to look up to. A lot of them come to me for advice, even some gay guys. It is a small community, the few friends that I have, but it just keeps growing and my name is everywhere; I don't know how come.

In my office, everybody knows I am gay. And they are accepting. Nobody has come to disturb me. They know practically all my girlfriends, because every new girl I date visits me at work. We go to weddings together. If there is a wedding in the office, my girlfriend goes with me. Any office party, I go with my date. If my office is having an event and I have a plus-one invite, I don't say, 'Okay, I am going to go with a guy.' Either I go alone or I go with my girlfriend and everybody knows she's my girlfriend. I have never experienced any homophobia at work. There is homophobia, but they exhibit it to others, not to me. Why, I don't know. They exhibit it to guys. If they suspect that a guy is gay, they avoid him and start acting like he is going to rape them, but they are okay with the girls. Sometimes, when the guys in my office want to go drinking, they call me. They'll say 'we the guys'. Like when they were planning a bachelor's eve, I was included. When some of the girls wanted to come, I was like, 'No, it is just for us boys.' So when they contributed money, they included me as one of the boys. Everybody has become accepting but they do not want you to come and pretend with them. If they don't know you, and they know you are gay, they might be homophobic towards you. But they know me. We have been together for years. They accept me. I had to remove some people from my Facebook because they were too open. I am openly gay, but I am not in their faces. I don't throw myself. I don't go out with my girlfriend and start kissing her in public. That would be going too far. They have accepted me but it doesn't mean I should throw it in their faces.

I don't have any gaydar. I have to ask people all the time. I meet girls at community parties, community events. I can't just see you on the road and walk up to you. If I do not see you at a community gathering, I will not talk to you. I am a very shy person. I wouldn't want to embarrass myself. Even back then, they always approached me. From secondary school, to university, to church; they came after me. I would rather stay on my own and read my book. If you become too friendly with me, I will figure out that you want something with me and attempt. If I attempt and she doesn't want, I pull away. I do not want to be embarrassed. I do not want anyone to start saying shit about me. I love my name so I won't do that. Even in the community, if you tell me you have a girlfriend, I pull out. I won't continue.

I think one of the problems we have in the community is that tomboys want to be boys. They want to be men. They want to act and behave like men. They feel that they are God's gift to women. They feel they are men and all the bad things that men do, a lot of women do too: have two girlfriends, beat up their girlfriend, cheat, go drinking, get drunk, stay at home and be the king while the girl cooks, serves the drinks, washes their clothes and stuff. We do a lot; we are misogynists. I let my girl do most of the stuff at home but I help out. If she wants me to go to the market, I will take her to the market. If she wants me to wash the plates, I do. But a lot of tomboys will rather sit down and be like men. The first time I washed my girlfriend's clothes, she was too surprised. Her ex used to beat her and treat her badly. She would beat her, take her to the hospital for treatment, bring her back home where they would settle, and then start the beating again.

We have a lot of violence in the community. My girlfriend's friend showed me a scar on her body. She said her girlfriend broke a bottle on her or something. I wondered, *Why do you stay in such a relationship? Why? Why would you stay in a violent relationship? Why do people act in the way they do?* I dated two people who I was warned against. I was told they'd been violent in the past. I think you have to give violence to get violence back. If I don't act violent towards this person, why would she bring violence to my doorstep? I have never experienced violence but I hear about it all the time. It is rampant everywhere, among old and young.

We abuse substances as a community. There are some who feel that they can fly. Those are the ones who sag. I counselled some people one time. I was like, 'Why would you want to sag your pants? You are sagging as if you are a boy. You are not a boy. You are a girl with nyash. Why are you sagging? What normal girl will date you, if you are sagging? If my younger sister were gay and she brought you to my house, I would throw you out. What company would you want to work for with your sagging trousers? If you come to me now, I won't employ you.'

They will pull up their pants in front of me and then when they leave they will sag again. But I just ask myself, *How many people do I want to talk to?*

I was telling my friends that people outside think our community is loose. The only thing we do is sex, alcohol and substance abuse. And this is so wrong. Yes, I hang out with my own friends and we have parties all the time at friends' houses, but the only thing we do is smoke cigarettes and take alcohol. And because everybody is driving home, we are all very careful. We do not really hang out with the younger ones. Because they come there and they want to start speaking slang: done it, darn it and all that. You'll see someone who has not passed the shores of Nigeria coming to do 'done it, did it, innit' to us. They don't even smoke cigarettes. They smoke weed. They go to the shrine there and smoke. I don't want to hang out with the younger people because they are wilder. Back then, the community was not so wild. I never smoked Indian hemp. Among all my friends, only about two smoke Indian hemp, and they have started reducing it.

Everybody thinks lesbians coming up right now are just into the money. People think they are dating other girls because it seems to be the in thing. Back then, we didn't know if it was the in thing; it was our life. You didn't see gay people, you just saw a few people and you would be so happy to see a fellow gay – someone like you. Now they are everywhere. Here in Lagos, they are everywhere. Everywhere you turn. Before, you wouldn't see a gay person. You would have to call for your people to be at a gathering, but now you go to Shoprite and you see everybody. Tomboys everywhere. You don't know them but you see them, you look at each other and turn your face away. You don't want to get mixed up in that. You see tomboys who are sagging, you see them wearing jallabia, sometimes looking dirty. You know how guys wear slippers halfway and drag their legs? Some tomboys are just like that. Those are the people who give us bad names. Now it is all piercings and tattoos. I saw some tomboys who I have known for a while and they had piercings and tattoos. Piercing their eyes in Nigeria. Everybody wants to be like the Americans. And I look wild, I behave wild, but I don't have tattoos. My office people are very surprised that I don't have any tattoos. Every day, I thank my God that I grew up in my own era. I am not comfortable now. I don't like it. I do not like this exhibitionist style thing. How many people will give you jobs when you have tattoos all over?

I am lucky because I am in the entertainment industry and everybody dresses like I do. Everybody wears jeans and trousers. I would have had issues if I was working in a bank where I would have to wear skirts. If I asked my bosses if I could wear pants, they would say no. If you go for marketing, they want you to show off your legs. Most bosses employ the type of female staff members who would make an impression if they introduced them to men coming to do business in the company. I do it too. I have an assistant and I want to borrow something from another department, I won't send the boy.

I will send the girl. I will say, go and shake your booby in his face. So, if you are not on your own or if you don't have a job that accommodates your dressing, it is very difficult. I know tomboys who dress as girls. They dress very feminine to be able to work and when they are home they switch. I even know one who keeps a change of clothes for immediately after she closes work. If you want to look for a job and you don't dress well ... Some tomboys just wear feminine clothes. They don't look for something that suits them. Just like they wear baggy pants, they will wear baggy skirts and go for an interview.

I would tell young lesbians to stop exhibiting themselves. It is too much. Stop showing off. Stop bragging. This is not our world. We come from a different world until they accept us into their world. This is a heterosexual world. And until they come to realise that we are not going anywhere, that we are as normal as they are, stop exhibiting yourselves. Because if somebody reports you to the police, the police will either rape you or tell you to bring money. Nobody is gonna come there to help you, so you help yourself. So stop exhibiting yourself. You need to pipe low. This country is too volatile. Gay people fighting back – we won't win. This is Africa. This is not America. You have no rights. Even as a straight person you have no rights in this country.

You have no rights as a human being in this country. When you report issues to the police, you will be the one who has to pay them. Why should we fight? There is a subtle way we have been doing it. Let that subtle way continue. Reasoning with the government is a battle you can't win. I don't know if it will get better in this country, at this age and time. Other countries are moving forward. In the countries that our leaders travel to, even China, you see openly gay people. My friend's husband was so homophobic when he relocated to America. He saw a lot of gay people. Recently, he said even his boss is gay, so right now he is very okay.

So you can't tell me that our Nigerian leaders have not met any gay people, any politicians or heads of state who are gay, and communicated with them. They know the gay people in this country. Maybe 70 per cent of this country is gay or bisexual but they will not come out. I have a friend who is married. She goes to events and I know about three women she has dated over the years. But on her Facebook page, she is so homophobic! She is covering up and that is what everybody is doing. I know a guy who works with an airline. He is gay and married to a woman. When he talks about gay people, it is as if he could stab them, but he is one of us. So if we are homophobic, what war are we fighting? You will see them killing a gay guy and another gay guy will go and stab him too just because he doesn't want people to know what he is. Our own people are killing us so what do you want to do? There are even men raping trans people and other men in the name of corrective rape. Isn't the rapist gay too? Me, I insist that any man who insists on having anal sex with his wife is gay. It is because you did not see any guy; that is why you are ramming into your wife's ass. I once heard the story of a guy who was arrested for being gay. When he was taken to the police station, an officer raped him. Until the community is ready to stop all this, we are not ready to be taken seriously. There is too much gay-on-gay violence.

In the next twenty years, I want to have my own company, my own home, my own family and have a kid. I will have a partner because I definitely can't raise a child alone. Probably not in Nigeria. Somebody my age in another country would have a Masters, PhD and subsidised school fees. In other countries, somebody my age would be planning retirement, but in Nigeria, life is just starting. I want to be happy, and I want to have my peace.

– KZ, age 40, Lagos

Who I Have Sex With Is Not Part Of My Identity

'I am a queer woman and this is not because I have sex with other women. All my partners have been heterosexual men so far. Being queer does not depend on whether I have had sex with a woman or not.'

Content Note: Depression

I am a student majoring in public health. When I graduate, I want to start preparing to move out of my parents' home. I plan to go to grad school so I will have to find funds for that. I aim to become a physician's assistant so I can be financially stable. I also want to run non-profit organisations on the side to help with people's health and improve their quality of life. I have a passion for volunteering and I want to volunteer for humanity, to help people rebuild their lives. I like to read. I like to go shopping. I like to hang out with my loved ones.

We are a large Igbo family based in the United States. I am the oldest to three boys. I have so many uncles and aunts from both my mum's and dad's sides. I have fifteen cousins on my mum's side alone. We are a very religious family, the sort that goes to church every Sunday.

My earliest memories consist of reading and kissing a boy

and girl. I was 4 years old. I do not know where I got the idea of kissing them from. I just know that it happened. My childhood was good from my point of view. I grew up with two parents who lived in a decent house. We had a backyard. We had a roof over our heads. We got to play. My mum would take us to places like Washington DC to sightsee. I was kind of sassy growing up – that was the not-so-good part of me. Whenever I misbehaved or was not obedient, I would be tagged as sassy. But at the same time, I was pretty obedient and obeyed the rules. I did what I was told because I did not want to make anybody angry.

I started noticing girls probably around fourth grade, when I was around 9 or 10 years old. I was small-chested and I noticed other girls who had bigger boobs than mine. That was interesting to me. I did not know why I felt that way but it drew my attention. I was not really as into girls until I grew older but girls were the first that I noticed.

I did not know anyone who was attracted to the same sex until sixth grade, when this new girl called Lily came to our class. She was Salvadorian and she was bisexual. That was the first time in my life I knew somebody, of any age, who was not straight. Before that, it never really entered my mind. I thought, *Oh, this is very strange*, and talked to her about sexuality. This did not last long, however, because I had to leave that school after sixth grade when my mum could not afford to keep us in private school any more.

In high school, when I was in either eleventh or twelfth grade, and maybe 17 years old, I fell for my best friend. She was my first love. I felt really different around her. I knew it was not just friendship. She was going out with a different friend of ours. We came out to each other at the same time.

Around the time I started questioning my sexuality, she wanted to come out to me because she saw me as a good friend. In that high school, I did not know many people who were not straight, apart from my best friend. I did not take my attraction to girls further in high school. It was not something I thought about then. Girls were really pretty and just there. As for guys, I would feel different around them. It was in college that I started wanting to find out more about the LGBT community.

My first kiss was not anything meaningful. It was something that happened recently, a few months ago. Although I am not in a relationship at the moment, I have been contemplating it. For a long time, I did not see the point of a relationship. I have strict Christian parents and my mum always told me not to focus on boys too much and instead to concentrate on my grades. At the same time, I was like, I am not trying to be in a relationship anyway. Besides, my parents are divorced and I do not want to enter a relationship that will end. It was not until the beginning of my first semester that I felt I needed to find a relationship.

A relationship to me means, first of all, that they have to be attracted to me. We have to like each other. They need to be supportive. We have to have similar points of view on certain topics. They cannot be homophobic or Islamophobic. They can have their own opinions, sure, but I do not want to be in a relationship with somebody who has those sorts of views. Before entering a relationship, we have to get to like each other. I have to get to know them for like half a year or two years to get an idea of who they are. I am only 20 years old and marriage just does not sound right for me at the moment. If I have kids, I will raise them to counter homophobia, Islamophobia and other prejudices.

When I first started out, sex was an exciting thing. As time went by, I realised that it is not that interesting. I am not that focused on it right now. Sex is not as important as it used to be, although it does have some importance. I find that I am not necessarily adventurous, but I am open to new ideas. If I were in a relationship, I would want the sex to be good, but it is not essential. I am discovering that I prefer to be submissive in bed. Maybe it is because I am lazy. I would rather not use so much energy, so I let them do the work.

I do not believe that who I have sex with is part of my sexual identity. I am a queer woman and this is not because I have sex with other women. All my partners have been heterosexual men so far. Being queer does not depend on whether I have had sex with a woman or not. I am a constant. When it comes to gender, however, I am not sure of my identity; I have not thought about that in a long time.

At school, I watch who I speak to about my sexual orientation. I do not always say that I am a queer woman; it depends on the person asking. I only come out to people who I think are safe. A good chunk of family knows about my sexuality. I came out as bisexual to my dad. He was okay with it and believes I should live my life. My brothers got to know later. Most of my cousins know about my sexuality because if they ask, depending on who they are, I will respond. The rest of my family reacted very harshly to my being queer, so I do not talk about it.

I am into something called queer camp, a programme sponsored by my school. Queer camp mostly comprises freshmen, queer kids from different demographics who get together. It is a way of bringing diverse people together and connecting with other kids who are not straight. When I wanted to go to queer camp, I had to ask my mum first. I initially told her, 'Oh mum, if I get a certain grade, can I go on this trip for this organisation?' She did not really say yes or no. She was like, 'We will talk about it later.' Then she found out what queer camp really meant and she did not want me to go. Her finding out was not something I was afraid of, but she warned that if I went there, there would be consequences. I still went to queer camp and I enjoyed it a lot. It was a really great experience.

I consider myself to be spiritual. I am not tied to Christianity because of its beliefs. There are a lot of things about the Bible that I am not sure about. I believe in God but I do not actively pray. Religion is awkward. I want to be religious but I do not know how to go about that as a queer person. I feel like the Bible is against me and I cannot reconcile faith with sexual identity. I do not want to have to make one more significant than the other. I want to do both but I do not know how to go about that.

I am mentally ill. I have depression. I have been traumatised before. Maintaining my health is of utmost significance to me. I need to ensure that I remain stable so that I can be productive, graduate from school and do the things I need to do. The fact that I am comfortable with who I am is important to me so I can reach out to other queer people.

– *UE, age 20, Maryland, USA*

Some Things You Do For Your Heart

'As the father of the family, I'm the one to dictate what happens in the relationship.'

Content Note: Controlling Behaviour

I am a full-time, professional footballer. I play football because it's my profession but also because I love it so much. Nobody taught me how to play. I just developed it. If I have children, there is no way they will not play football. I love it with a passion. I can't explain why, I just do – and I thank God for that.

I support Chelsea FC but they are not in their best form this season. I'm surprised in one way and not in another. You cannot decide what human beings do. They play great football but things turn around. You just have to wait it out. But, as a big club in Europe, they have to step up. It's not possible that a big team like Chelsea will be playing Europa League. They need to be playing in the Champion's League. They need to catch their form and qualify. If they don't, how will the sponsors continue with the team? But, no matter what happens, they're your team. You need to keep connected with them via social media to support them.

I grew up in ___ State. It's not big and we were not even in the state capital but in one of the little towns around it.

That place is very local. I wanted to plan big and make moves so I wouldn't remain in the same spot. Even now, any time I am at home, I soon think of travelling elsewhere. I dream of becoming big in Nigeria. Even if you're a local politician, nobody knows you. It's when you roll with politicians outside your state that people know you. It's the same with football. You have to be moving outside your state. I want to become somebody who people know. Without becoming big, nobody knows you are something. I know if I achieve success with football, my future will be brighter.

Even though one of my parents is from ___, they have been in Nigeria a long time and I am Nigerian. I am the last born of my family. Well, I am the only child, but I have cousins who my parents took as their own children, so they're my older brothers and sisters. I was closer to my mum growing up, but both our parents used to talk to us and give us advice early in the mornings. Even when I was away playing football as a child, I would keep coming back to visit them. My dad died around the time I got admission to my first football team. Since then, I lived my life with the help of God and the people around me. That's what made me who I am today.

My mum is the most important person in my life. She is a trader selling provisions. She loves children. She taught us all to be God-fearing. She said that once you have good character and behaviour, you can cope with anything you meet outside. She told us to focus on where we were going and how we live our lives – if we did that, nobody could change us except ourselves. She suffered a lot because of us. She struggled for us after my dad died. She was moving helter-skelter to cater for our needs. Anything I needed, I could tell her. She would sell her own clothes to look after us. My mum owns a big part of my heart.

As a child, I was gentle and cool. My childhood friends liked movies and reading. Most of their dads and mums would not give them enough chance to play around. Any time I went to visit them, I met them watching movies, reading novels or watching history that taught them something. I used to stay with them and learn. When young, I stayed away from trouble but I played very well. The main thing I can remember from that time is those days where the little guys and me played, ran around in the compound, up and down, and played football. I was the only girl among them. It's from there that I developed my football skills. Playing with those boys in the compound led me to a career in football.

In primary school, I had male and female friends but I liked the boys the most because we played football together. In secondary school, everybody liked me a lot, because I'm a female and I play good football. I was the only one out of a hundred people who was female and knew how to play very well. They included me among the prefects.

I developed a liking for women in secondary school. I don't want to talk about what my sexual orientation is. I've never had a relationship with a man. I only have relationships with women. There were others like me in that school but it was not something people will admit is going on.

There was this girl, one of my seniors. When I was in SS2, I was the assistant senior girl, so our senior girl was my friend and I liked her. She liked me a lot. Any time she couldn't get in touch with me, she would look for me. I showed her love and told her how I felt about her. She accepted, but there was no chance for us to share love. I was staying with my parents. She was staying with her parents. Any time I went to visit, her parents would be there. Any time she came to my place, my parents would be there. So there was no time. We showed each other love, bought things for each other, hugged each other and that was the end. But, one day when I was in SS3, there was nobody at home and she came over. That's when we shared love for the first time. I was so happy to do that.

It was not the first time I had kissed a girl though. Earlier in SS3, we had played a football competition. Back then, I had never been to Lagos because there was nobody to visit. I kept thinking, *One day I'll travel to Lagos.* I was tired of the area, the little compound. When they told me we were going to a competition in Lagos and I had the opportunity to travel there, I was so happy.

I couldn't sleep till daybreak. When we got to Lagos, I was so excited, so happy. I didn't know how to express my feelings to anybody. Now, Lagos has become somewhere I go like I go to the toilet, but that first time, it was a fine place. Seeing all those three-storey buildings, all those cars you've not seen before, all the white men you see there, so many things like that. Sha, I was just so happy to be there. It was so different from ___. It's a big city. It's a civilised town.

They had said they would give fifteen buses to any school that got to the final. We got to the final and we won. They gave us jerseys, caps – so many things like that. When we finished that match, they told us that there was a woman who had a female team in ___ State. She wanted to choose fifteen players. It meant you would be playing for her and collecting a salary. Fortunately, I was included. They called us and told us to come to the camp. I was told that the professional league was the best league in Nigeria. I was so happy to be chosen.

You are so excited at first but it's not as you expect it to be. If you are down, you are down. If you are up, you are up. You have to do everything yourself. You have to hustle to do it. Camp life in Nigeria is hard. They will not provide anything for you. They tell you that you need to provide for yourself from the salary they give you but they will go three or four months without paying you. How can I go home and ask people for money? They wonder what it is that I'm playing football for. Once you get injured, they abandon you. When you were playing for them, they didn't give you any money so how are you to pay for medical bills when you are sick? Life is rough as a result. You need to hustle, hustle, hustle.

The first time I kissed a girl was at this football camp. She was a footballer too. I liked everything about her. She was 15 or 16 and I was 13 or 14. When you like someone in that way, it's inevitable that you will at least try. When I have something on my mind, I have to free my mind by acting on it. And, when we met at the camp, we were free to do anything we wanted to do. Everybody there had matured. There were some girls in town who already knew about these things. Through seeing them and having motivation for happiness, I moved closer to her and told her I liked her. I really showed her I loved and cared for her. She accepted my proposal.

At the time I met her, I had done nothing like this before. For me, it is difficult to practise what you have never done before. I thought about how she felt. When I finally tried, it came easy for me. Fortunately, when I made the attempt to kiss her, I noticed she already had it in mind. I only did it a little because it was not what I had done before. We started dating at the same time I started properly playing football. That was when I went deeply into the game. I had time to share my love, to do anything with her. I was free then and that was how I continued to live my life: without any fear.

Unfortunately, we were together only for two or three months before she travelled to meet her parents. I was lonely. I decided to stop dating. I felt so bad because the person I loved was not with me any more. People around me in the camp told me to stop feeling that way because there were a lot of girls outside. I had a sport mum, an older footballer who looked after me and advised me. When I travelled to ___ to play another team, she would tell me that I'm a handsome somebody, that I should make moves to date, that if a girl doesn't accept, I should mention that she's my sports mum. She was a popular footballer back then, so there was no way any young footballer would not know her. When she encouraged me in this way, I changed my mind and decided to keep dating.

Time passed. I was the youngest player of them all. When I clocked 14 years, they told me not to sign to a professional team because I was too young. I was just training with them. When I turned 15, I was so happy. They included me in the team and I played for them. Everybody liked me a lot. They would tell me so many things: that they loved the way I played and I should keep it up.

At that time, I met a girl. Another footballer. I loved her attitude, character and the way she interacted with people. My heart decided that I should choose this girl as my love. I didn't want to long for her. I made inquiries. I went straight to the point and told her I loved her and wanted to date her. I asked her out and she accepted.

We dated for two to three years before we separated. The relationship was very good. We were in the same team. We cared for each other and looked out for one another. We did so many things together. The feelings were so strong. The love was moving every day. Even now, I would say she is the best person I've ever been with. But we broke up. It wasn't that we fought or anything happened. As a footballer, you have to go to another team so that you'll make progress. When you are not staying with them, girls decide you are sleeping with another person. After some months, I let her know that I knew this was the way she felt. If she were mine she would stay, but if she were not mine she would go. I tried to show her how much I loved her and tried keeping in constant contact but she couldn't cope with a long-distance relationship. That ended our relationship.

I had dated someone I loved with all my heart. She fucked me up. I loved her with everything and she departed. Afterwards, I dated a lot of girls. I would meet someone at a party and just flirt.

When you are playing, they tell you to stay away from sex. As a footballer, once you have sex with a man, you lose skills and fitness. I can see it in some women. When they have sex with men constantly, you can see the results of it in their bodies. They will not be fit. They won't do things the way they did before. They won't be as good. If you put ten European players and ten Nigerian players together, their structures will be different, because European players are having sex with men and we are not.

For my friends and me, being unfit is not good. We prefer to do it with women as a result. If you have sex with a woman, nothing happens to your form. Knowing this made me like women more than men. Since then, I developed the moral of having sex with women. Having sex with women will not affect you the same way. I can't explain why. It does not take too much strength and, even if it does, we know how to handle each other in ways that you don't know how to handle men. Instead of looking for men outside, it's better to make a move with someone you are playing with so that you can release the feeling from your body.

Sex boosts my love in relationships. Sex makes me stronger. The more I have sex with my girl, the more I love her. That's me. I don't know about any other person. Sex is unexpected sometimes. It's not something you make plans for. It may not work out. The feeling there is very strong. Once you are in the mood and that person is with you, if someone decides to distract you, you won't even listen to that distraction. That's why I say that feeling is very important.

My feelings are so strong. The most important things in relationships are belief and trust. Once you believe in whom you are dating and you trust them, nothing can happen. If I believe you, nothing will happen. Nothing will bother my mind once you are telling me the truth all the time. If that is missing, it will shake. For example, the lady I am with now is working in ___ State. If I don't believe in her, I'll think she's with somebody or she'll think I'm with somebody. Once you have developed trust and belief right from day one, there's no way that can happen. They can tell you, 'Okay, your boo is doing bad,' and I will say, 'No, it can't be possible.' I normally have strong belief in my relationships.

I count myself as the man in the relationship. I'm the pole, the head of the relationship, definitely. As the father of the family, I'm the one to dictate what happens in the relationship. No matter how busy you are, you have to tell me in advance that you are going out. In any relationship, there has to be a man and a woman – even if it's between two women. In Nigeria, they believe that once you call yourself a man, you have to handle everything in the relationship. Even if your woman has responsibilities, she will expect you to say something before she does it.

I'm the one who carries the large part of the relationship.

She is included in some things but out of 100 per cent, I carry 99 per cent with only 1 per cent left for my babe. We share our problems and solve them together but I carry most of the relationship. It's not possible for me to watch my woman find something hard for herself. I have to do it for her. I have to work harder to take good care of her.

In this Nigeria, if you are working somewhere, they may owe you four, five, six months salary without paying. When she's not working, I can't expect her to steal. Once I'm working, I have to take good care of her. All her responsibilities, everything she needs, I have to take good care of, pending the time that things will be better for her. If she's working and I'm not working, she may help – and I will bear it. But I will have it in the back of my mind that any time I can pay her back, I will do it times ten. I have to show her that she's the one who brought me up.

It's this way because in Nigeria, if you don't work and take good care of your baby, they'll look for another person outside. I've not experienced this myself but I've heard from my friends that their girlfriends went outside because they were not providing. I take good care of my girlfriends to make sure it doesn't happen. If I don't do it, another person will, so I have to take my own responsibility. Let me take good care of this person for her not to feel bad. Her own happiness is mine.

I've been with my girl about eight months now. It's fine. It's beautiful. It's lovely. I love her so much. In Nigeria, people believe a female should get married when it gets to a particular time. There is no way you can be with parents over the age of 25 and they will not tell you about marriage because women have a limited time. Nigerian people have it in mind that, since you are female, you will marry a Nigerian man. Every time we meet, my mother tells me, 'You have to bring your husband because you have to settle down as a woman.' You can't tell people you would want to marry a lady, except those who are in this game.

For now, I'm not interested in marrying a man. I don't know what tomorrow will say. I want to get married and have children – but with a woman. I love children so much. Of course, I would like to have children of my own. I would raise them to be open-minded and tolerant. There is no way I can have children in this country though. If the chance were there to marry a woman, I would love to, but I'll leave this country and go abroad. If you do it here, they will threaten you. Outside, things will be free. It's possible. With God, all things are possible.

From the time I started, I have been focused on my football. Back then, other teams told me they wanted to sign me, so I worked harder to make sure they were interested. In Europe, if they see your video clips and the manager likes you, they sign you. Here, you have to go to their trials, and if they like the way you play, they sign you. They sign you monthly rather than annually. If you collect two months and you are not pleased with the team, you can leave. But now, they've changed their rules and regulations. Once you sign with a team, you have to stay with them until you've finished your contract. The longest contract you sign is for a season. If they sign you this season and you don't want to go, you can stay. Or, you can go to another club. I played two seasons for my first team before I went to another team. I played two seasons there before I moved again. There, I played four seasons before I got admission. I played for so many teams but I wanted to further my education. I went to ___ and read physical and health education there. I was playing football and schooling the whole time until I graduated.

Without football, there is no way I could have completed my education. Most footballers are like me, from poor families and struggling to make it. They hope it will be better for them one day. Some footballers play but don't have an interest in the game itself. They just like it as their career. It's a job for them. They take wherever they are playing as their base.

After graduating, I started playing football again. At the end of the day, women have little time. You have to make hay while the sun shines. In Nigeria, you cannot depend on football alone. What you get is not enough to take care of yourself, your girlfriend and your family. I looked for a job and started working with ___. My salary from playing football and working gave me enough to support myself but it's not easy to work and play football. The team doesn't allow you to work. It caused so many disturbances. I would be late for training practices or have to miss them altogether as I needed to be at work. I was dropped from the first team. I had to choose. I stopped working and went back to footballing to continue struggling. I am now concentrating all my energies on football. You have to manage with what little money you collect.

We have a good, strong relationship in my team. We play jokes. We buy things for each other. If you are down or sick, they will care for you. I love my team so much. They are mature players. They encourage the young ones coming up. If they had encouraged us in bad ways back then, you would see it in the way we are behaving now. I thank God that everybody around me advised me in a good way when I was young.

Everyone around me knows about this gay. Out of 100,

99 per cent of footballers know about this gay. Of the people I know, 75 per cent know that I date girls. Some in my family know about it too – my parents, my neighbours and the people in the place I'm staying. The first time they caught me, they called me, preached to me and advised me, but I told them I would continue to do it. When they disturbed me, I would normally answer that they could ask me to stop doing it when I stop playing football. In sport, there is no room to give any man the chance to do rubbish with you. They accepted this explanation once I gave them the reasons and allowed me to do it. Now, they are fine. They are cool. I have a nice relationship with my family and friends.

I'm a strong Christian. I believe in praying. With prayer, all the yokes are broken. I go to church all the time. My mother taught us to be God-fearing. Whenever you go to church, they tell you so many things about homosexuality. When you read your Bible, you see it is not allowed. But some things you have to do for your heart. It's hard to drop something you have inherited. You don't have the option to go back, since it's the thing that makes you happy. You know you'll pray for forgiveness later. People say this thing is bad. Once you are doing something that people say is bad, you pray that it is good for you. I continue to pray for forgiveness. With God, I believe all things are possible.

– JS, age 26, Kwara

I Don't Believe In Love

'I am not scared of people. It is more like I am scared of myself.'

Content Note: Child Sexual Abuse

I have never been heartbroken. In secondary school, I used to be ridiculously emotional and everything used to make me cry. Before I left, all my friends were like, 'You need to stop being as soft as you are, you need to be harder than this, blah blah blah,' and I guess I took that to heart cos I never let anything bother me after that. Even when I like someone and the person does something, I think, *Yeah, whatever.* I feel being heartbroken is something really serious where you cry and you are sad but I really didn't give a shit about anything. I was just like, *Whatever.* This started at about 17 and I can't remember being heartbroken before then.

I do not know if I believe in love. It is too magical to be real. I believe in really liking someone and really caring for them but love just sounds like this word meant for parents and their children. I do not believe in love at first sight but I believe love starts at first sight. I have never been in love; maybe that is why. Or maybe I have been in love and I have never admitted it to myself. I will probably just be like, I really like this person and there is not a lot there.

But if your friends can break your heart, then yes I have been heartbroken. At about 15, I was in an all-girls school and my best friend, K___, broke my heart. We were really close. I don't even remember what we did when we were together. We weren't even in the same house so it is not like we were always seeing one another, but we were in the same class. And then even in class she had to change seats so she wouldn't get into trouble, because we were always talking. It didn't make sense how close we were. We saw each other almost first thing in the morning and last thing at night. We would hang out in class, break together, lunch together, prep together, and go to the hostel together.

I fell ill a lot of times in secondary school. One of the times I was ill, I went home for like two weeks. When I came back, I found out she was always hanging out with this other person. I tried to talk to her and she was like, 'No, we are just friends.' I don't know why I found it more serious than it was but I was awkward about it. I had a group of friends who were all like, 'She is messing you up. Just leave her and let her be.' And I was like, 'No, she is just talking to this person and this person is helping her with her spiritual life,' and they were like, 'No, that is not what is happening.' But it really messed me up and I don't know why. It was ridiculous. I cried a lot. A whole lot. After that, I was like, *No, it is not happening again.*

Looking back at it now, there is a good chance my feelings were more than friendship because it sounds like we were more than best friends. I mean, a normal best friend will not mess you up like that. It was bad. Really bad. I had other friends so it was not like she was my only friend. But she was special. Then she just wasn't there any more. It happened when I was not around so I started blaming myself, that maybe if I hadn't fallen ill it wouldn't have happened. I couldn't have controlled that but still, it was really sad. I have not been in anything remotely serious since then.

I do not like commitment. I have nothing against it. I appreciate people who are in serious commitments or relationships. I just do not think I am the person for it. I don't see myself being with one person forever and ever and I would rather not have to answer to anybody again after my parents and maybe my child. I do not want to be in any relationship at all. Not even if I can be with other people while I am in that relationship.

I do not think I want a relationship. I just do not get the concept. Or I get it but I don't think I have ever been in one serious enough for it to be a proper relationship. And I would feel bad. Let's say I am busy throughout the day and I don't have time to call someone before I go to bed. I would feel guilty. In my mind, when you are in a relationship, you are supposed to always keep tabs on and talk to someone and make sure the person is alright. Most times, I don't even like talking to people so it is going to be really complicated and I just can't be bothered.

I do not want to get married – either to a man or a woman – but I do want to have kids, one or two. I think marriage is good but I don't think it is for me. It comes down to the whole commitment thing. I am not willing to let anyone control my activities or feel bad because I have not interacted with a particular person. In the future, it will be me and my dog and my son. I do not want Dangote or even Adenuga money. I just want enough so that when I want, I can go to the airport, buy my ticket and go wherever. I want to wake up with my money when I am 45 and go to China and have no one telling me, 'But we had plans for this night,' or 'You can't just up and go.'

No. I want to be able to do that without anything restricting me.

It's not that I don't like people. I do like people as far as I think you are fine. I can't like you if you are not fine. If I think you are fine and not a dick, I will have some sort of crush on you. Guys. Girls. Everybody. But most people just have this box where they write you off if you are not so and so.

My longest relationship has to be this guy TR___ in my first year of university. He was in his third year and I was in my first. I saw him at an event during fresher's week and I told one of my friends that I thought he was very cute. She told him and he came over and said hi. From then on, we became close. I really liked him. I think that was the closest I have been to a relationship. We were together unofficially throughout my first year. People knew I was with him and he was with me but we weren't particularly together. I was with someone else and he was with someone else while we were together and we were both okay with it. We liked each other but I don't know if that is enough to think of it as a relationship. Then he changed cities for his Masters and I was like, 'No, I can't do distance.' We were still in each other's lives in my second and third year. We are still kind of in each other's lives even now. He wasn't my boyfriend but I think he was my first remotely serious relationship.

Last year I was in a situation that was sort of serious with a girl named D___. She initiated a conversation online, then we met up. It was casual, then grew into something else. We moved offline two weeks after we made contact. We went to Instagram first, then Twitter, then phone numbers. We were talking for about three months and decided to make it official.

Two weeks after that I cheated on her with another girl so I guess I messed up. I wasn't getting 100 per cent from her and

I didn't want to be that person who would push her. I knew she liked me but I didn't know in what capacity so I had never initiated anything physical with her.

We had only kissed once, then V___ came up. I am not going to blame anybody else but there was a lot of external pressure saying D___ was probably not interested in me the way I was interested in her. 'Maybe she really likes you, but not anything physical, and V___ is talking to you ...' And V___ knew about D___ but didn't mind ... So, I jumped at it.

After it happened, I told D___ about it even though there was no way she would have found out on her own. To be honest, I still don't know why I told her. Everybody was like, 'You really do not need to tell her.' But I felt guilty. I derived pleasure from something that could make someone else unhappy. If I had to do it again, I am not sure I would confess. Knowing what I know now, I still would have had sex with V__, and I would not have minded feeling bad.

I was exposed to sexuality very early. At age 4. Obviously not consensual. I remember every single thing. My senior brother was having lessons. I had just started nursery school so we were all there. There was this guy, short, black, with his white shirt, teaching us. After a while, he gave my brother money to buy biscuits. There was a shop not too far from the house. My brother dashed out, then it was just me and him. For the most part, when I was younger, everyone was busy. I remember him putting me on the dining table, then trying to finger me. It was really messed up. My brother must have been very fast because he came in and screamed. The neighbours heard and came out. They called my mum and my dad and told them what happened. My mum is very quick to act. She beat him then my dad locked him up. He went to jail.

But the first person I was attracted to, two different people actually, were a guy and a girl when I was about 8 or 9. This was at two different times. I don't remember who came first. We were neighbours with the boy, who was about a year older than me. There was a lot of rubbish on TV and we said, 'Let's do what they are doing.' We would make out and sometimes it even went beyond that. There were trousers going down but we were 8 so nothing too serious. With the girl, she was about two to three years older than me. I was living at her house because we moved far and I couldn't be commuting that far for school. I didn't want to move schools so my parents made an arrangement where I stayed at her house Mondays to Fridays. Her younger sister was my classmate.

She was in secondary school and she came back for midterm once. I don't even know how it started. I was sleeping and I felt someone touching me and I was like, *Oh, okay, I know there is something happening.* The first night I was still. I didn't move. I didn't know what to do. The second night I was more aware. I realised she was not going to stop. By the third night, I think I started it. It was a massive bed. My friend was actually on with us at the time so I do not know how she never noticed. Well, we were meant to be asleep.

This went on whenever she was at home. I was there for the whole of Primary 6. It happened maybe once or twice during the day, but most times were at night. We would make out, take off our clothes and hump. I didn't have breasts but there was breast involved as well.

I do not know exactly what we were trying to do. It was not like I had ever seen anything with a girl on TV. I have never talked to her about it even though we are still in touch. I want to talk about it with her but I do not know if she will answer.

Then, when I was 11, there was this family friend who

used to sleep over and we messed around a bit. Besides that, I went to an all girls' school but I was very much to myself. Then came that best friend, K___, who was the first person I got close to.

Since then, I don't think I have changed much. I was always not girlish enough and not boyish enough. I am not really boyish, apart from the way I walk and the fact that I cannot be bothered with a handbag. I do nothing exactly boyish. I have been like this for as long as I can remember. I have had this walk, dress sense and everything. It is not something I can just change and I don't want to change. If you are going to like me then you are going to like me the way I am.

I have a brother who is five years older. My next sibling is two years younger but she was really sickly so I didn't interact much with her. I have two other siblings, twins, but they are seven years younger than me so I didn't spend much time with them either. It was always me and my brother. We did everything together and he liked me so much. We ate together and played together. I liked everything he did so I was very much a tomboy and not a girly girl at all. The toys I remember playing with were boys' stuff like cars. I remember I had way too many injuries for a girl. My mother would say, 'Do not go and play football with your brother' and I wouldn't listen. Then I'd scrape my knee. I would have to hide it so he and I would take care of it together.

I still get along with my brother like that. We hang out. Only now, he still thinks I am young. Sometimes he treats me like I am 12. I don't know why. He is the most oblivious person. I can be by his side with a girl sitting down on my lap exchanging looks and he will say, 'Oh that is just my sister and her friends. Nothing there. Nothing to see.'

The first girl I shagged, I met online. When I started university, I realised I liked girls and there was no way I could hide it. Well, I could hide it but I wanted to find out what these feelings were. I started watching loads and loads of YouTube videos. Right now, anyone who picks up my laptop and opens my YouTube channel will definitely know that I am not straight because there are way too many LGBT videos for me to just be a curious straight girl. I had to unsubscribe from some so it wouldn't be like that was the only thing I was ever on YouTube for.

I did my research because, for a long time, I wondered if I was just bi-curious or trying to find things out. Then I would flash back to when I was younger and it didn't seem so. But I still avoided being in close contact with friends, because I knew whenever I hugged them or we slept in the same bed, I felt a certain way. I was not sure if that was the way I should feel towards them so I avoided all of that up until my third year. And I thought, *You know what? Fuck it, I am just going to tell.*

I told one of my friends that I was talking to this girl online and we were going to meet up. My friend just started laughing, then she was like, 'Oh my God, I knew.' I told her she didn't know anything. There was nothing to know. But she was really supportive for the most part. She asked me many times if I was sure and I was like, 'Yeah, what is the worst thing that could happen? I won't enjoy it and then that is it. It can't be that bad.'

We met up, had drinks, talked, then had sex. It was different from what I had with guys, very different. I enjoyed it but for the first ten minutes, I was like, *Wow. What are you doing right now?* But after the initial awkwardness and weirdness, I was just like, *This person is cool*, and we had sex.

We kept in touch but she didn't live in the same city.

After that, I became more aware and willing to be myself. She was the first adult girl I was with. And the sex was very good. Before that, I had had sex with a number of guys but not like this. This, hands down, was the best sex I had ever had in my life. The other guys, it was not like they were bad. I mean, I liked a few of them but she was the best. After that night and during the next weeks, my friends got tired of me because I kept calling them like, 'OMG I just had the best sex of my life.' They were like, 'WTF, you told me this story yesterday.' I would be like, 'Yeah, I need to tell you again. I do not know what she did but it was that good.'

The second person I had earth-shattering sex with ... I do not even know how to describe it. We met through a mutual friend, then started talking. One day, out of the blue, she sent me a nude picture of herself. Till now I do not know why I deleted it. Maybe because my family members do not mind their business and they go through my phone. But she sent the nude and I sort of had the house to myself. It was just me, my brother and my aunt, who already knew about my sexuality.

So, I invited her over for the night. I got shwarma and drinks. We smoked some weed and eventually, at about ten, we headed to bed. I do not know how this big brother of mine didn't get that there was something up cos I do not go to bed at ten and we went up to the room together. I was wearing boxers and a shirt, lying on the bed staring up, thinking, *Please I do not know what to do.* She was watching something on her laptop, then luckily her battery went out. We stared at each other. Then she said, 'Are you really not going to do anything?' I was just looking at her like ... But then she moved closer and it took everything ... I don't really know what I was scared of or why, but I eventually kissed her. I think she needed me to make the first move, then she took control.

I don't think I have ever had bad sex. Mediocre yes, but not bad. In my third year, while my friend TR__ was doing his Masters, I went over to his city for the weekend. We had had sex many times before but this was a craving: something we had both been wanting and we had to satisfy ourselves. We did not leave the room except to get pizza and wine and maybe we watched a show once or twice. I don't know how his flatmates felt about us not leaving the room but we had fun. I arrived on Friday night and left on Saturday night. Out of all the guys I have had sex with, he was one of the few who really, really satisfied me. It was basically regular sex, but maybe because it was him and I was comfortable with him.

It is easier meeting people online. Offline you meet people and you are not sure, especially in Nigeria, and you don't want to not be sure. Online, you don't even have to exchange numbers. You can just decide not to talk to the person again. The first girl I met, I met on Whispers. You can post stuff anonymously and people can comment on it. I can't remember what I wrote but then she sent me a private message and we started talking. Then we got to Instagram, then Twitter, then exchanged phone numbers. And I met V__ on Twitter so yes, the Internet is a good way of meeting people.

I had been going to the lesbian website on and off for two years before I decided to join. I am not particularly active there. Every once in a while, I check in and check out. I identify as LGBTI and I don't know that I have a community in Nigeria. I haven't actively tried to find one and I do not want one. I would go to a community event if invited but not on my own.

My best friend is gay and we are each other's beards, for

lack of a better word. He is very effeminate but most people do not ask him questions because they see him with me. They assume we are together. When I go to a wedding or whatever, I go with him. It is not intentional. I told myself that I am never going to lie and say I have a boyfriend. If you ask for my number, it is better I tell you or I give you someone's number.

I don't fear so much for myself but I get really scared and concerned for him because I feel like people are going to take advantage or he is going to get into some sort of trouble. I want him to get out of Nigeria. He is very skinny and soft. When we come back from a night out, we blast music on the highway. With the most feminine song, you will see him being all handsy and I think people go, 'WTF is wrong with these people?' There are times we are out and it gets uncomfortable. That is when I start playing with him, hitting him and throwing myself on him. Sometimes it feels like I am doing it for other people but I am mostly doing it for him, to make him more comfortable. I think he has a thick skin when it comes to words that people throw at him but I still get scared for him.

I am not really out. In my family, the only person who knows for a fact is my aunt. My younger brother, who is 17, has an idea. Once, he came to me and we were talking about something random and he said, 'You know, if you tell me you are a lesbian, I will not be surprised.' I was like, *What?* I never responded. I just laughed and left the room. He has said this twice but I still haven't answered him. Out of all my siblings, I am closest to him now, so he probably knows. Maybe one day I will confirm it to him. I always talk about LGBTI issues in my house. Everybody is like, 'We don't care. Stop.' He is the only one who really indulges me and keeps on talking. Randomly, when we are out together, he will say something like, 'See that woman going? See that woman's boobs!' I am like, 'You are 17. You should not be looking or talking to me about a woman's boobs.' I think he is 90 per cent sure but doesn't know for a fact. I might tell him when he is done with secondary school.

He could tell my parents. I don't really know how they will react. I imagine it will not be positive. My parents like to think they are very cool and I don't think they will be particularly shocked but I really don't know.

My mother is the parent I see every day. I always bring up LGBTI issues to see her stance. Recently it has been leaning towards neutral as opposed to negative. My dad thinks I am 14. He has said nothing to me relating to boys. Ever. He is not ready to talk about me being sexual. I am his favourite child and he still sees me as that little girl. I do not know how he is going to react. It is going to be serious ...

I know they will not make me move out. Best-case scenario will be, whatever, carry on. Worst case, they might take me to hospital. My mum may think it is medical or go to church.

I was raised Catholic. I attended church for my confirmation so I am an active Catholic. I go to church willingly maybe once a month. Unwillingly, I go whenever my mum is around. She doesn't let you skip. Most times, I try to stall and when they see they are running late they might say, Whatever, let's leave her. I can get away with that maybe once a month. I end up going to church three times a month and maybe it's once that I really wanted to go.

As much as I enjoy and like the doctrine teachings, there are a lot of things I do not agree with. One is supposed to receive Communion every Sunday. You don't have to. It is when you feel like you are in a state of grace. Sometimes I am listening, then I see someone or flash back to a time when I was with someone so I just sit down and skip Communion for that day. It is hard to align things. I would rather believe in God and find that nothing exists but oblivion, than not believe then leave here and find that there is actually a God. I would rather have my faith. I believe that, regardless of any other thing in the Bible, the ultimate law is to love one another as Jesus loves us. Any other thing is secondary. I think that if I am a good person and I don't worship other deities, then I am fine. I know a lot of good people. The fact that they are gay, lesbian, bisexual or whatever cannot be why they are not making heaven.

I did not know any queer person growing up, not even on TV. Ellen was the first person I saw on TV, when I was much older. Although ... I remember this senior who had a girlfriend she really liked. The school was doing everything to tear them apart and she kept on saying she loved her. This was a Catholic school so you can imagine it was a scandal. I think they might have been seen making out or whatever, once or twice. They tried to break them up but one told the other that she should not worry and when they graduated, she was going to have a sex change and come back for her. Everyone was like, they need to pray for them, do this, do that. For the most part I was like, 'You people should leave them alone. Whatever happens to them, it is their choice.' I thought they were so cute. They were suspended for a while, then they made one of them sleep in the convent with the Reverend sisters to keep them apart until they left school. I loved the Reverend sisters, but they could be mean so I can imagine what it was like sleeping in the convent, especially when you had done something wrong.

I did not want to be the person everybody was talking about. I am not scared of people. It is more like I am scared of myself. The feelings I have are too intense and I do not know what to do with them. I think those types of feelings are the ones that make one want to kill an ex-lover or something. Such strong feelings!

– *FR, age 26, Lagos*

I Can Still Love More

'Allah is full of mercy and forgiveness. I now know that God did not make a mistake in allowing us to love men and women and that the silence of the Qur'an on this matter says a lot.'

Content Note: Bereavement

My earliest memory is of a funeral. I think I was 5 years old. I came back from school and there was a lot of crying and many, many people in our house. I tried to find my mother but she was not there. I started crying. My brother Y___ held my hand and took me aside. He gave me his school bag, then took it back. He asked me if I understood but I was still confused. Then he told me God had given our mother to us for a short time but now had taken her back and I shouldn't be too sad.

I remember that day very well. I think I will remember it until the day I die. I remember the uniform I was wearing. I remember the colour of his bag. I remember the way he was trying not to cry. I started crying and my father and stepmother came to console me. There were so many people but it was mostly my family around us.

My mother was the second wife and I was her last-born.

There are eight of us children in my family. My stepmother YD___ had three of her children before my father married my mother. Then my brother Y___ was born, followed by two other children before me. I am number seven in the whole family with one brother after me, but I am my mother's last. Y___ and I are very close and that has not changed, even up to now. My other brothers and sisters, from the same father but not the same mother, are close too but not as close as I am with Y___.

Growing up, our household was peaceful and quiet most of the time. We went to school, we came back, we ate and we performed prayer. We went to Islamiyya every day except on Thursdays and Fridays. Those days, there was no Islamiyya so we stayed at home with our friends and played. Up till now I love Thursdays and Fridays because I think of them as days of playing and resting.

I was not a very obedient girl but my stepmother treated us like eggs. It was very different from how she treated her other children. I remember every time they needed something, they would tell me to go and ask YD___ because she would give me anything I asked for. She would say, 'You are my little pony. How can I refuse you?' Y___ was very stubborn. He would go out to climb all the trees, chase all the animals and beat other children. One Eid when we were young, he painted himself with the blood of the ram that my uncles had slaughtered. My father was very, very angry. He beat him every morning for three days. Me, I wanted little trouble so I did not do the things that Y___ did and my father was always proud of me.

My father was a huge presence in our lives. He was attentive and most evenings after prayers, he would sit with us to settle quarrels and talk about the news, school, his work, everything! Then immediately after the sound for the network news started, we were all chased to go to sleep. As I grew to be a teenager I think he became more focused on religion and discipline because one of my brothers, the first, was getting into a lot of trouble in school and at home. B___ would get into everything, from fighting on the street to insulting his teachers. My father was not happy at the example he was setting for Y___ and the rest of us, so they sent him to military school. Everyone cried when B___ left, but we also liked when he came home in his uniform. Everybody on the street called him 'soja' and he became more responsible, very disciplined.

The first time I felt attracted to a girl, I was around 17 years old. Before then, I liked one of my cousins who lived in M___. He was very tall and handsome and would jokingly call me his wife when I was very young. At 15, when my sisters and I went to stay with his family, I was very much in love with him. He was definitely my first love. He was studying in university then and came home for holidays. He knew all the Indian movies, all the good songs. He liked to dance and he used to say he could sing and dance better than Amitabh Bachchan. I thought he could.

The first girl I had feelings for was my eldest brother's wife. B___ was in his thirties when he got married – very late – so I was old enough. My father was very proud as that was his first son getting married and he did everything big. His wife was from Gombe and their marriage rites were very different. There was a lot of dancing, traditional ceremonies and they kept hiding the wife. They made him pay a bit of money so they could reveal her head and talk. Before then, we – the groom's sisters and cousins – had never met her because only two of my aunts went to the gaisuwa and leffe, which is when the families officially meet, exchange gifts and set a date for the marriage. In those days, they did not do pre-wedding pictures, calendars and all that. At least, our people didn't do all those things.

When they revealed her head after B___ and his friends had paid the money, I couldn't stop looking at her. She was so pretty. She kept smiling and looking away from everyone. Even now, I remember how pretty she was and how I felt that day. I tried to maintain eye contact but I think, as the bride, she was meant to be shy so she did not look at anyone. Not even B___.

That night, they brought her to B___'s side of the house, which my father had built for him, and I was very, very happy. I was happy she was going to be living in the same house as me and I was going to see her all the time. I couldn't stop looking at her. I wanted to talk to her, to be friends with her. I wanted to be around her and keep looking at her. When her sisters and aunts went back home, I was the youngest girl so I was expected to help her with chores. That was how I started spending all my time at their side of the house. Every day, when my brother left in the morning, I would wash her plates even though she would tell me not to. I would clean the house for her, go on errands, do everything that was expected of me.

Looking back now, I wonder why nobody noticed or commented. Even Y___ never said anything to me until I said I wanted to go to the same school as my brother's wife. I know he was disappointed but he did not say anything. And my father, Y___, and everyone was happy B___'s wife would be living with family while she was schooling. They worked an admission for me and when school resumed, we went back together. I wanted to spend all my time with her, talking, gisting and laughing. All that made me very happy. I was only less happy when B___ was in town, which was every two or three weeks. At those times, she had no time for me. She would cook big meals, shine and dust the whole place, dress herself up and beam like the king was coming. I was never jealous, only less happy that she did not have time for me.

I spent so much time with her, at home and in school and we were very close. One time she asked me about my love life and I told her about my cousin S___, who was married. She told me I would not be anybody's second wife and that we would find me a husband amongst the good boys. I think she knew how I felt then and wanted to discourage my feelings and push me towards men. That was the period when I really realised my feelings for her, and for girls in general I guess. It did not feel wrong or right. I just knew that I liked her. I never even knew what being gay or lesbian was.

I now think I must have been very sheltered. Just before I met my husband, there was an Igbo boy who liked me. He knew my background and that it was not possible, so he would send his friend N___ to talk to me. N___ was very nice to me in class and it took me a few weeks to notice that every time she spoke to me, he would come over and say hi to her then smile at me or say something. Small time, my course mates started calling me his wife. I think everyone in class knew so it was no secret. One day, I asked N___ if she was talking to me for herself or for him and she said, 'No, I am a lesbian but it is my brother that likes you.' It was later that I put two and two together to understand what a lesbian was. I was so surprised and curious.

I tried to speak to B___'s wife about it but she always said to leave it alone. She said luadi was a sin, that the earth turned every time anyone did it and God would never forgive it. I continued to be friends with N___, but shortly after that I met my husband. He was Y___'s friend from Ahmadu Bello University and one day they came to visit together. At that point, I had never had a boyfriend. He kept smiling at me and Y___ but I didn't take much notice. Maybe everybody knew and approved him before he was even allowed to be friends with me. He was my father's friend's nephew and very smart. He and Y___ would visit often and he would bring me gifts when coming to town. He would hang behind to walk slowly and talk to me and I very much liked his company.

In less than a month, I was looking forward to their visits and I asked Y___ if he had a girlfriend. Y___ said, 'No, only you.' I was very surprised and happy. One day he told me his family wanted him to get married and asked if he could tell them to come and greet my family. I was scared but happy and I nodded yes. Later, he kissed me and I shook inside with fear, excitement, love, everything.

The introduction, courtship, everything went fast and before I knew it, we were married. He was a wonderful man. He was my first in everything. I moved to his house. Before the year was over, he had been transferred to Abuja and I went with him.

I have been living here since then. The old Abuja was not too different from the Abuja of now. We have always had good roads, big houses and big men. Sometimes I felt like Abuja was another country. I was happy as the city was quiet and clean, everywhere had street lights, there were many bridges and everything was new and fresh.

He was a very, very good husband and we were deeply

in love. I do not remember if he ever said 'I love you' but he would always call me 'mata na', meaning 'my wife', with such affection that I knew how he felt. I was still schooling but the rest of the time I was in Abuja. We made friends until Y___ moved to Abuja and got married too. They lived close to us and we did everything together. I had a very good marriage and life was happy and simple.

Before I knew it, I finished school. My father called his friend and I got a place to do my NYSC. I had just started working in the ministry when my husband fell sick. At first, it was just a headache but he did not feel better after two days. We went for tests and they said he had small malaria in his blood. He started malaria treatment, but he did not get better. You know how God works. Exactly two weeks after our fifth anniversary, he died.

I do not like to talk about it. It was a very difficult time for me. For all of us. We were so happy, then he was gone. Just like that. I was by his bedside in the hospital every day. I kept praying for him. It was obvious something was wrong and it was not getting better. He was buried here in Abuja. This was his land, as they say. He was a very, very good man.

I don't remember when I stopped loving B___'s wife or when I started loving him. I think it overlapped at some point. I don't think I have loved two people at the same time. Most of the time people think you are a cheat when you say you are bisexual. Yes, a lot of women think so. I haven't ever told any man what I do with girls so I do not know what they think. I met a girl online last year and I told her I was bisexual. She said she didn't think bisexuals could be faithful so nothing could happen between us. I wasn't too surprised. She was not the first to think or say it.

The first girl I had anything with was somebody I met through Facebook in 2009. After I finished reading a link on someone's profile, I saw her comment. I clicked on her profile and saw that she liked both men and women. I sent her a friend request. It wasn't my intention to even meet her. I didn't think I could actually do anything with it but we started talking and becoming close. One day I told her I thought I liked girls and she said she knew. She was going through a break-up with a girl at that point and was very honest about it. I was happy to just be friends with a lesbian. Finally.

We talked all the time on Facebook, on free night calls, then one day we decided to meet. She was coming to Abuja and I said she could stay in my house, no problem. The first two days, nothing really happened, but on the third day, we started. Before she left, we started sleeping together. We did everything. I was just discovering that side of me and I really liked her. We were in the relationship for over a year and she came back to Abuja two more times.

I am still close to all my family but I am not out to anyone. Well, only Y___. He keeps asking me when I will stop this nonsense and marry again and I just laugh and tell him that will happen when he gives birth to my husband. He only has two daughters. Lovely girls who I love dearly. I still live in my house. I own it full. It came with my inheritance. I think my husband's mother wanted it, but she is comfortable where she is. I see her, his brothers and sister, his whole family sometimes.

Do I want children? Yes, but maybe my window of opportunity has passed. If I marry again, I don't see myself having any children. I don't think I can marry a woman because I can't have children with another woman. If I marry again, it will be a man. But I do not think I will. I am happy with the relationship I am in now. We haven't talked a lot about the future. She is younger than me and knows what she wants in life. She is a lesbian and has only dated women. I believe everyone can love many people during their lives. I have loved three people deeply and I can still love more. My father loved two women at the same time and that did not change anything in his life.

– NT, age 41, Abuja.

Why Do I Have To Ask You To Consider Me Human?

'They keep us busy so that we don't demand our power back. Somebody has to be vulnerable and victimised so that they, who feel powerless in other aspects of their lives, can feel powerful over others.'

Content note: child sexual abuse, sexual violence, deliverance sessions, verbal abuse, controlling behaviour

My sexuality is my sexuality. You are either accepting or you buzz off. It's nothing special. It's nothing new. It's nothing I should be advocating for people to understand. But, due to religious and mostly political reasons, some people have decided to demonise others to make them less than human. It all boils down to money or power. The 1 per cent who own the wealth need to keep everybody so busy they won't notice. These guys have been around for years. They are in charge of everything. So, what do they do? They keep us occupied. They keep us busy so that we don't demand our power back. Somebody has to be vulnerable and victimised so that they, who feel powerless in other aspects of their lives, can feel powerful over others. Unfortunately for me, I face the conundrum of being a woman, a black woman, living in a country like Nigeria and being of a certain sexual orientation.

In view of the revelations about Sugabelly and Mustapha Audu, I've come to realise that we have a long way to go in Nigeria. People you'd expect to know better have been saying, 'Oh yeah, she was not raped.' They don't understand that a 17-year-old is a minor and that rape doesn't just happen when somebody grabs you off the streets and tears off your clothes. Rape can also happen within marriage and within relationships. I'm thinking about how many women get raped on a daily basis by these so-called intellectuals and elites on Twitter and Facebook. I don't want to think about it because it's scary. I just don't get it. Why do I have to ask you to consider me human? Can't you see I have the same body features as you? How am I less of a human because I'm a woman, because I don't have sex with people who you have sex with? What does that have to do with you? Does it affect the money you spend when you go to the market? How does it affect the price of rice?

I grew up in Ibadan, Lagos and Abeokuta. I had a fantastic granddad and grandmother who taught me everything I know about Yoruba culture. My mum taught me how to read. She bought books. She gave me a gift for loving books and reading. She bought me my first diary – so that she could read it.

My mum was fond of getting married. She likes men and so does my grandmother. My great-grandmother too. They have three to four marriages and in between they have lovers. They like changing men. My stepdad, who was the most fantastic guy on the face of earth, raised me. Then my mum ditched him, saying, 'I'm done with getting married, I want to be on my own now.'

I have two sons. I had the first when I was in my mid-twenties. I met his dad when I was 17 or 18. We used to hang out. He had a flat. He was this wise, cosmopolitan dude in Lagos. So, any time I was on holiday in Lagos, I was in his flat. He never made any inappropriate advances. He was my absolute best friend. Then, one night, we got drunk and had sex.

I fell pregnant. That was the end of that relationship because he wanted me to have an abortion. I was at a point in my life when I didn't know what to do with myself or what I wanted from life. There was something wrong with me. I tried very hard but I just couldn't fit in. I thought maybe a baby would help somehow. It was either that or commit suicide. It was the stupidest reason for having a child.

Now, I know why I felt that way. Hindsight is 20/20, but back then I couldn't put words to all the confusion. I still don't feel I belong anywhere. I don't like cliques and gangs and groups. Back then, I think that the way I saw the world was different from the way the world expected me to be. I was supposed to think in a certain way. I was supposed to talk in a certain way. I was supposed to behave in a certain way. I tried so hard but I was in suspension. And I was affected by all these things from my childhood ...

When I was young, I thought my mum was poor. But thinking about it, that was not true. We didn't have a dining table but we always had food. My mum was enjoying her life. I went to good schools. I was actually quite privileged. I had a stepdad I loved. I had two brothers and stepbrothers. They're all fantastic. One of my brothers died in a car accident about twenty or so years ago. He was my best friend. He bought me my first bra, my first lipstick, taught me how to shave my pits and ride a bicycle.

There was this maid who looked after me and let me do whatever I liked. During the holidays, I would wake up, go to Y___'s house, stay there until she stopped paying attention to me, then leave and start playing with the boys. We used to play all sorts of games. There was this small stream where we would go and hang out. We played pirates, monsters in the wild ... I'm sure that place was just the bush with a few trees but in my imagination, it was a jungle.

In primary school, I was rough and tumble. I remember yanking the heads of the dolls my mum used to buy – blonde, blue-eyed Barbies. I used to take off their hair. There was this girl I quarrelled with. I beat her up. From Primary 1, she would order me to bring her lunch every afternoon. When we got to Primary 3, I told her I wasn't going to give her my lunch. She said, 'Okay, wait after school.' We had a big fight – and I won.

School was torture for me. I didn't know how to do half of the things they taught. We used to have needlework. That was the worst. My work was the dirtiest, most horrible of the class. I would score minus 2, minus 3. I enjoyed English. Yes, let's read! I loved Social Studies because we had to learn about history. We got to read. But I didn't want to work on maths, or do General Science. I didn't want to sit in class from morning to night. I wanted to play. I wanted to make up words and tell stories.

I also remember Y___, my first female crush. It was all-consuming. I was about 6 or 7. I used to go to her house and stay all the time. Y___ was absolutely gorgeous. She was dark-skinned and chubby. I liked the way she talked. I liked her skin. She was all girl. I didn't want anything from her. I just wanted to sit near her and be everything she was – smart, well brought up, very polite. I wanted to be that special friend she would talk to when she was sad. When she lost her brother, she talked to me and I listened. I wanted to be her special person.

We attended the same primary school. I would walk down to her house. We would go to school together, then I would wait for her afterwards and we would go home together. I would just want to be near her. But when we went to the same secondary school, she stopped talking with me. She became distant and cold. I totally understand. By then, my weirdness was becoming obvious. She was with this group and I couldn't fit in. Y___ broke my heart.

In Primary 6, we all got concerned about growing breasts. We used to climb the fence that separated the primary and secondary schools. The girls looked so grown up, so cool and sophisticated. They told us, 'All girls in secondary school have breasts. You're in Primary 6 and you don't have breasts. What are you doing being alive? You should just find a way.' So we would catch beetles, put them in a box and carry them home. They had to be alive. In the evenings, we took them out and wrapped them around our chests or put them on our nipples. They were supposed to make you have breasts. If they say that you need breasts for secondary school, you do what you can to get them. And, if that requires having bloody breasts, you do it. We did this every night in Primary 6 for a week. It didn't work. After that week, we gave up.

One of our distant cousins molested me around that time. I was 8 years old. He was a tall, handsome guy and best friends with my brother. I admired him. I was so proud of him. I loved talking to him. My neighbour had raped me earlier so he was the second person to molest me.

I will never forget that day. I had gone to the house and there wasn't anyone around. He didn't penetrate, unlike the neighbour who tried to and said, 'Oh, you're so tight. You're so dry. You're so green.' I will never forget that. This cousin was rubbing his penis between my thighs whereas the neighbour was actually trying to penetrate, because he was jamming. I can still feel him trying sometimes ...

This guy was just masturbating. I never went back to his house again. I knew it was wrong. I knew it was bad. I knew it was the same thing that my neighbour did to me. I totally avoided both of them.

After it happened, whom could I tell? My mum, who travelled a lot for work and came back with all this happiness and gladness, giving out chocolates and telling stories? My older brother was in a boarding house. My stepdad went to work in the morning and came back in the evening. He was tired. He just wanted to eat and sleep and watch TV on the weekends.

You don't want to tell anybody because if you do, it's going to spoil and they're friends with the parents of the guy. You don't want them to think you're a bad child. You don't want to spoil their happiness because, somehow, you feel responsible for their happiness.

And, of course, the men tell you that you are ashawo. That it's your fault that they're raping you. That if you tell anybody, they are going to kill you – and kill your parents. That sticks. I didn't want them to think I was ashawo. An ashawo was that woman who lived a few houses down from us. She was a single mother, wore lipstick, drove a car and your mother hated her. Ashawo was the worst thing anybody could ever say. I didn't want my stepdad to look at me like that. I wanted him to see me as his little daughter. That's why it was shocking when people were saying, 'Why didn't Sugabelly tell?' Because she couldn't, especially not if she loved her mum, if she felt her mum had gone through so much and she didn't want to add to it.

Although I remember my childhood being mostly fun, it

was also traumatic because the person who raped me was our next-door neighbour. I had to see him every day. I never told anybody what happened. I don't like talking about it. These are things I buried for so long.

In secondary school, I stuck out like a sore thumb. I couldn't fit in with any of the groups. I couldn't feel comfortable with girls because of my experiences. I got tired of plaiting my hair and went to the barber and got my hair cut off. I was one of the few girls who wore a skin cut in secondary school. I would hang out with one group this week and another the next week. When the boys came to the school, all the girls would line up, crowds of them, and yell, 'Boys!' I never did that. I thought they were mad.

B__ and I__ were my secondary school friends. We didn't really click until we got to class 2. I__ was tall and butch and loved girls. She was a flaming lesbian. She was never shy. She later became a second wife to a married man – and born-again. I've had to block her from my Facebook.

We had a boarding house at the school and it was obvious some of the girls were dating each other. At least, among the student populace it was known. I don't know about the teachers. The boarders were the ones who got to date. Nobody thought it was weird that two girls were walking down the road and holding hands, kissing and saying, 'Oh, it's my wife.' But we kept it away from school authorities. It was none of their business. It was our business. Those girls were not treated any differently. In fact, they were seen as gods. I tried to go to boarding house my final year so that I could get a girlfriend, but it didn't work.

In Form 1, I had my first lover. I was 12 or 13. It was one of those long holidays and there was nobody at home. D__ was my next-door neighbour, a girl my age. We would go to her house and sit on the bed together, read and talk, then go to my house and do the same thing. One day we went to my house and instead of going to my room, I said, 'Let me show you something.' I took her to my brother's room and pulled out *Playboy* magazines from under his mattress. We were giggling. We did the same the next day. By the third day we were making out.

She wanted us to kiss but that didn't work. We didn't know how to do it. It was like biting each other and squashing teeth. It was really her breast I needed to touch. She had these really nice breasts and I asked if I could touch them. She really liked it so I touched her body. It wasn't really anything. It was more rubbing skin against skin. After we broke through that first barrier, it was something we looked forward to. Every time we had a chance, we would go there and do that. This went on for the whole holiday until my mum came back earlier than usual and caught us.

She was furious. She beat me and beat me. She said that instead of having me as a child, she would kill me. That she was going to put pepper in my pussy. She told me how Elton John was gay and had to wear pads. After she travelled, she would come in with piles of newspaper and show me all these horrid people who were gay. That's what I remember most vividly. She was very homophobic. She didn't mind me having male friends but she wouldn't let me bring female friends home.

We started going to child deliverance sessions. We went to the babalawo who would give me stuff in a pot to eat. Now, when I look back, I realise why, but at the time, I just thought my mum was a horrible person who wanted to kill me or maybe thought I was a witch. From my point of view, she had just started taking me for deliverance, to the babalawo, to the herbalist and I had no idea why. Every time, I tried to talk to her, even now, it always descends into 'You don't respect me', so there was no way I could talk with her then.

At deliverance, they would pray for me and beat me with a broom. At some point, my mum sent me to live with her friend who was a celestial. The herbalist was the mildest of them all. He said, 'Leave her alone. She's just a child,' but my mum was insistent so he made a concoction, which my mum forced me to eat in the middle of the night.

I was this angry teenager who didn't even know why she was angry. I had a book in which I wrote angry, confused poetry. Writing and music were the only spaces I could escape to. They are still what give me most joy. To please my mother, I started hanging out with boys – smoking, drinking and playing snooker.

After D___, I had one night with my mum's friend's daughter when I was about 17. She came visiting and we liked each other. In the middle of the night, we started kissing and touching each other. The next morning, there was a mutual looking forward to seeing each other again, but she never came back to my house.

The only time I ever told my mum I was raped was when I was violently raped at 18 by a friend of mine. He was this older guy, perhaps 28. Whenever he came home on holiday, a bunch of us would go over to his place. We would play Scrabble and chess, hang out and smoke. He raped me violently. Beat me and raped me. I had to be taken to a hospital.

When my mum came back from her travels and I told her, she got upset and said, 'Oh, you are just a stupid girl. You shouldn't tell me you've been raped. What do you want me to do? You want to tell me you've not been having sex all this while? I don't want to hear about this.' So having sex makes it all right for some guy to rape me? She did take me to the hospital and have me checked for STDs. She did that at least, but that was the point I divorced myself from her.

I was about 22 when I had my first boyfriend. He was such a gorgeous man. He was all chubby and had breasts. He wasn't much for penetration, but he taught me about my body, about my skin. I really enjoyed having sex with him. It was fun but it would always get weird for me when we had penetration. I still enjoyed him because it was more foreplay most of the time. He thought I didn't like penetration because of my trauma. I had told him I'd been raped and he was understanding.

His mum didn't like me though, because I was a wild child. It all came to a head one night when we travelled to Eruwa and the car broke down on the return journey. By the time we got back, it was already after 1am. My mum was outside waiting for me. She had called his mum and they had had a big fight, claiming that the other one's child was the bad influence. That was when we officially broke up, but we were still friends. We were together for two years before I slept with the father of my first son. That was the end of that.

So, my childhood … I took my first female lover when I was about 13. I was molested and raped when I was 8. Which I never resolved. I was just a typical Nigerian child. You get abused. Nobody talks about it. So, you can understand why I was in the state I was in when I became pregnant with my first son.

After I gave birth to him, I found Jesus and became born-again. I went to church every day. For ten years, I didn't have any relationships. I had a crush on a woman in church. She was married but I was in love with her. Every Sunday, I would go home after the service with her and her husband.

She would send me on errands. I was her little slave. I didn't see my behaviour as odd. I thought it was something everybody did.

Going to church was part of me trying to fit in, trying to belong. I became the pastor's friend. I would see him and ask him lots of questions. I found the Bible so racist and anti-women and I didn't have a name for what was wrong with me. Homosexuals are men who have sex with other men. I'm not a man. I don't have sex with other men. I didn't have a name for girls who have sex with other girls. All the books I read were about men and women falling in love. Somewhere in the book there might be this homosexual guy who is the fun person everybody likes. You don't see yourself in books. You see a lot of white people having fun.

So, in my mid-thirties, I was in church. I was also online searching desperately for girls. I was all over the dating sites. At first, I listed myself as lesbian. Then I thought, maybe there aren't any lesbians in Nigeria, so I listed myself as bisexual. Then I tried dating sites abroad. It was difficult. I was in church praying for Jesus to stop me from doing this because I was obsessed. I would wake up in the middle of the night and check if somebody had sent me a mail. I was in church praying to be saved, calling my friends, making up stories about having sex with men to convince myself, and trying to find women on dating sites. I was on lesbian sites but I didn't think I was a lesbian.

I found a woman. She was the only Nigerian who responded to me on the sites. We would have phone sex, Internet sex then we finally decided to meet. I went to Lagos and met this wonderful, gorgeous ex-nun who told me all about her sexual exploits – but she wouldn't let me touch her. At the beginning we were holding, kissing – then suddenly she said I couldn't touch her breasts. That just killed it.

That's life for you. You want to meet a girl you can touch but she doesn't want you to touch her. I want us to touch each other. I was just turned off. The next morning, I said, 'I will never see you again – obviously, I'm not really a lesbian.'

When I got back from Lagos, I went back to being depressed. I turned myself to work. I took myself back to church. I was a member of the choir. I was everything. There was something wrong with me but I didn't know what that was.

Then somebody put a name to it. My brother's best friend took an interest in me. My mum went to him and said she had a child who was not romantic enough with guys. He asked me, 'Are you a lesbian?' I said 'No, I'm not a lesbian,' then had sex with two of my male friends who I could trust and found someone to marry to prove it.

So, I dated a guy, we got married, I had a child for him and he left me. He said I didn't know how to behave like a proper wife. We used to have sex and I'd be dry most of the time. I was broke when he left me. He took the car I had spent almost a million Naira fixing after an accident on the Lagos–Ibadan expressway (not to mention the money I put into the purchase of the car itself). He left at the time I miscarried our second child. I was going to die. I was the one who said leave – and he actually left. But it was fantastic because we had my second son.

I tried to divorce him and he refused, saying it was unnecessary because it was just a piece of paper and he never wanted to get married again. When he was about 3, my son learned other children had fathers so he started saying he wanted to see his daddy. I asked him to come around for a couple of weeks. That's the kind of relationship I have with the father of my older son. He's the most irresponsible father you'll ever meet in your life but he'll take his son every holiday. He will say all sorts of stupid things to him, then I need to work on the boy's head when he gets home, but at least he has a relationship with his father. Anyway, my ex-husband tried to kidnap my son, saying he was a brat and needed to be broken. I had to do a lot of Nollywood drama before I got my son back.

While I was married, I was talking to a woman I met through a friend. She was openly lesbian and living abroad. We talked for about a year and a half. She knew all about my marriage and how it was breaking up. Then, one day, months after my husband left, she told me she was coming to Nigeria. I was so happy. After we met, she asked me, just before we were about to go out, whether she could kiss me – and we kissed. I was in my late thirties. That kiss was my first. That kiss did it for me. I just crawled to her. I was in Lagos every week to see her. It was the most nourishing sex I'd ever had. It was healing sex.

I broke up with her three months into the relationship saying I wasn't really a lesbian. I broke up with her the second time, saying, 'It's just you I feel this way with. I'm going to try men.' I tried a couple of guys. I broke up with her for the fourth time to sleep with other girls to check if I really was a lesbian or if it was just her. I went back to her.

I don't think she knew how to do relationships either. Relationships in Nigeria are weird. There is always an element of control. You are trying to do 'Who is the guy here?' At the same time, I was growing in my feminism. The dynamics of power really played out between us. She was the one with all the money. When I met her, I was broke. I've never needed much money. As long as I have money to have nice things once in a while and put good food on the table, cars and houses are not important to me. But she was cautious about status and station. She wanted me to dress in a certain way and behave in a certain manner, carry myself with more dignity and all that. I think it's all middle-class bullshit. Seriously, why should I carry a designer bag when I can buy something cheaper? I tried though. Sometimes I would want to go and see her but I couldn't afford to – I would have to choose between leaving money for the kids while they were with my mother and seeing her. Why would I want to make that kind of choice?

I was really dependent on her in the beginning. She had all the power. In my relationships with men, I never gave that power to anybody – but I didn't know how to behave in a relationship with a woman. I didn't know how to express my love. How could I show her what she'd done for me by allowing me to know myself? I was truly in love and wanted to worship her. That was the first time in my life that someone would ask me who is the man and who is the woman in the relationship. She was obviously comfortable in a position of power over her partner and it didn't sit well with me. I handed my power over to her. That was one of the major reasons I kept breaking up with her. The last time I broke up with her, I really broke up with her.

That was when I had my crisis. That was when I hit rock bottom. I locked my door and sent my children off. I sat in my room and cried. I thought about how I have always been the way I am. I looked at my monsters and brought them out one by one from the place I had locked them – the guys who abused me, the guy who raped me, my first love. I permitted myself to remember all these things. I realised I'd never been straight. It helped me become a better person. Once I recognised the thing that was wrong with me, I realised there was nothing wrong with me.

I resigned from my job. I went away for six weeks. For the first time in my entire life, I was alone. I didn't have a child. I didn't have a mother. I didn't have brothers. It was just me in a room by myself. It was the most liberating time in my life.

That was five years ago. Now, I'm in a much better place, a much happier place. I'm more confident. I know myself better. I've become a stronger feminist. I have a voice. Nobody can silence me.

But I have found it really difficult to raise my sons. I love them, but if I had known then what I know now, I'm not sure I would have kids. Having my first son as my responsibility pushed me to be stronger. I was earning the same amount of money in my first job as his school fees so I got another job. It also made me consider what kind of parent I wanted to be. My mum wasn't perfect but she raised me to like books. She allowed me to breathe. She wasn't this overbearing, sit-on-your-face kind of mother. So, he has a phone and I don't call him even when he goes out. I only call him when it's important. He'll call me and know I'll pick up his call because it's important and relevant.

Even before I came out to myself, I never raised them to see gay people as different. My oldest son learned how to cook and keep the house from age 7 or 8. He would come home with stuff like, 'Boys shouldn't cook but I'm a boy.' I would ask him what the difference was between a boy and a girl. It got him bullied in school. I'm this weird woman in jeans and a T-shirt. I'm not like other parents. For a long time, he wished I was some other woman he imagined as his ideal mother. When he was in JSS1, he came home and told me about this fag he met at school. We had this big blow out because we had that conversation on sexuality.

It became worse when he discovered I was a lesbian. NEPA[1] had taken light and I was in a room with a woman. We were both naked and I was sitting on top of her. He was 15 and he came in. He asked me, 'Oh, why have you decided that you are a lesbian now?' I told him, 'I didn't decide. I've always been.' He told my mother on the phone. She didn't make it easy for him. She ranted and I had to throw her out of my house.

It was a really difficult time – a lot of crying, a lot of yelling at each other. There was a day he said he was going to report me to the police because I was a lesbian. I had to tell him, 'My sexuality is none of your business. I'm an adult. I've raised you this far. I've not changed. Whoever I have sex with, I still pay your school fees. I still put food on the table.'

He's partly homophobic to me but it's much better now. I worry, especially when they go to visit my mum. For a while, I didn't send my kids to see her but she's old. She's lonely. I don't want to stop them visiting her. We have these conversations and I noticed it affected my oldest son – but he shut this off by focusing on his WAEC exams, which he passed with distinction.

In Yorubaland, girls have sex with girls all the time, especially while growing up – your next-door neighbour, your cousin. I have had all kinds of sex. I have had sex with men and sex with women. I like men but not in a sexual way. I love all the men in my life – but I'm not attracted to them. I refer to myself as queer because I'm more emotionally attached to women.

When I met the woman I'm living with now, she made me realise how much I love and enjoy talking with women. I really liked her. I said, 'Let's have sex and see if we enjoy each other's bodies.' When we moved to this area, we were formally dating but after we had lived together a few months, I realised she didn't like children and that neither of us could have the kind of relationship we wanted. We are both still sexually attracted to each other and have sex but we are not seeing each other. We are just friends. I know she sees other people. For me, if I find somebody, that's great but I can't deal with a lot of the women I meet.

I have no idea if people around us know about the two of us. When we first moved to this area, we sat down in a bus and some random woman sat down beside us and said, 'Awww, the way you treated your wife is so beautiful.' I said, 'She's not my wife. She's my sister.' Some okada riders have said, 'This your girlfriend is fine o.'

In my circles, we have long debates and my friends are pro-gay rights. They are feminists. I choose my friends well. All my male friends see me as an adventurous girl. I think they thought I was just experimenting about two years ago. I don't know what they think now. When I meet them, I always go with her. Everyone thinks we are dating and it's good. It's like I'm making a statement. They tease us and they're fine with it. On the other hand, I've lost jobs because of my sexuality. I got a job two weeks ago that I lost because somebody told them I was a lesbian. I was banking on that money.

Things have really changed on this issue since I was young. People weren't so religious back then. They weren't so corrupt. We use 'lakiriboto' to describe women who go against the grain, women who won't sleep with men, including those who go with other women. The first time I saw two girls kissing was in my grandmother's house – my aunt and one of the girls. They were all sleeping on this long mattress they would spread on the floor. The two of them would have sex and nobody would turn. My grandmother's younger sister lived in Ghana for a long time. When she became old, she went to the house of this young girl who lived in the next compound and said she wanted to marry her. She promised to take care of the girl, send her to school, take care of all her expenses – and they gave her out in marriage. She married her so the girl could take care of her. They're both dead now but the practice of women marrying women was common in the past – and I think it still is.

This is one of the reasons I love living in this neighbourhood. People are still living the way they were. Technology is not as fast here. They use old phones. We have a man who dresses obviously as a woman. Everyone knows him. They call him Baba Sango and think he gets possessed by the spirit of Sango. We have girls who dress like boys. Nobody looks at them in a weird way. We have all sorts of people and there's still the polygamous way of life, which is a great way to cover a lot. Two women, best friends, would say they are marrying the same man, then they would marry other women for their husbands. They would say 'I'm marrying a woman for myself and my husband can have part of it.' A lot of these things are covered up under the Agbole system. You don't know who has children or who does not because there are always children in the compound and everybody's called by some child's name. Nobody cares if you are married or not. The compound system really worked for them.

They still have it here but it's changing. People are moving out of their compounds and becoming individuals. Now people have a really bad name for it. People are seen going to churches and mosques. Imams are saying that the women who sleep with women or the men who sleep with men are all going to hell. They pretend to be moralistic. They don't remember that, when they were boys, they used to have sex with each other in all these corners. They still have these 'all boys' clubs' where men meet. We all pretend to be religious and moralistic so that we can be accepted.

I want to see a community that is stronger, more educated, with people coming to knowledge of themselves. A community that is bolder. I want to tell people that they should be themselves. It's when you are yourself that you can accept other people. I always say that it took me almost half my life to get to this point.

When I talk to young people, I tell them, 'Don't waste years struggling with yourself. Just accept yourself the way you are.'

– DK, age 42, Oyo

---

1   NEPA = National Electric Power Authority

I Convinced Myself I Wasn't A Lesbian

'I had to remember to change the pronoun of my lover so nobody could tell she was female ... making up pictures and stories of how we met and why I couldn't introduce "him" to any of my friends. It was exhausting.'

I grew up in a normal northern-Muslim household in Jos. My parents were well educated and worked government jobs. We spoke Hausa and English interchangeably in a five-bedroom house with my three siblings and four cousins. Each room had a double bunk and people running in and out, so we learned early in life to share everything, especially personal space. We woke up every morning at 5am, we ate lunch at 2:30pm and dinner at 7pm and were in bed at 8pm I attended an Islamic primary school, returned home to extra lessons, then attended evening Islamiyya school to learn to read the Qur'an and write in Arabic. Our lives had a comfortable routine and life was easy.

I attended the same school as my siblings and I remember having a crush on my teacher Ms. S___ when I was in Primary 3. She was pretty. She was female. She was political. I don't think she did anything different or special, I just enjoyed being in class and watching her while she taught. I loved going to school. I excelled because I was super attentive and always trying to please her. As an adult, I learned that my reaction wasn't unique as most people have a crush on their teacher at some point. Mine just turned out to be female. This was mildly disappointing; I thought we had something special.

As much as I loved school, I was severely bullied because I was young, small and generally easy to pick on. People knew what was going on. There was this tall girl who had a little clique. I can't remember her hitting me but I was deeply afraid of her and if she ordered me to do anything, I quickly obeyed. When we had a test in class, I would crawl under the tables and my classmates would make space for me. I would give her my paper to copy off, then crawl back to my own seat. She would ask what I'd brought for lunch today I and if she liked it, she would say, 'Okay, I'll have that one. You have mine.' She told me that if I ever saw her carrying anything, I should come take it. So, if she had a bag on her, I would take it to her desk.

One day in Primary 4, when I was about 8 or 9, I was sitting on the windowsill in class. She was late. Her car drove into the school compound. I could see it from where I was sitting. She got out with her bag so I jumped out the window and went to take it for her. Unknown to me, the teacher was there and wondering what the fuck was going on.

All hell broke loose. There was a whole lot of trouble for everybody – most of the people in class, her and her gang, and other teachers – for not having said anything. They started watching me and it became annoying. I became that person that everybody knew was being bullied so I convinced my parents to let me stay home and write the Common Entrance exam. They bought me the form and put me in extra lessons. I wrote the exam and got admission into the same secondary school as my sisters. I was very excited!

I really loved secondary school as everybody was friendly. After being brought up in such a regimented household, I was used to going to bed early. In school, I would get punished often for sleeping during prep. The punishment was to jump for thirty minutes or so to wipe the sleep from your eyes. But I was so notorious that I perfected the art of sleeping while jumping. So many nights were spent in front of class, jumping and sleeping. After prep, I would not even remember walking from class to the hostel. Immediately I got to the hostel, I would sleep, half the time in the clothes I wore because I was so tired.

I can't point to the first time I liked a girl. I have memories of so many women who drew a strong reaction from me. From Ms S___ to these older girls who took care of me and whom I was attracted to. There was a rotating number of women whom I had a thing for.

In boarding schools in Nigeria, women are allowed to show affection and love. There was a kind of coupling up that was generally allowed. It wasn't a big deal. A chokkor or a lifey was just someone special to you. Sometimes the person was in the same class as you and sometimes they were in a higher class. And the relationship was romantic in nature. There was even a whole economy around Valentine's and buying gifts for your chokkor.

So, we grew up accepting that it was okay to love another girl. It was even celebrated. In our uniform, there was a code. If you tied your belt backwards, it meant you were in the market for a chokkor. A person would be like, 'Okay, I like this girl.' Her friends would go and talk to you or your friends and ask if you had a chokkor. You would say, 'No,' and they would reply, 'Okay, we're going to connect you with someone. Thursday night, you're going to wear your best outfit, and we're going to come take you from your room to your chokkor's room.'

Sometimes, you would have no clue who she was. Other times, you knew because she was sort of picking on you or gave you extra food or said hello to you one too many times during assembly. They would take you to your chokkor's place and leave you there for the night. That was totally normal.

There was drama when some girls were snatched from their chokkors. We would hear things like 'Amira was just going steady with Nneka and the next thing, Bola came into the picture and now Amira no longer hangs out with Nneka. They stopped going for break together and now she goes for breaks with Bola.' We would all be scandalised that such a thing had taken place.

Throughout secondary school, almost everybody had a lifey but there were only four people who had girlfriends. They were not just in love but had kissed, made out or had sex. They were all known of course. You're teenagers, you talk to your friends and nobody can keep a secret. When I was in JSS3, there was this huge outrage about two girls being lesbians. One was in SS2 and the other was in JSS3. They spent all their time together. At some point, they kissed and someone found out. They told somebody who told somebody who told the school administration. They were both suspended. I thought it was weird that people were allowed to be in love, but never to take it to the next stage.

Years later, people who knew me in school would tell me

how homophobic I was. I wasn't homophobic but people around me were and I didn't do anything to speak up. At school, I was so sure that I was not a lesbian. To be a lesbian, you needed to have held a girl's hand, kissed a girl, made out with her or had sex with her. I had done none of those things. Then secondary school finished. My childhood passed really quickly – one day I was a kid and the next, I wasn't.

University was fun. I found studying a breeze. But socially, few girls played any kind of sport at that level so I kind of stood out. It also didn't help that I liked to wear men's clothes. Everyone I knew became super feminine and conversations became about clothes, parties and boyfriends. I wasn't into clothes nor did I like any boy but in my bid to fit in, I decided I needed a boyfriend.

H___ was the first boy I kissed. It wasn't unpleasant. It was almost exciting, but not quite. I would talk about the fact that we were not really compatible and he always told me that my expectations were built around watching too many Bollywood movies and that, actually, we were fine.

I had doubts but I didn't want to rock the boat because I was very comfortable in the relationship. He was a good friend, he lived and schooled in another city, and we saw each other once or twice a year. We relied on writing each other letters as no one had cellphones then. After about three years of this, we broke up when he started dating another girl in his school. I was relieved and moved on quickly.

Around that time, I was coming into myself and trying to figure out what was different about me. I knew I liked girls but I was still convinced I wasn't a lesbian. I concluded that there must have been something wrong with H___ and I just needed to find the right boy.

This led to the beginning of my wild stage. I started partying every weekend, hanging out with a lot of boys and I had no problem kissing anyone and everyone. I was determined to find the right person with just the right chemistry. I made out with a ton of boys. There was tons of heavy petting and that was it. And my friends were fascinated. They would joke about it and help me keep score. We only stopped counting after about a hundred.

In all those hundreds of boys and men, I never found anyone mildly exciting and I never dated. But it made me feel normal to have a boyfriend and be out there kissing everyone. I was slowly realising that I was only attracted to women, but I was in deep denial!

It was around this time that my family went on Hajj. I remember trying so hard to pray away the gay. It might have even been my sole aim in Hajj. I would include it in salat, during tawaf around the Kaaba, during my walks on Safa to Marwa, and it was my consistent prayer when I stood on Mount Arafat. I prayed every day, deeply, sincerely, that I would no longer be in love with girls, that I would no longer be a lesbian. I wanted nothing more than to be straight, to meet a man, fall in love with him, get married and have a family. I just wanted to fit in, to be a good daughter, to be a good Muslim.

Then I met this girl on the website Hi5. My status had 'interested in girls' and hers had the same thing so we started talking and flirting. She told me she had a boyfriend, she had dated girls before, she was fascinated by northern girls and she would like to meet me. I told her I would definitely like to meet her too.

Her name was N___. She was schooling and living in

Ghana. We decided to meet when she was in the country. I went to Lagos because she was there for one night before flying to Kumasi. We hung out that night and the next morning I flew back to Abuja. I was so excited: *Oh my God, I can't tell anybody. I met this girl and she's cute and she's also into women and she likes me and I like her and we are going to date.* When she got back to Ghana, we had a conversation and decided to date.

We would talk on the phone all the time. I told my friends I had met this boy named Nathan. After about three months, I bought a ticket to Ghana to visit her. We had agreed we were going to take everything slowly but after three hours at her place, she asked me, 'So, can I kiss you?'

The world stopped. If I said yes, I was going to be committing a sin. If I said no, all of this was kind of useless. I would never find out if I really like girls like that. She kept on asking, 'Can I kiss you?' I told her, 'If you keep asking, I'm never going to answer you.' So she reached over and kissed me – then we had sex.

And ... the sex was awful. It was awkward and very weird. I was too into my head and watching myself have sex with her. I was overthinking everything, and I was riddled with guilt. We had sex a second time and just cooled it off. We would write long emails to each other and talk all the time but that was it. I went to Ghana on three different occasions. We would kiss but we never had sex again.

Then Facebook came along and destroyed Hi5. We all moved to Facebook and stopped meeting people who could put 'interested in girls' as their description. Internally, I was settling into self-acceptance. I had already had sex with a girl. I knew I was completely into women and no man was going to change that.

At the age of 26, I fell in love. I was sooo in love, I wanted her to meet everyone. I wanted to shout from the top of every building how much I was in love with her. She was the first person I could walk with on the streets holding hands. We would talk about everything, anything and nothing; honest, frank conversations. We were friends and we were lovers. For the longest time, it was perfect. I experienced the awesome freedom that was the ability to love myself, to love another person and be okay with it. I didn't know where it was going but it felt good. I wanted to keep going and figure it out whenever.

Shortly after she and I became official, I moved out of home and started living with a flatmate. I knew in my heart that I could not live in the closet. I was flirting with the idea of coming out, and I knew that I was likely to lose friends and family if that happened. I was already living a double life: free and out when I was with my girlfriend, hidden and sad when I was back home or at work. I felt like I was choking. I couldn't take the pretence any more so I started to cut ties with a lot of people. I stopped spending time with friends and buried myself in work. I would tell them I was too busy. I would travel without telling anyone and spend weeks away. I had decided that I would shut out everybody before anybody alienated me. I even stopped communicating with my family and told them I needed to be an adult.

One day in 2012, I sent a message to my mum saying, 'I want to introduce you to my girlfriend and don't you dare act surprised.'

With my heart in my mouth, I waited for her reaction. Deep down I was ready for the absolute worst. She replied saying, 'Where's she from? And are you girls getting married?'

I said, 'Slow down woman. I said girlfriend not fiancée. Do not try to U-haul us.' I was flabbergasted. I took a screenshot and sent it to all my queer friends. I was shocked, relieved, happy and convinced that my mum was the most amazing person on the planet.

Then fast forward to 2014 after the Same Sex Marriage Prohibition Bill passed. I was so angry that it had passed into law that I wrote an article about being lesbian in Nigeria, stating how the law couldn't criminalise sexuality. Immediately I published it, everything changed. There was a lot of abuse, a lot of online bullying and a lot of threats. Some type of stupid semi-hisbah board from my state put out an APB to find and prosecute me.

My mum went crazy on me. 'How could you? How dare you? How could you say you're a lesbian?'

'Why are you acting this way?' I asked her. 'We had this conversation years ago and you were fine with it.'

'I regret the day I had you,' she told me. 'You're a disappointment to me. In fact, you're not my daughter.'

My sisters said, 'Why are you doing this thing to her? Are you trying to kill her?'

I asked them, 'What am I supposed to do? Am I supposed to take it back? Lie? Just say what you guys want to hear? Because it's not going to change anything.'

The entire family went ga-ga. Everyone was calling me, trying to 'talk sense into me'. All they wanted me to do was take it back and tell them what they wanted to hear. They sent me all these preachings and scriptures to get me to change.

I stopped picking up their calls and replying to their messages. But to put their minds at ease, I told them I was a lesbian but I had never dated anyone. I thought it would be easier for them if they thought I had never had sex with a girl.

Throughout all of this, it was just my baby sister who was supportive. She asked, 'What does this mean? What has this meant for you all this while?' I told her, 'Well, that's it. All these lies, the pretending and faking. I'm tired. I am a lesbian and that isn't going to change.' She asked me why I never told her, and then just listened to all my experiences as I ranted about how hard it was. She stayed on the phone and cried with me and I felt very guilty. She was barely 21, all her friends were talking about it and there was nothing I could do to protect her from the outpouring of hatred that also came her way.

But I stuck to my decision, continued to reiterate how gay I was, and remained open to engaging with people both online and offline. I was determined to show everyone that gay people were everywhere and we were just as regular as they were. In that time, I had to answer some invasive, probing and insensitive questions, but I was determined to stay the course because I didn't see any other way. I was determined to get through the rudeness, the curiosity and get to the mundane. Friends and even strangers would ask questions about how two women have sex, if we use sex toys, if we were lesbians because we were corrupted by white people, and if I thought we were going to hell. I answered as often as I could, until they grew tired of asking or were shocked by my reply.

I also found a lot of friends were more supportive than I thought they would be, not to mention the large new family of queer people who found me from that article. Hundreds of people reached out to me through emails, Twitter DMs and some even called me. A few were out but most of them were closeted. They showered me with love, shared their stories, held me up when I had doubts, and checked on me every day to make sure I was okay. I can't even begin to explain how helpful that was. At that point, I had cut off contact with my family so this showering of love was everything!

I think one of the main reasons I was able to come out was the fact that I was financially stable. I had a job, I lived in my own apartment, and even though my office was unaware of my sexuality until that time, they quickly changed the office culture and security policy and were very supportive of my decision. I missed my family but luckily I was 100 per cent independent from them. I missed my mum. I missed my siblings. I missed my culture. I missed the religious rituals with the family.

Now I feel like it has been a lifetime since I came out publicly. I have never been happier or more comfortable with myself, and I have slowly started having my old friends back in my life. I remember the person I pretended to be when I was closeted so that no one could tell that I was different. I lied about who I was talking to, who I was hanging out with, and had to watch myself lest I let something slip. I had to remember to change the pronoun of my lover so nobody could tell she was female, had to change her name from N___ to Nathan, making up pictures and stories of how we met and why I couldn't introduce 'him' to any of my friends. It was exhausting. And heartbreaking. I remember thinking, *I can never tell my mother that I like girls, I can never tell her that I fantasise about marrying a woman, I can never tell her that all her wishes for me – a good man, 2.5 kids, and a 'good civil service job' – are my biggest nightmares.*

I think about that fake version of me and look at how much I have grown. I'm much happier with the person I am now and

I think my friendships are more meaningful in that they can experience all parts of me without any pretence. We're very honest and blunt with each other. I don't lie about who I'm with, who I'm seeing, what my life is like. A lot of times, they pray for me and try to talk to me about choices but we're still able to be honest with each other.

Looking at the future, I know that I want to continuously engage with the LGBTI community in Nigeria. I want to be more out there, more open and more visible. If more people come out and normalise our existence instead of pretending there's only a handful of gay/bi/lesbian/trans people, the faster everyone will come to terms with it. I am well aware that not everyone is in the financial, emotional or physical place to do so, but for those who can, I can't wait to see them step out of the closet and experience the love and freedom!

Right now though, the community is a bit haphazard. I know tons of queer people who are Muslim and northern and I know different groups of queer people who are not Muslim or northern. These two groups don't meet. They don't socialise. They have so little in common. I feel like non-Muslim, non-northern people are more independent. A lot of them move away from their original place of birth or are away from their families so they are more able to assert themselves and live their authentic lives. It's not the same with most northerners. Ninety per cent of us still live at home with our families. Whether we identify as lesbian, queer, bisexual or whatever, most of us are resigned to getting married to the opposite sex and toeing that line. It sometimes feels like a lot of queer northerners are experimenting because almost every queer person you know eventually gets married.

Two women or two men in love have no model to base their

love on. We haven't seen anyone living, working, and raising children with their same-sex partners in Nigeria so we think it cannot be done. Many women bow to pressure and marry men. Many of them end up having affairs while married and this leads to new levels of complication. In fact, I hear a lot of people complain that they cannot date bisexuals because they are only in the relationship with a woman until they find a man. Most people with such views forget that not only bisexuals marry men. And until we become visible, until we show women that it is okay privately and publicly, until we discourage this notion of marrying straight or gay men to hide our sexualities, queer people will continue to think that they have no other options.

And that takes movement-building, fighting for our right to exist, telling our stories, and reaching out to other people like us. Unfortunately, that isn't happening, as many people keep saying, I don't want stress, I don't want a big deal to be made of my sexuality. It's heartbreaking but I hear it a lot. Too many people just want to party, hook up and never rock the boat.

The queer community does not engage with the few queer organisations and the organisations don't necessarily know how to go out and find our people. So we end up with a situation where 20–50 people are making decisions about what happens in the movement of maybe 17 million queer people.

I don't think there's going to be a change in the law or the lives being lived in our generation but I know the next generation is going to be completely different. We live in a globally connected world where we can't just put people in a vacuum and pass on false information. Straight kids will watch Ellen changing lives with kindness on TV, they will see Mpho Tutu famously married to a woman and accepted by her father, they will see Caster Semenya breaking world records, they will listen to Frank Ocean sing soulful songs about a man, they will watch Laverne Cox charm the world, read Binyavanga Wainaina's stories and be lifted by Chinelo Okparanta's words. Our young people are going to continue to have direct interface with LGBTI folks and find for themselves that they are just like everyone else and acknowledge that our lives and our rights are just as important as everyone else's.

– HA, age 30, Abuja

Biographies

Azeenarh Mohammed is a trained lawyer and a queer feminist, holistic security trainer who spends her time training not-for-profit organisations on tools and tactics for digital and physical security and psycho-social well-being. Azeenarh is active in the Nigerian queer women's movement and has written on queerness and technology for publications including *This is Africa, Perspectives and Premium Times NG*.

Chitra Nagarajan is an activist, researcher and writer. She has spent the last 15 years working on human rights and peacebuilding and is involved in feminist, anti-racist, anti-fundamentalist and queer movements. She currently lives and works in Maiduguri, Nigeria, focusing on conflict mitigation, civilian protection and women's rights.

Rafeeat Aliyu is a writer, editor and content development consultant. She is also a documentary film producer. Her first documentary, 'Things We Carry' was produced in 2017 and centred on the impact of death, grieving and loss on young Nigerians. Rafeeat's fiction has appeared in *AfroSF: Anthology of African Science Fiction, Expound Magazine, Omenana and Queer Africa 2*. Her story "58 Rules To Ensure Your Husband Loves You Forever" was longlisted for the 2017 Writervism Short Story Prize.

Acknowledgements

We want to thank, first and foremost, all the narrators for telling us the stories of their lives and opening up about their past experiences, fears and dreams for the future.

Without publisher Bibi Bakare-Yusuf and her excitement, belief and patience in this project, there would be no book. She took an idea we shared with her and brought it to life through her support.

The High Commission of Canada made it possible for this project to happen through their funding, enabling us to travel all over Nigeria and ensure a wide diversity of narrators.

There were many who gave practical support throughout the project. The staff of The Initiative for Equal Rights partnered with us and were there from start to finish. The folks at Advocates for Grassroot Empowerment, and the Women's Health and Equal Rights Initiative connected us with people and put calls out on their platforms. Many human rights defenders went out of their way to introduce us to people in their communities, even giving us places to stay when we visited their towns. Unfortunately, we cannot list their names, but without them we would have had no narrators. We also want to thank Lauren Smith for her excellent copy-editing.

And finally, thank you to our friends, partners and families for their support and enthusiasm.

Azeenarh Mohammed, Chitra Nagarajan & Rafeeat Aliyu
Abuja, June 2017

Support Cassava Republic Press

We hope you enjoyed reading this book. It was brought to you by Cassava Republic Press, an award-winning independent publisher based in Abuja. The more you support us, the more contemporary African writing we can produce for you. Here's how you can help:

Recommend it. Don't keep the enjoyment of this book to yourself; tell everyone you know. Spread the word to your friends and family.

Review, review review. Your opinion is powerful and a positive review from you can generate new sales. Spare a minute to leave a short review on Amazon, Goodreads, Wordery, our website and other book buying sites.

Join the conversation. Hearing somebody you trust talk about a book with passion and excitement is one of the most powerful ways to get people to engage with it. If you like this book, talk about it, Facebook it, Tweet it, Blog it, Instagram it. Take pictures of the book and quote or highlight from your favourite passage. You could even add a link so others know where to purchase the book from.

Buy the book as gifts for others. Buying a gift is a regular activity for most of us – birthdays, anniversaries, holidays, special days or just a nice present for a loved one for no reason... If you love a book and you think it might resonate with others, then please buy extra copies!

Get your local bookshop or library to stock it. Sometimes bookshops and libraries only order books that they have heard about. If you've read something you've loved, why not ask your librarian or bookshop to order it in. If enough people request a title, the bookshop or library will take note and will order a few copies for their shelves.

Recommend a book to your book club. Persuade your book club to read this book and our other titles and discuss what you enjoy about the book in the company of others. This is a wonderful way to share what you like and help to boost the sales and popularity of the book. You can also join our online book club on Facebook at Afri-Lit Club to discuss books by African writers.

Attend a book reading. There are lots of opportunities to hear writers talk about their work. Support them by attending their book events. Get your friends, colleagues and families to go to a reading and show an author your support.

Thank you!

Stay up to date with the latest books, special offers and exclusive content with our monthly newsletter.

Sign up on our website:
www.cassavarepublic.biz

Twitter: @cassavarepublic
Instagram: @cassavarepublicpress
Facebook: facebook.com/CassavaRepublic
Hashtag: #SheCalledMeWoman #ReadCassava